ST. CLARE OF ASSISI

NESTA DE *ROBECK*

St. Clare of Assisi

FRANCISCAN HERALD PRESS
1434 WEST 51st STREET • CHICAGO, 60609

Reprinted with permission of Bruce Publishing Company who first published this book in 1951; copyright ©1980 Franciscan Herald Press, 1434 West 51st St., Chicago, Illinois 60609.

Library of Congress Cataloging in Publication Data

De Robeck, Nesta.
    St. Clare of Assisi.

    Reprint of the 1951 ed. published by Bruce,
Milwaukee.
    Bibliography: p.
    Includes index.
    1. Clara, of Assisi, Saint, d. 1253.
2. Christian saints—Italy—Assisi—Biography.
3. Assisi—Biography.
[BX4700.C6D4   1980]   282'.092'4 [B]   80-19555
ISBN 0-8199-0808-8

To My Friends
With Love

"Non vox votum, non clamor sed amor,
 Non cordula sed cor, psallet in aure Dei,
 Lingua consonet menti, et mens concordet cum Deo."

(Inscription in the choir of San Damiano)

"The tower which guards the shrine of Saint Clare is tall, and strong and beautiful, even as she was; and the pearly grey and rose of its stone reflect all the light in the sky. It catches the first rays of the sunrise, and its bells ring for the new day. Throughout the hours it waits upon God's pleasure in sunshine and storm, and its mid-day bell recalls us to His Presence in His world. Its face is turned to the sunset, and while many birds fly round it singing, it joins with all the other bells of the valley in echoing the Angelus; the time for rest has come. When the moon rises the tower is still watching, for perhaps some new star may be born this night. Thus pass moments, centuries; the tower of Saint Clare remains tall and strong and beautiful."

Contents

ST. CLARE OF ASSISI

I

Lights and Shadows in the Background

ASSISI is a city with two faces: to the south nothing disturbs the serenity of the valley of Spoleto; the diaphanous lines of the hills are so gentle, the light so translucent and tender that often it is hard to tell where the hills and the sky melt into one another. As there is no harsh line in the landscape, so there is none in the upward slope of the city against the background of Monte Subasio; light seems to emanate from its very stones as the colour changes from hour to hour until it becomes a rosy reflection of the sunset. But what a different view we see when, from the castle hill, we turn towards the north! The steep slope plunges down to a narrow valley through which winds the river: other hills rise rugged, and grandly defiant to enclose it; everything speaks of solitude, effort, and strength in assault as in defence, while the wind rages down the gorges and over the hills.

These two aspects of Assisi are reflected in its history and in the character of its people; and this is true of both Francis and Clare.

We know nothing of the centuries during which Etruscans and Umbrians glared at each other across the twenty miles of valley between Perugia and Assisi, when the boundary of the Etruscan kingdom was marked by the Tiber. Recorded history begins some three hundred years before Christ when the

Romans arrived and Assisi became a beautiful city with green terraces facing southwards, with aqueducts, forum, baths, theatre and amphitheatre, and though it was not renowned as a religious centre as was Gubbio or Todi, nevertheless Assisi was a city of temples, and the memory of the Roman gods lingers on in many a name of gate, hill, and village. Communication with Rome was assured by the road along the valley, and a number of well-to-do families owned villas in which life was civilised and pleasant, and the literary-minded no doubt read all the best authors and invited the local poet Propertius to recite his verses. Assisi possessed all the amenities of Roman life, and those people felt that their civilisation was assured, even when it was already being undermined by its own inherent defects and by the vast movements of Barbarians many hundreds of miles away.

Civilised Roman Assisans can hardly have been seriously impressed when they heard that an old man, Felicianus, was preaching the doctrines of the new Christian sect to anyone who would listen to him in the fields and even in the streets. The Consul Lucius Flavius, however, was a devout pagan, and a savage persecution began. Felicianus, then nearly a hundred, gathered his followers together on what is now the hill leading down to San Damiano: he set up a cross saying: "Remember in this place to venerate and adore the cross which I have planted in honour of the Lord Jesus Christ. Here you shall pray to Him and praise Him in the morning, in the noon day, and in the evening. Praise Him, and offer Him your hearts." Felicianus, the first bishop of Assisi, died on his way to his martyrdom in Rome: and over the place where that cross stood a chapel was built, and round it tombs have been found inscribed with the names, and sometimes with the professions of their owners, ordinary men and women in whom the martyrs kindled a like heroism to their own.

Assisi had numerous martyrs, among them the Bishop Vittorinus who baptized a great number of people before he suffered together with many of his flock. He was succeeded by Savinus during the reign of Diocletian, when the Prefect Venustianus was eager and zealous for the Emperor's favour. Everyone knew that Savinus was an intrepid Christian, and he with two deacons was brought to trial in the forum. The interrogation began: "Who are you?" "Savinus, a bishop and a sinner." "Are you a slave or free?" "A slave of Christ, free from the devil." He was offered the choice either to burn incense to Jupiter or die; and a precious image of the god was brought made of coral and gold. "Is not this a god?" they asked. "No, and that you may know the truth of what I say, let me do with it what I will." Savinus took the image and dashed it to the ground where it lay smashed. His hands were cut off, but he could still encourage his deacons in their martyrdom before being imprisoned, and the threat of death did not prevent eleven more people from being baptized. Venustianus became blind and was ready then to listen to a converted blind man whose sight had been restored by Savinus. At last the Prefect was taken to Savinus who ordered that the fragments of the image of Jupiter should be thrown into the river; Venustianus and his household declared themselves Christians, and at the moment of baptism his sight too was restored. He went to live in the Bishop's house until the Emperor's order arrived that Venustianus and his family were to be beheaded, while Savinus was taken to Spoleto and there scourged to death.

Then there was Rufinus who with his son Cesidius had first been imprisoned in Rome for preaching the Gospel. Two women were sent to tempt them, but on the contrary these were also converted, and suffered so valiantly for the faith that, in their turn, they converted their executioners. Cesidius was killed, but Rufinus left Rome and reached Assisi where he became bishop, and more citizens were baptized. Eventually he and some of his followers were arraigned in the forum before the Pro-Consul Aspasius, and he answered the same questions as Savinus, and was offered the same choice. When they refused to burn incense to the gods a number of the Christians were flung down a deep well, while Rufinus was scourged and thrown into a furnace. The flames subsided, the heat became as cool water, and the Bishop emerged, unsinged. He was accused of sorcery: "Christ is my magic," he answered: he survived many tortures, and at last on August 11 he was thrown into the river bound to a block of stone, "glorifying the Father, the Son and the Holy Ghost."

These stories were repeated by every generation of Assisans, enshrined in many popular legends, and especially Rufinus became the beloved and venerated Christian hero and protector.

All down the valley the same struggle went on between Christianity and paganism, and every city had its martyrs. Christian hermits settled on Monte Luco behind Spoleto, one of the first European imitations of the Thebaid, and in the basilica of San Salvatore there still exists a fourth-century frescoed representation of the cross.

An ancient tradition, which at any rate cannot be disproved, ascribes to this period the building of the little chapel of Santa Maria della Porziuncula, in the valley below Assisi. The story is that it was the work of pilgrims returning from the Holy Land filled with devotion for the Blessed Virgin. The subtitle "della Porziuncula" may have come because someone gave a little portion of land on which to build, but very early the chapel was also called St. Mary of the Angels for it was an angel-haunted place. Thus the chapel so dear to Francis and Clare was probably the earliest Assisi sanctuary of our Lady, directly connected with the age of the martyrs.

Christianity had become the religion of the empire, but it was threatened at every moment by heresies and corruption, tossed hither and thither in political upheavals, and yet the one stable light in the world. Like many another small city Assisi shared in all these vicissitudes.

Italy had become familiar with invasions even before Christ's birth, and the fifth century saw the beginning of a long series of conquests. Alaric the Visigoth besieged Rome three times and sacked it; Attila and his Huns overran all northern Italy while the Vandals threatened the empire in northern Africa. Vacillating and decadent emperors were no match for the Ostrogoth leaders, and yet the conquerors were themselves conquered by the might of the Roman civilisation, and though Ataulph might wed the Roman princess Galla Placidia, he never aspired to make himself emperor. The greatest Ostrogoth, Theodoric, ruled in Ravenna as a Gothic king, but he died defending the empire. The Goths were Christians, but also Arians, therefore opposed by all the Catholic bishops of Italy, and their presence gave rise to bitter theological controversy. Yet the Goths could claim that they did not proselytise, that no Goth converted to Christianity was penalised, that the civil service was left in Italian hands, and Roman law respected and upheld. Had the Gothic domination survived would it have saved Italy other and worse conquests? The forces of the Western empire would certainly never have turned the Goths out, but Justinian in Constantinople was determined to expel them from Italy and Belisarius was put in command of the army. There were still regions of southern Italy which were Greek-speaking colonies favourable to the Byzantines, and for twenty-eight terrible years — from A.D. 527 to 565 — the struggle against the Goths continued. At one moment it seemed as though the imperial victory was assured, but under Totila the Goths made a new stand and recaptured a good deal of lost country, and it was at this time that they besieged, took, and sacked Assisi. Then the forces of the empire were reinforced under Narses, and his victory in 552, at the battle of Gualdo Taddino only a few miles distant, drove the Goths north and Assisi was occupied by the victors.

Through prolonged and bitter experience Italians were learning how to survive invasion, either by armed resistance, or when that was not possible by bowing to the storm and subsequently reasserting themselves. Besides the actual storm of the fighting they were assailed in far more insidious ways, for instance, by having to offer "hospitality" to foreign troops for long periods; no invasion was rounded tidily off, but inevitably each one left behind numbers of people who had had to be absorbed into the local population in the country districts as in the town. As always happens, each invasion left a deep mark; and no other country bears the impress of so many varied cultures and races as does Italy in her whole stretch from the Alps to Sicily.

Officially Italy was free of the Gothic rule, but the worst was that the empire proved unable to rule; the imperial garrisons shut themselves up in the cities while sporadic fighting continued. The sufferings of the people were terrible. Earthquakes, famine, and pestilence seemed to have combined in the work of destruction; and to add to all this, the way into Italy was unguarded, and Alboin with savage hordes of Lombards poured in to ravage cities and countryside. This was A.D. 568. To men like St. Gregory the Great it appeared indeed as though, humanly speaking, nothing of civilisation could be saved in such a cataclysm, when the civil order had crashed, and the appalling trials of multitudes made death seem the only remedy. In a former generation St. Augustine had felt the same, and his *De Civitate Dei*, begun in A.D. 410, was the Christian answer to the sack of Rome. More than ever his words seemed justified, and the only consolation in such disaster was the vision of the heavenly Jerusalem beyond all the material ruin of civilisation. And indeed the Christian Faith proved equal to the test; men still had the vitality to build up an art so rich and beautiful that what we see of it in Ravenna, for instance, is like the rising of the sun; St. Gregory still had the valour to send missionaries to England as well as having at heart the conversion of the Arian invaders; St. Benedict had already founded his abbeys and written his rule headed by the quotation: "Turn away from evil and do good: seek after peace and pursue it."

The next centuries were dark; Rome sank into squalor and degradation and corruption, and outwardly there must have seemed no authority that could avail to save the Church's organisation from perishing. Yet through all these disasters, despite the conquest of Christian Africa by the Arabs, and with Saracens threatening Rome itself, the Church was spreading and acting as a great unifying force between peoples of the most varied races. The light of sanctity was everywhere. A world of wars and violence could not kill the sense of Christian unity as it had been conceived by St. Augustine and all the great Christian thinkers: the urge to unity is the counterweight to the evil that divides men.

The Assisan chronicles describe the Lombards as "exceedingly fierce and terrible": with their hair dyed green these marauding northern tribes devasted all they found, and naturally struck terror into Italian hearts. The conquerors divided Italy into new principalities, and Assisi was included in the important duchy of Spoleto. The Lombards, too, were Arians, but Paul the deacon tells how in 610, Ariulfo, duke of Spoleto, was converted from "idolatry" — by which he may mean heresy — to the Catholic faith through a miraculous apparition of St. Savinus the martyr-bishop of Assisi. In the course of time many Lombards became Catholics, and gradually through the inevitable daily intercourse and intermarriage between the occupying race and the native population a certain degree of fusion came about. Each race influenced the other.

The Lombard predominance lasted a good two hundred years during which time the duchy of Spoleto was repeatedly a centre of disturbance; at one time it was at war with Perugia whose Lombard ruler had submitted to the imperial exarch in Ravenna; at another Lombard forces from Spoleto besieged Ravenna and marched south on Rome and Naples. During the earlier period of the occupation they were the Pope's enemies, but later his supporters against the iconoclast emperor of the East. On one occasion Liutprando, king of the Lombards, came to Spoleto to quell a revolt among his vassals, and in all the violent political cross-currents the smaller cities were involved together with the greater.

By the eighth century, history was preparing to take another turn. The Carolingian dynasty had established itself with the Pope's approval. Pippin the Short had been anointed king by St. Boniface the English apostle of Germany, and the ambition of the Lombard King Aistulph in Italy brought the Pope and the Frankish king into a growing alliance. Aistulph was not satisfied with threatening the imperial exarchate of Ravenna, but he also wished to rule Rome with the result that Pope Stephen appealed to King Pippin; the Lombards were defeated by "liberating" French forces, and the cities taken from the Lombards were handed over to the Holy See. The Lombard Duke of Spoleto decided to make common cause with the Franks, and this brought the Lombard King Didier to the valley of Spoleto, sacking and burning what he met out of revenge. Sporadic fighting went on throughout the country, confusion was everywhere, no authority could keep order, there was no security for life or property.

Twenty years later, in 773, Assisi again suffered. King Didier's ambition was not satisfied with attacking the imperial exarchate in Ravenna; he also wished to subdue Rome. Pope Hadrian, a Roman patrician, appealed to Pippin's son Charlemagne, and again the Franks defeated the Lombards, and the Frankish King took for himself the iron crown of Lombardy. Assisi was besieged, and the Frankish soldiers found an entrance by the Roman Cloaca Maxima which had either been left unguarded or was betrayed to the invaders. All the inhabitants were massacred, and the city was destroyed. A chronicle describes the situation: "Thus Assisi bereft of her citizens found herself an unhappy widow. Then was the most clement ruler grieved, and ordering that the city should be rebuilt, he placed therein a new colony of Christians of the Roman faith, and the city was restored, and in it divine worship." Oliver the Frank became a hero of a later Assisan legend which tells how he slew a monster called Occhialone who lived in a cave behind the castle hill and murdered all who approached. Arianism may have disappeared from Assisi with the coming of the Franks, but despite these political changes quite a number of Lombards must have survived and stayed on in Umbria, for well into the Middle Ages Assisan chronicles register Lombard names and Lombard customs.

Even this Frankish triumph did not bring order into Italy, and twenty-five years later Charlemagne again intervened to protect Pope Leo III against the violence of his enemies in Rome. To everyone the King of the Franks appeared as the only person able to guarantee stability, and already the Patriarch of Jerusalem, despairing of protection from Constantinople, had sent him the keys of the Holy Sepulchre. Charlemagne came again to Italy in the autumn of 800, the Pope took a solemn oath on the Gospels of his innocence of the crimes imputed to him by his enemies, and Charlemagne was crowned emperor on Christmas day in St. Peter's. Latin Christianity had found its champion, and there was again an emperor in the West.

Even after Charlemagne's death fourteen years later the Frankish ascendancy in Italy continued: the duchy of Spoleto passed into the hands of Franks; but this is an obscure period in Assisan history. Local power was shared by the bishops and counts assisted by judges chosen among the citizens. There must have been an interval of at least relative peace and increasing prosperity, and this coincided with a new wave of veneration for the city's martyrs, and especially for St. Rufinus, whose body had hitherto lain in an obscure sepulchre outside the walls.

It was the people of Assisi who wished that a new and grand church should be built in the saint's honour; they did not wish his body to rest in the old cathedral of Santa Maria Maggiore which had risen over the ruins of a Roman temple. The place they chose was a part of the city where the people habitually met for public discussions, and St. Rufinus' body became a political symbol as well as a relic. According to St. Peter Damian there were quarrels, there was bloodshed, there were miracles, but anyhow the first record of donations for the new church is dated 1007, and this date makes one think that perhaps the decision to build a new church was at any rate partly the result of the panic over the year 1000. The end of the world had then seemed imminent; everywhere people prepared for their end, and when the sun rose as usual and nothing happened, a new church and greater honour for the martyr would not have seemed too great a thank-offering.

The remaining crypt of the first church is Carolingian in style; and a document of 1045 states that Bishop Ugone, a powerful man who was later sent as Roman legate in Germany regarding the election of Leo IX, was consecrated "in the house of Blessed Rufinus." This indicates that the new church was already regarded as the cathedral under the double title of Santa Maria and San Rufino.

A century later this first church was already felt to be inadequate by a city that was being rapidly enriched through expanding commerce, and in 1140 Giovanni di Gubbio was commissioned to rebuild it. Only the crypt of the original church remains; and Giovanni's façade is still one of the glories of Assisi, as is the bell-tower which rests upon a splendid Roman cistern. The final solemn translation of San Rufino's body to its present resting place beneath the high altar took place in 1212 when Francis was already famous; it was the year in which Clare left her home to follow him.

San Rufino was not the only church built and rebuilt in Assisi in the early ten hundreds: there was the Benedictine abbey on Monte Subasio, the abbey and church of San Pietro, the church of San Paolo, that of San Masseo; a war with Perugia in 1054 did not apparently interrupt this desire to build which was so characteristic of the age. Like most of their contemporaries the Assisans built with skill and splendour. Romanesque architecture had come to its perfection, so had Romanesque sculpture which, for all its beauty and grandeur, never lost sight of the facts of cruelty and violence. How often did it not represent men destroying men, human backs being broken by the weight of the pillars resting on them, beasts devouring men or each other, and this at a time when the friendship of saints and beasts was being recounted in endless charming stories. The façade of San Rufino is an example.

Violence and corruption, spiritual illumination, aspiration and achievement walked side by side through the eleventh and twelfth centuries: in 1064 Rome was again sacked by Robert Guiscard and the Normans, and some years later the voice of Peter the Hermit rang out, followed by that of St. Bernard summoning Christendom to the first Crusades. Who could remain unmoved by the cry of *"Jérusalem qui plainte et pleure pour le secours qui trop demeure"*; from all countries men set out, some saints, many idealists, many adventurers, the single-minded and the calculating, those who were ready for martyrdom, and those whose ambition was for power and money. Then in 1099 all the bells were set ringing for the news that Jerusalem was free; the Latin kingdom was established in the Holy City protected by the Knights Templars and the Knights Hospitallers, the Holy Places were accessible to pilgrims, and the Crusaders' castles appeared on the hills of Palestine. It was a moment of *Te Deums*.

This new opening of the East to the West was of incalculable advantage to commerce, learning, and the arts, and soon the Western missionaries would realize the immense field which awaited them. The educational impulse given by Charlemagne was strengthened; and the first flowering of national cultures was beginning within the framework of a united European Christian culture. And what a richness and diversity and individual inspiration that unity was able to produce! There was enormous unifying strength in the Church's liturgy, not only in the Mass and Divine Office, but in everything connected with them, in all the arts. From Scotland to Sicily the same liturgical dramas were being performed, the same Gregorian music was being sung in all its perfection, some of the most beautiful religious poetry was being written, the

Arthurian cycle of legends was about to emerge, the great tales of chivalry were being told, while poets had started singing the praises of our Lady and the saints in the vernacular. Every court and castle was the haunt of troubadour and trouvere and minne-singer singing of a knight's lady and his love: no wars and dissensions could stop genius which everywhere was at work praying, thinking, writing, singing, building, carving, painting, busy with every art and every craft. Each generation handed on a wonderfully increasing inheritance in the small cities just as much as in the great, and the world was being enriched by something very rare and beautiful.

The unity of faith proclaimed by scholars and artists of the Middle Ages was roughly that of every man; and it shone luminous and radiant in the lives of many saints. Many great orders had been or were being founded: St. Romuald was the father of the Camaldolese, St. Bruno of the Carthusians, St. Bernard and St. Stephen Harding of the Cistercians, St. John Gualbert of the Vallombrosans, St. Norbert of the Premonstra-tensians; St. Anselm had kindled an inextinguishable light with his soaring realisation of God, his love of the Passion of Christ and of the Blessed Virgin, St. Bernard had done the same; there were great visionaries like St. Hildegarde, St. Elizabeth of Schoenau, St. Mechtilde, St. Gertrude, and all these men and women gave something divine to their fellow-men creatures. Everywhere scholars were "fighting the devil with pen and ink," and Montecassino, Bobbio, St. Gall, Cluny, Bec, Chartres, St. Victor, York were centres of spiritual life and thought whose influence was felt from one end of Christendom to the other. None of this was theoretical; it was all intensely living and being expressed through most powerful and dynamic personalities.

The drag-away from this unity came through schism, heresy, and corruption. The whole of Christendom was wounded when in 1054 the Eastern Church declared its autonomy and threw off allegiance to Rome. Popes and antipopes repeatedly defied each other; the Church was rent by political intrigues, and even in

Rome the Pope was constantly subjected to violence and insult. Even such a great constructive reformer as St. Gregory VII had difficulty in imposing his rule on the warring Roman factions, as on the schismatic Patarine Lombards; and all this happened in an age of very many saints and wide-spread acceptance of Christianity.

Lombardy — the province of Italy which had taken its name from the Lombard invaders — was the breeding ground for the Catharist heresy which taught that everything not pure spirit was created by an evil power, denied the sacraments, and opposed the whole outward organisation of the Church. There were many degrees among the Catharists, some being content to preach and practise poverty and penance, while the inner circle abominated marriage and all earthly happiness, and hastened death by self-torture and starvation. Catharism and its various offshoots spread all through northern and central Italy, took its firmest hold in southern France round Albi, and had devotees scattered throughout Europe.

There were other sects of both men and women who were all attracted by the idea of the evangelical life; some of these like the Poor Men of Lyons led by Pierre Valdes fell into schism, others like the Beguines and Beghards and the Umiliati of Lombardy remained within the Church leading a communal life of voluntary poverty and charity under a rule sanctioned by the Church. These people took the literal words of the Gospel as their ideal, but the world was still waiting for St. Francis to sweep thousands off their feet with his vision of what it means to follow Christ.

Abelard's disciple, Arnold of Brescia, also preached poverty with an enthusiasm akin to that of St. Bernard; he wished to reform and reduce the organisation of the Church to its primitive simplicity, while his political passion made him wish to crown the people's majesty on the Capitol. To many Arnold was a heretic, to others a heroic reformer, but the revolutionary who wished to destroy the power of the Pope, Emperor, and nobles in favour of that of the people, finally faced a coalition which was too strong for him. Rome was placed under the interdict; Pope Adrian IV (Nicholas Breakspeare) appealed to Frederick Barbarossa, king of the Germans, whose first expedition into Italy in 1154 was to "liberate" the Pope from the violence of the new Roman Republic. Arnold fled but was recaptured and burnt.

These were the circumstances which brought the red-haired Frederick of Hohenstaufen on to the Italian scene. As soon as he had risen to power in Germany he dreamed of himself as the heir of Constantine and Charlemagne, the ruler of the Holy Roman Empire, and perhaps he thought of his troops as the Roman legions. He talked of "our Roman laws," and the jurists of Bologna supported his claim. His only rival in power was Henry II of England, who far surpassed him as an organizer and administrator, but was nothing like so romantic and adventurous a person.

His second expedition into Italy was in 1158 when he entered into the long swaying struggle with the northern Italian communes which involved also the rival claims of the Papacy and the Empire. It was another violent tangle full of knots and loose ends with many conflicting loyalties, sympathies, and interests. As a result of trying to throw off the imperial rule Spoleto was burned in 1160 and Barbarossa sent a warning declaration to Assisi that he considered the city and its territory as imperial property, and forbidding anyone to build a new castle in the district: on these terms the Assisans could consider themselves free and could count on the Emperor's favour. An interesting document of that year makes mention of a donation by a priest of the cathedral who made over all his possessions for the use of "all free men and of the churches," asking that they should be defended by the people of Assisi. Here we catch a glimpse of the self-consciousness of the people, as well as a deep-seated wish to be free on their own terms and not on the Emperor's!

Not very long after this—about two years—Milan fell to the imperial troops, its walls were razed, and the bodies of the

Three Kings were carried off in triumphal procession to Cologne. The Holy See at that time was divided between a pope and antipope, but when the Emperor invited both to a synod in Pavia presided over by himself, Pope Alexander III retorted that no emperor had the right to preside over a council of the Church and Barbarossa was excommunicated. Barbarossa descended upon Rome and was crowned emperor by his antipope, but the Roman son fought for Alexander, the Germans were laid low with fever and had to retreat, and the antiPope fled: the advantage was with Alexander.

All this heartened the Lombard cities, the walls of Milan were rebuilt, the northern city-states, the powerful Norman rulers of Sicily, the rulers of the Byzantine empire and the Pope were all drawn together in their hostility to Frederick who suffered his most severe defeat at Legnano in 1176. When he met the Pope in Venice in the following year, Barbarossa knelt to receive the kiss of peace, and for the moment it really looked as though the question, "Does the Emperor hold his crown as the Pope's vassal?" had been at least temporarily settled.

Three years earlier the imperial Chancellor had been sent to take possession of Assisi, which he did by force of arms. Evidently Barbarossa did not feel sure of the efficacy of his earlier declaration, and wished to keep the valley of Spoleto firmly in hand. On his next visit he came to Assisi in person and occupied the newly enlarged and fortified castle. The overlordship of Assisi was conferred on Conrad of Luetzen, a kinsman of the Hohenstaufen who was created Duke of Spoleto; and he too established himself in the Rocca Maggiore from which he ruled the city as an imperial fief. But the people of Assisi, who always delighted in nicknames, called the German troops "La Mosca nel Cervello," the fly in the brain.

Luck was on the Emperor's side again when his son Henry married Constance, the heiress of Sicily, which the efficient Norman rule had provided with a strong army, navy and exchequer, and though the results of this were not immediate, they were far-reaching. The rest of Italy found itself sandwiched between the German forces coming in from the north, and an imperial stronghold in the south. More than ever the city-states were torn between rival powers and alliances which changed according to the varying fortune of each side: Guelph and Ghibelline had become realities.

Another reality was also coming into the foreground, for the victory of Legnano was a warning to feudal Europe that a new fighting class had arisen, ready when called on to defend its rights. Another most powerful "C" had been added to the two already existing capital "C's": the life of every man and woman in Europe was being formed within the tremendous realities of Church, Castle, and Commune, each full of ideals and problems, each commanding its own loyalties, and they all affected every city and every citizen.

Such roughly was the state of affairs when Francis was born in 1182, just twelve years after the murder of Thomas à Becket. He was the child of the civilisation that surrounded him, absorbing much from it, and making a huge contribution in return. Socially he was the child of the Commune and of the rich commercial class that was growing up as one result of the Crusades, the child of a highly creative period, but some at least of the immediate influences were summed up in the prayer taught to Umbrian children, "Save my soul from the heresies of the Lombards, and my body from the ferocity of the Germans."

Those children spoke a mixture of Umbrian-Italian and Latin, and Francis learnt French, for otherwise he could not have continually broken into French songs as is reported of him. The Assisi that little Francis knew was the typical mediaeval city enclosed within its walls, yet in close contact with the countryside, dominated by its castle the Rocca, its artists and artisans and merchants kept busy by the city's self-sufficient life. For the children the year was punctuated by the colourful festivals of the Church and the Commune, they certainly joined in the Calendimaggio revels which ushered in the month of May, and played in the streets as the boys do to-day.

Those streets provided varied entertainment with strolling players, fairs, broils, and processions, and Francis may have heard that wandering preacher to whom the Tres Socii allude, and who greeted everyone with the words *Pax et Bonum*. He was probably a disciple of Joachim of Flores, the famous Calabrian prophet and visionary who had predicted terrible disasters would precede the reign of the Holy Spirit, the age of peace. Many people were terrified and fascinated by Joachim's apocalyptic visions, but not so many heeded his words when he insisted that the only remedy for the present and future ills was a mending of life, and individual sanctity. He gave his followers the one command, "Love one another." Joachim's influence was great, but that of Francis was to prove far greater and thirty years later the greeting *Pax et Bonum* would be repeated all over Europe by all kinds of people because the spark of charity in the heart of one small boy in Assisi had been fanned into a great fire of love of God and of men. Francis claimed later that his greeting of peace had been revealed to him by God. In his day the Assisans were commonly divided into "Buonuomini" and "Uomini." It was a social distinction, but to Francis every man was "good," and his greeting was the same to all: "Good people, the Lord give you peace."

Before the coming of Francis, Assisi was not a distinguished place; it was one of many ancient and small Italian cities, yet in little over a hundred years Dante was to write of it as the Orient, so great was the light it had shed over the world, a light which still continues. Much remains of the city that Francis knew; and after seven hundred years we still expect to meet him at turns in the countryside, and in the terraced streets where the brown houses are intersected with vine trellises and are bright with flowers. Most precious of all surviving objects is the font in San Rufino where he and St. Clare were baptized, and which is still in use; and they too must have prayed before the ancient Pietà which is still venerated in the cathedral as La Madonna del Pianto. Almost certainly they saw the same façade of San Rufino that we see; they too knew the churches of Santa Maria Maggiore, San Pietro, Santa Maria della Minerva, a former Roman temple, and San Giacomo di Muro Rupto; they too climbed the castle hill to the Rocca Maggiore and to the smaller fortress of the Rocchicciuola; from the purely material point of view we often tread in their steps and see much of what they saw. The woods in the valley and on the hills, alas, have disappeared; the view remains, and it was while looking at these hills that Francis learnt to sing — for all of us — the Canticle of the Sun.

The blessing which he gave Assisi on his last journey to the Porziuncula is still active; how otherwise can the pervading sense of peace felt by multitudes be accounted for? It is not only the beauty, the light, the art, or anything material; it is a gift from Christ Himself given us through Francis and Clare.

II

The Early Years

IT WAS on July 16, probably of 1194, that a daughter was
born in an Assisi palace to Ortolana, the wife of Favorone.
Before the child's birth Ortolana had prayed fervently in church
before the crucifix, and had received the assurance, "Fear not
for thou wilt safely give birth to a light which will shine on all
the earth." And so, when the baby was baptized in the
neighbouring cathedral of San Rufino, she was named Chiara.
About that time the Empress Constance dreamed that she
would give birth to a fire-brand which would make of Italy
a lighted torch, and on December 26, perhaps of that same year,
either in Assisi or Jesi, her child was born, the son and heir
of Emperor Henry VI. By some the baby was hailed as a future
saviour. Merlin prophesied that he was the king who would
unite East and West; but Joachim of Flores, that he would be
the world's scourge and antichrist. He was entrusted to the care
of his kinsman Conrad of Luetzen in the castle of Assisi, and
three years later he was baptized Frederick, also in the font of
San Rufino in the presence of fifteen cardinals and bishops; and
one reason for so much ceremony may have been a wish to
placate the Pope, for the child had already been recognized
as king of the Germans. There were great festivities, and
although the citizens looked on the castle with rather a sour
eye, no doubt they were quite pleased to share in a "festa,"

and fifteen-year-old Francesco Bernardone was not the lad to sit at home in the background.

No one that day could have dreamed of the closely inter-woven destinies of the Assisi boy and girl, or how the life story of the baby prince would constantly touch that of the other two.

Favorone was a feudal noble but the surname of Scefi given him by later biographers has no historical sanction: indeed authentic information about Clare's family is scarce. Favorone is known to have been lord of the castle of Coccorano on Monte Aldone above the Chiagio valley on the boundary of the Assisan territory; he has also been called lord of Sassorosso on Monte Subasio, but if his family ever owned that castled crag it was before 1177 when Barbarossa gave the property to the Ghisleris.

There is frequent mention of a Monaldo, probably a brother of Favorone, who appears as the head of the family and a leader in political and domestic affairs. These people "were rich in all things that were accounted riches in the land wherein they dwelt," and they also owned a palace in Assisi within a few paces of San Rufino. Pietro di Damiano, a witness in the cause of Clare's canonisation, says that "Madonna Chiara was of noble birth," and that the family included "seven knights, all noble and powerful," to which Messer Ranieri di Bernardo adds that "Madonna Chiara belonged to the most illustrious families of Assisi, both on the side of her father and of her mother." The family name of her mother is uncertain; tradition has called it Fiumi. All these feudal nobles were of very mixed descent; there may have been a Lombard strain in the families of Favorone and Ortolana; at any rate the Lombard women were famous for their wonderful golden hair, and such hair was one of Clare's beauties.

A family with seven knights was immersed in the full tide of chivalry, and its counterpart could have been found in any part of Europe, living by the same code, with the same ideals and prejudices, enjoying the same sports and songs, having the same defects. Politically the feudal nobility of Assisi favoured the empire of which they were the vassals, and their loyalty was reinforced by an iron determination to maintain their privileges against what they considered the encroachments of the other citizens, merchants, and artisans, the Populo Minuto, who were becoming so conscious of growing power and widening needs.

In 1198 Innocent III became pope, with his heart set upon reforms in the Church and upon opposing the imperial rule in Italy, a worthy follower of Gregory VII. A year previously Henry VI had died, and at the age of four Frederick was crowned king of the Sicilian kingdom, with the Pope and his mother as his guardians, but the latter also died in that same year. Innocent therefore found himself regent of Sicily for Frederick the golden-haired "Boy from Apulia," who, even as a child, "would only follow the dictates of his own will," and learnt to assert his independence very early.

For the moment, however, Innocent could direct events; his cry was "Italia" and one of his first actions was to call upon Conrad of Luetzen to renounce the duchy of Spoleto in favour of the Holy See. Conrad appears to have made no difficulty; perhaps he realized that resistance would have been ineffective; anyhow he fled, and the Assisans enthusiastically seized the opportunity to tear down part of the castle as a protest against the imperial claims, economically using the stones to build a new city wall. The first consul of Assisi, one of the Bombarone family, issued a decree, dated 1198, which was announced in San Rufino no longer in the name of the emperor, but in that of the Blessed Trinity.

This was but another assertion of the growing power of the Commune; and desultory fighting went on throughout the countryside between the opponents and supporters of the new regime, and the feudal Ghibellines could no longer count on immediate imperial help. Things came to a head when in the January of 1200 Girardo di Gislerio, the lord of Sassorosso, made his submission to the Commune of Perugia. It was a tremendous

insult to Assisi that an Assisan nobleman should join the heredi-
tary enemy; and when a number of other nobles followed suit,
tempers rose to boiling pitch. The castle of Sassorosso was sacked
and destroyed by the Assisans who also vented their fury on
every feudal possession they could reach. In the alliances and
counter-alliances of its cities the valley of Spoleto became a
miniature picture of the whole of Italy, and the feudal nobles
who had gone over to Perugia did their best to foment the
feeling against Assisi.

Among the list of these there is a Monaldo, and considering
that the family property of Coccorano was on the boundary
between Perugia and Assisi, it seems certain that he was indeed
the brother of Favorone. It follows logically that none of the
family could have remained in Assisi, and the first care would
have been to remove them to Perugia: this seems to be irref-
utably confirmed by the contemporary documents.

In Perugia the children whose fathers were brother knights
and of the same political opinions, naturally became playmates;
and it is extremely likely that thus began the friendship of three
little girls, Chiara, Filippa di Gislerio, and Benvenuta, who
belonged to a noble family of Perugia. Let us enlarge the circle
and look at these children grouped round Ortolana: besides
Clare and her two friends there are her sisters, Penanda, Agnese,
and Beatrice; perhaps her brother Martino; as well as two kins-
women, Pacifica and Bona Guelfuccio. They little dreamed that
they were the nucleus of a great religious order, and that all
of them except Martino, Penanda, and Bona would end their
lives with Clare in San Damiano, the first convent of
Poor Clares.

In those early days, however, Ortolana was still the central
figure in the group, a great feudal lady, devout, expert in ordering her household, and with considerable experience of life.
She had travelled to the Holy Land, probably following her
husband on the Crusade, for the crusading armies were habitually encumbered with crowds of non-combatants. She had

seen Jerusalem and Bethlehem before they were lost to the Christians, a disaster which filled Europe with dismay and strengthened the will to recover them. She could describe the Holy Places making the children see them through her eyes; she could tell of the great leaders, Richard, Tancred, Godfrey, and of how and where they had fought; she knew the disunion of the Crusaders, their dangers and difficulties, at first hand. Like many others those children of Assisi and Perugia must often have played at Crusades, the most wonderful adventure in the world which had the cross as its banner and as its war-cry, *Dieu le veut*. Every crucifix pleaded for the liberation of the Holy Places as well as for the virtues of Christian chivalry. It was as a knight of the cross that feudal children heard of St. John Gualbert of Florence who, when his brother's murderer appealed to him for mercy in the name of Christ, forgave the injury. At that time John Gualbert was a knight, and when he parted from the murderer and entered the church of San Miniato, the Figure on the cross bowed Its head before him. Christ had bowed His head because a knight had obeyed Him and for-given his enemy: could it happen again? Each carved or painted cross the children saw must have seemed to answer "yes."

Besides her journey to the Holy Land, Ortolana had also been in pilgrimage to the tombs of the Apostles in Rome, and to the sanctuary of St. Michael on Monte Gargano. This round was the chief recognized pilgrimage of that time referred to collo-quially as *"Deus, Angelus et Homo."*

Mediaeval people felt the battle between good and evil spirits as a tremendous reality going on all round them, and St. Michael was not only the leader of the hosts of heaven and men's most powerful protector, but also the patron of every Christian knight and warrior. Rome had been saved once from the Barbarians when St. Michael appeared on the wall of Hadrian and the Castel Sant' Angelo bore his name: and when in the fifth century he appeared in a cave on Monte Gargano in Apulia it became one of the chief sanctuaries of Europe to which people flocked from France, Spain, Portugal, England, Ireland, Poland, Hungary, Germany, and even from much farther afield. The immense veneration for St. Michael made it customary to fast for forty days in his honour during August and September; every country built sanctuaries to the Archangel; France had its Mont Saint Michel, England, Saint Michael's Mount.

Ortolana directed the education of her daughters according to that of their time and class. The advice given to parents by Lapo di Ser Pace was "if the child be a girl set her to sew and not to read unless she wishes to become a nun." Clare does not seem to have had any thoughts of being a nun but she certainly learnt to read, and judging from her letters, to write, and we know what a needlewoman she was, for the alb made by her and preserved in Santa Chiara in Assisi is one of the most beautiful examples of mediaeval handiwork, only possible to fingers which had always held a needle.

Clare was also talented for music to which she remained very sensitive all through her life. Like Romanesque art, the music of the Church had reached a wonderful fullness of beauty; and besides that of the actual liturgy there were many lovely sequences and songs, for instance those of Gauthier de Coincy which she certainly must have known. There were also the songs of the Troubadours, both French and Italian, there were the popular songs of Umbria, and melodies and dance tunes played on little portable organs, on the vieille and the lute and the pipes. It was an age of much singing and much playing.

No chronicler has thought of telling us how far little girls of the castle were allowed to go scrambling after flowers in the spring woods, but certainly flowers were another love of Clare's, and one which she carried with her to San Damiano.

As Ortolana looked at her daughter she must often have wondered how the prophecy about her would be fulfilled. The child was naturally pious and inclined to prayer, even to solitary prayer, though she does not seem to have been a spiritual prodigy. She liked to count her prayers — as was a common custom — upon stones strung on a cord for that purpose: such strings were called *Pater Nosters* and probably Ortolana and the children would recite these prayers together. Almsgiving, too, came naturally to Clare: she was sensitive to the needs of others, and always ready to give her sweets to poor children; this generosity grew on her and became proverbial.

The war which had uprooted Favorone's family ended with a victory for Perugia, and it is quite possible that the first time Francesco's name was mentioned in Clare's home was when someone repeated the boast of one of the Assisi prisoners who was asked why he was so gay in the Perugia prison and answered: "Because I see the day when the whole world will bow down before me." If there was any comment, it would have been a gust of scornful laughter for that young wind-bag, Francesco Bernardone. Yet something else had also been noticed — his power of reconciling people who did not get on together.

In 1203 a peace had been patched up, not only between Assisi and Perugia, but also between the conflicting Assisi factions of the Majores and Minores, and a couple of years later the self-exiled Assisi nobles returned to their homes. It had been stipulated that the Commune was to restore their property and indemnify them for damages. Clare was then nine, already lovely and radiating the joy of spring-time, a characteristic which remained with her all through life.

The household of Monaldo and Favorone and Ortolana had returned to the palace in the Piazza di San Rufino, and Clare saw her own city almost for the first time. Her home was mediaevally luxurious with lavish entertaining: visitors came and went constantly; and the children grew up accustomed to the talk, happenings, and amenities of feudal life. Tournaments had come into fashion, and Folgore di San Gimignano gives us a picture which more or less would fit into the setting of any city:

Provencal songs and dances that surpass,
And quaint French mummings: and through the
hollow brass
A sound of German music in the air.

In other words, troubadours and jongleurs from France and
minnesingers and minstrels from Germany were everywhere
welcome, and something of the pleasures of the grown-ups
trickled through to the children.

The Rocca of Assisi was empty, Barbarossa already a legend,
but the Pope and German princes were still wrangling over the
regency of the Two Sicilies which Innocent claimed as Frederick's guardian. The Norman Walter de Brienne was in command of the papal forces in the south, and to many he appeared
as a hero fighting for the Church and for the final overthrow
of the German rule in Italy. Among the Assisans who set out
to join him was Francis Bernardone: probably everyone knew
of the fine kit given him by his father, and how he had handed
it on to a poor and very shabby knight.

Nothing is known of the sympathies of Clare's family during
those years, and whether any of the seven knights were with
the crusading armies which busily sacked Constantinople instead
of trying to free the Holy Places. Local excitement was aroused
in 1204 when the Assisans elected Giraldo di Gilberto as
podestà, regardless of the fact that he was an excommunicated
heretic: and as a show of independence they decided to keep
him in office notwithstanding a protest by the Pope. This in-
furiated Innocent who laid the city under an interdict, whereupon the Assisans reconsidered the matter, got rid of the heretic,
elected a new podestà, and fifty of the most important citizens
did homage to the papal rector of the duchy of Spoleto. The
interdict was raised, but Innocent passed Assisi by when he was
next travelling in the district. An interesting detail of the quarrel
is that the precocious Frederick II sent the Assisans a message
of benevolent encouragement, a sign that local politics were
watched with interest.

Something else, however, was happening which began to capture the interest in Assisi where everyone knew everyone else.

Pietro Bernardone the upright and successful cloth merchant was a familiar figure, respected by all, and indeed he was described by his contemporaries as "reipublicae benefactor et provisor." His son was a "king of the revels," conspicuous for his princely extravagance and also for his courtesy to everyone, and there must have been plenty of gossip when having set out as a would-be warrior he suddenly returned home from Spoleto. Soon there was much more to gossip about, for young Francis appeared completely changed and was behaving in the maddest fashion. His squandering had taken a new line; he was going about dressed like a beggar, pursued by jeers and stones, and someone in Monaldo's household may easily have seen a simpleton fling his cloak on the ground for Francis the beggar to walk on. The whole of Assisi was roused when Messer Pietro sued his son in the Bishop's court for the restitution of his stolen goods, and the son had answered him by throwing not only the money, but all his clothes at his father's feet. No doubt there was considerable sympathy for Pietro when he left the court "full of anger and sorrow for he greatly loved him."

Was Clare's imagination first touched when she heard of the naked, rich young man wrapped in the Bishop's cloak, and then going out penniless into the world to start a new life?

Other news followed, for the young madman was constantly met begging for stones to help with the restoration of country chapels. In later life Clare recalled one particular scene so vividly that one feels the impression it had made in her young, enthusiastic mind. In her Testament she thanks God for the blessings which reached her both before and after her conversion "through his beloved servant our Father Francis. Quite soon after his conversion before he had any disciples or friends, he prophesied concerning us what God in due time brought to pass. It was when the man of God was restoring San Damiano,

the church in which, completely entranced by divine consolation, he had been impelled to leave the world and worldly things,
enlightened by the Holy Spirit in a transport of joy he leaped
on to a wall, and from it addressed some peasant folk who were
standing near, speaking in a high tone and in the French tongue,
'Come and help me in the work on this convent, for here there
will dwell devout women, and our heavenly Father shall be
glorified throughout the length and breadth of His Church by
the sweet odour of their conversation.'"

Another great stir was made among the Assisans when Bernardo di Quintavalle gave away all his possessions and became
a beggar like Francis for love of Christ. And this first follower
of Francis is described as "one of the richest, wisest and most
noble citizens of Assisi." Many rich and powerful people would
soon be following this example. The next recruit was Pietro
Catani, a canon of the cathedral, who chose to leave a position
of established authority; Sylvester, a priest, and Giles, a peasant,
followed, and not long afterwards Favorone's kinsman Rufino
joined the new group. Giles spoke for thousands when he exclaimed, "Brother Francis, I want to be with you for love of
God." Francis had drawn a good deal closer to the palace in the
cathedral piazza, but no one in that house can have dreamed
of the impending threat to the family's ambition, and that it
would come through the eldest daughter.

By that time Clare was sixteen, and a beauty: her "face was
oval, her forehead spacious, her colour dazzling, and her eye-
brows and hair very fair. A celestial smile played in her eyes
and round her mouth, her nose was well fashioned and slightly
aquiline; of good stature she inclined to stoutness, but nowise
in excess." That was how her contemporaries described her.
She charmed all with her looks and with her kindness, for
everyone in trouble knew that this radiant girl would always
help them if she could; in this she was following her mother's
teaching and example, and probably the men of the family did
not mind her reputation for charity. None suspected the hair-

shirt which she wore beneath her fine clothes. Wherever she passed, people turned to look at her, and all wondered whom she would marry. Knowing what an asset they held, her family were determined she should make a "magnificent marriage to some great and powerful lord of her own rank." There was no reason for delay; but Clare strenuously opposed any such plans. She was born to love with the whole strength of her being, but when repeatedly pressed to make up her mind, "she gave an evasive answer and committed her virginity to God."

Messer Ranieri di Bernardo, who was her cousin and a witness in the cause of her canonization, declared "since Clare was beautiful the question of her marriage was discussed, and many of her relations pressed her to marry, but she would in no wise consent; and having myself pressed this on her repeatedly she would not allow the matter to be mentioned." Another neighbour, Pietro di Damiano, adds, "she would in no wise be persuaded."

In afteryears successive popes were to find themselves no match for Clare's tenacity when once she was convinced of the rightness of her cause.

It is difficult to establish exactly at what moment Clare came into personal contact with Francis; we have to bear in mind the double story of the girl in the palace and the doings of the new fraternity.

In 1210, having received a first permission from the Pope for their way of life, the brothers were wandering through the countryside preaching, and everywhere the listeners were struck by their light-heartedness. When asked who they were the brothers' answer was, "We are men of Assisi who live a life of penance." Those were the days when Frederick's rival, Otto IV, passed down the valley of Spoleto on his way to Rome where he hoped to be crowned. Francis felt entitled to send him a warning of the evanescence of all earthly dignity: within two years Otto had to hurry back to Germany in a vain attempt to save his crown; and Frederick was elected German emperor. Francis' warning would then have been remembered and quoted.

In Assisi itself the tide of mocking insults had ebbed; and Francis was being invited to preach in San Giorgio, where he had been to school, and in the cathedral. Some years later Thomas of Spalato described that preaching; "When I was a student in Bologna I saw Francis preach in the market place where nearly all the citizens were gathered . . . the whole of his discourse was to assuage enmities and to make for peace. His habit was dirty, his appearance insignificant, his face not handsome, but God gave such power to his word that many families between whom were old feuds and spilled blood were induced to make peace. All felt such devotion and reverence for him that men and women precipitated themselves upon him and tried to tear off bits of his habit, or even to touch its hem." Such scenes were probably often repeated. Other listeners reported: "He began to preach wonderfully of despising the world, and of holy penance and voluntary poverty, and for the desire for the kingdom of God, and the self-stripping of Christ in His Passion," while again others declared, "He seemed to those who beheld him as a man from another world, whose heart was set on Heaven, and his face turned upwards towards it seeking to draw others upwards with him." Even in reading the words we feel something of what that fascination must have been.

Francis once said, "What are the servants of God but His singers whose duty it is to lift up the hearts of men and women and move them to spiritual joy?" Unconsciously he had described himself, and the secret of his irresistible charm, for joy is the greatest gift one man can give to another. The hearers felt how that preacher saw each person, each creature as a unique creation, a child of God, and therefore a being worthy of respect, courtesy, and charity. Crowds flocked to see the former king of the revels, now penniless and ragged and happy; they hung on the words that tumbled over each other in his wonderful voice, and they knew that he and his brothers practised what they preached. They recognized that these men had every right to preach the beauty of poverty since they lived it, every right to preach charity since their chief care was for the worst cases among the lepers, every right to cry "peace" for they were at peace with all men "for the love of God."

"Good people, God give you peace" was their greeting to everyone, a greeting Francis claimed to have been revealed to him by God. Peace was the gift of Christ which Christians held in trust in an age of strife. In Assisi acute rivalry existed between the two classes of the Majores and Minores, but when Francis chose the name of Minores, the Lesser Brothers, for himself and his companions it was not out of any conventional humility, but because the way shown by Christ was to be "humble and subject to all." The Three Companions could later report, "Therefore all Assisi wept tears of compassion over the Passion of Christ, and nobles and plebeians, clerics and lay-folk threw aside the thought of passing things to walk in the way shown them." Through the influence of Francis and his fraternity the treaty of civic peace which had been drafted in 1203 was solemnly ratified in November, 1210.

All this gives us an idea of the place Francis had taken in Clare's life even before she met him: each knew the other by sight and by repute, and surely Rufino must have acted as a link. Of course, Clare wanted to know him personally, and Francis was equally anxious to meet her for Celano tells us, "He, God's huntsman, was minded to snatch this noble booty from the world and to offer it to his Master. And so he visited her and many times she visited him, coming forth from her home in secret with an intimate female friend."

This friend was her kinswoman, Bona Guelfuccio, who recorded how together they sought out Francis at the Porziun-cula "secretly so that no one should see her," which incidentally cannot have been too easy, and that Clare listened to him "with the utmost fervour whenever he spoke of the love of Jesus." It was his favorite subject and "always Francis was occupied with Jesus: Jesus he carried in his heart, Jesus in his mouth,

Jesus in his eyes, Jesus in his hands, Jesus in all his members."
Often he forgot where he was and what he was doing at the
thought of Jesus, "and with such glowing love was he moved
towards Jesus Christ, yea, and with such intimate love did his
Beloved repay this, that it seemed to the servant of God himself that he felt his Saviour almost continually before his eyes."

Everything spoke to Francis of his Beloved; Christ the
Corner-stone, Christ the Lamb of God, Christ the Light of
the world, Christ the Water slaking all thirst, Christ the Bread
and Wine of life, Christ the Vine, Christ the Way. He could
hardly bear to put out a candle or see bread carelessly wasted
or water polluted, all for love of Christ. He wanted a plot of
land set aside for the cultivation "of our brothers the flowers
so that all who see them shall remember the eternal Sweetness."
Christ, the creating Word, was in all creatures and shone in
all beauty, Christ the Pilgrim met him in every stranger, Christ
the Crucified in every sufferer, the Risen Christ in all life.
Francis must have talked to Clare and Bona very much in the
spirit of the prayer attributed to him, "I beseech Thee, O Lord,
that the fiery and sweet strength of Thy love may absorb my
soul from all things under Heaven, and may I die for love
of Thy love, even as Thou didst die for love of my love."

All the Gospel for Francis was glad tidings of love personified
in Jesus, and with what insistence he must have repeated to
those two the passages that had decided his own and his brothers'
vocations. He showed them how the Franciscan life was "to
observe the Gospel of Our Lord Jesus Christ owning nothing
and in chastity." It was Clare's hitherto half-conscious ideal
being put before her as a practical reality; and "enlightened by
the flaming torch of his speech, she caught, as it were, a glimpse
of the Beatific Vision. Forthwith the things of the world seemed
to her as dung, and dreading the allurements of the flesh, she
resolved to lay aside all thought of earthly marriage, and to do
her utmost to render herself worthy of the espousals of the

heavenly King, and henceforward she regarded Blessed Francis as, after God, the charioteer of her soul."

Clare's mind was made up, and she took her decision with the clear sight and single-mindedness of youth. How many martyrs were under twenty? Throughout her life she saw the wonders of God opening on earth to those men and women "who have the courage to leave on one side the goods of this world and its vanities." Courage was one of her chief characteristics.

In the bull of canonization Alexander IV says that, after the meeting with Francis, Clare sold her possessions and distributed the proceeds among the poor. She must have done it very cleverly, for even then it aroused no suspicion in her family: perhaps they thought it wiser to humour what they hoped was a passing whim. Bona Guelfuccio later related how Clare had once sent her to "the brothers who were working at Santa Maria degli Angeli in order that they should buy some meat." Perhaps someone was ill; anyhow this shows the same practical solicitude for other people that distinguished her as abbess of her own community.

A legend that she also begged in the streets seems quite incredible, for that could not have gone unobserved, unless we accept the explanation that an angel saved her from recognition. Otherwise her relations would certainly have risen in wrath against such behaviour.

One thing is certain and that is that Bishop Guido must have known what was preparing both in Francis' and Clare's minds, otherwise Francis would never have dared to act as he did. The legend of the Three Companions insists that he did nothing without the Bishop's permission and consent, which is entirely in keeping with his whole attitude towards the clergy. Bishop Guido was the proved father and friend of Francis and the Fraternity, and he must have been consulted about the very delicate matter of Clare's vocation.

She had reached the point when waiting was intolerable, and Celano tells us that "as it drew near to Palm Sunday the girl Clare came to Francis in ardent expectation desiring to know how and when her conversion could be finally accomplished; and he commanded her that, dressed in her habitual clothes she should go as usual to receive the blessed palm together with all the faithful. In the following night she would set out from her family home, and turn from all the joys of the world to weep for the Passion of Christ. When therefore it came to be Palm Sunday, she appeared among the women resplendent for the joy that shone in her, and merrily she entered the church with her companions. There it befell her according to God's providence for when the moment came for all to approach the altar and receive the blessed olive Clare was held back by shyness. Seeing this the Bishop came down the steps to where she was and put the palm in her hand." This gesture illuminates both him and Clare; and they must have felt how wonderfully appropriate the Palm Sunday liturgy was for what only they knew to be her marriage day. She was setting out with Christ, and, as the processional hymn echoed round the church, each verse must have lifted Clare's heart in a wave of worshipping love. "Thy praise in heaven the host angelic sings, on earth mankind and all created things, glory and praise to Thee Redeemer blest, Rex bone, Rex clemens cui bona cuncta placent, Hosanna in excelsis." Only the Bishop could understand her moment of shyness before what was so tremendous, and he placed the olive blessed to strengthen and defend in her hand, as the sacred sign of divine grace confirming her vocation.

Celano continues the story, "In the following night having prepared herself to obey the saint's command, she fled from her father's home with one trusted companion, and, not wishing to leave by the chief door, with miraculous strength she opened a side door heavily shut and barred with stones and wooden beams. Thus she left her family, home, and city, and with great fervour went to Santa Maria degli Angeli where the friars were keeping watch and singing the divine praises."

Other accounts supply some supplementary details. Her companion was Pacifica Guelfuccio, for Bona was away in Rome; and the Paschal moon was already full shining on the fruit trees in flower as the two hurried down the mile and a half to where Francis, Rufino, and Filippo were waiting with lighted torches. Singing the *Veni Creator Spiritus* they went into the chapel where the other Knights of Francis' Round Table were waiting, and Clare knelt before the altar and made her profession, "I want only Jesus Christ, and to live by the Gospel owning nothing and in chastity." To seal this vow Francis cut off her long fair hair, her fine clothes were taken off, and he gave her the rough habit of poverty and covered her head with the white veil of chastity and the coarse black one of penance. Clare had listened to the voice bidding her leave her people and her father's house: in the Porziuncula she met the Bridegroom who had chosen her. All present knew that the little ancient chapel had ever been a place of visions, where the presence of our Lady was often seen, and angels could be heard singing her praises and those of Christ. It was the perfect place for the consecration of Clare, and for the birth of the second Franciscan Order; and in the Porziuncula that scene is still alive, and the vibrations of it have never died. Immediately after the ceremony Francis took her to the Benedictine monastery at Bastia.

When Clare's flight was discovered the furious consternation of her family knew no bounds. They were not bad people, nor necessarily irreligious, but their values were of this world, and like Pietro Bernardone they were those left behind who could not keep up with the pace of saints. The scandal was enormous; and everyone said exactly what they would say to-day were the circumstances repeated. Except to the few who could understand, Francis, Clare, and all concerned appeared headstrong, selfish, and unscrupulous. It is curious that in the ensuing hubbub there is no mention of Favorone, only of Monaldo, and though there is no positive proof, this suggests that Clare's father was dead.

As soon as her whereabouts were known the men of the family besieged the convent, "their hearts torn, and greatly disapproving of what she had done, and what she meant to do." From their own point of view they were justified; they would not allow that Clare at eighteen had the right to choose something which they considered preposterous, and they tried persuasion, threats, and every means to get her back, "and make her renounce this dishonour which is bringing shame on our family, and has no equal in the whole neighbourhood."

Clare had to defend herself from being dragged away by force, and she clung to the altar in the chapel; there at least no one could touch her without committing sacrilege. At last to convince her relations that nothing would move or change her she uncovered her shorn head; after that Monaldo and his followers knew they were beaten and turned away.

The nuns may have been shaken by these scenes disturbing their Holy Week; anyhow Clare was removed to another Benedictine convent of Sant' Angelo in Panso, really Sant' Angelo della Pace, on the slopes of Monte Subasio. Francis, Bernard, and Philip went with her, and as they walked through the budding woods with the ground covered with spring flowers, something very like the Canticle of the Sun must have been on their lips, for there was never a moment when Francis was not praising God for some gift. Praise, preferably in song, was the life of the Fraternity. It would have been the first lesson he would have wished to inculcate into the Second Order!

Whether that walk took place by sun or torchlight, it may quite well have been an occasion for Francis' words: "In the morning when the sun rises, all men should praise God who created it for our use, for by it all things are made visible. Then in the evening we must praise God for Brother Fire who gives light to our eyes in the darkness. For we are all like the blind, but God gives us light by these two brothers."

Within a few days of Clare's arrival at Panso, she was joined by her younger sister Agnes, another runaway into the arms of Christ and Poverty; and their relations stormed with increased fury, as indeed was only natural. It was intolerable that these girls should throw away all their chances of advancing the family fortunes, and only bring shame on their clan by flinging themselves into a new-fangled movement and so-called fraternity with no decent standing, and associated with the lowest social class. If Clare and Agnes insisted on taking the veil, they could do so in a respectable Benedictine community of which in due course Clare could become abbess. It was bad enough that Rufino should join a company of beggars, but this was a thousand times worse, and the family pride and ambition were cut to the quick.

Again the men headed by Monaldo set out hot-foot and furious to fetch Agnes home. They entered the courtyard of Panso coldly demanding to see her, coldly and roughly asked her what she thought she was doing, adding a command to go with them. Agnes answered that she would never leave Clare. They dragged her to the gate while she screamed for help, "Christ my Lord, save me." Clare fell on her knees while the peasants came running up at the sound of the tumult. By this time Agnes was lying on the ground, hardly conscious, her clothes torn; but when one of the men tried to lift her to her feet, that fifteen-year-old girl proved to be so heavy that no one could move her. The men had to give it up; they turned away, and Clare knew the battle was over.

Francis' desire had been "that the dust of worldliness should not dim the mirror of Clare's immaculate spirit . . . and for this reason he hastened to draw her away from the darkness of the world." The first great step had been taken, and following him Clare, and now Agnes, had "abandoned the world," and started on a new life.

III

San Damiano

> *After her shall virgins be brought to*
> *the King . . . they shall be brought*
> *with gladness and rejoicing.*
> (Psalm XLIV, Office of St. Clare)

THE Benedictines were staunch friends of Francis: the abbot
of San Benedetto on Monte Subasio had given him the Porziuncula with the one condition that the chapel should always be
considered the mother church of the Fraternity, so Francis had
had that reason too for wishing Clare's consecration to take
place there. He had also received from the abbot the tiny
mountain chapel known as the Carceri which was used by the
Subasio shepherds and became one of his favourite and earliest
hermitages.

It was now the turn of the Benedictine Dames; and they
sheltered Clare and Agnes and gave them their first experience
of the religious life. The weeks spent among them must have
been of immense spiritual and practical help to the girls who,
however full of the enthusiasm of love of God, had still to
learn how a community was ordered.

From Francis' first meeting with Clare he had almost certainly
connected her with San Damiano, which for him must have
been as blessed a place as the Porziuncula, and where each sight
of the crucifix hanging from the vault brought back to him

the sound of our Lord's own voice, "Francis go, and repair my church." As usual he turned to the Bishop for help and advice: the priest who had been in charge of San Damiano was dead, the chapel was standing empty, and even materially Francis' work of restoration to the building had given him some sort of claim on it, had he ever wished to claim anything! Anyhow the Bishop put it at his disposal for the Sisters who were soon joined by Pacifica Guelfuccio, Benvenuta, Filippa di Leonardo Gisleri, and Cristiana di Bernardo da Suppo. San Damiano had become a magnet; and one after another the richest families of Assisi saw their daughters cast away all worldly advantages to follow Clare. In her own words: "Thus by the will of God, and our blessed father Francis, we came to dwell in the church of San Damiano, where soon the Lord, in His mercy and grace multiplied us in order that what had been foretold by His holy one, should be fulfilled; for we had sojourned in another place, but only for a short time."

At first Francis gave them a very simple rule, and it was only after a couple of years or so that Clare reluctantly took office as abbess, promising him obedience. Later she referred to this primitive rule saying: "Our blessed father moved by pity gave us a written form of life in this way"; and she incorporated at least a fragment of it in her own rule. In a letter to Blessed Agnes of Prague, Gregory IX described it as a "draught of milk"; but it was sufficient for the moment, and for Clare its most precious clause was that in which Francis promised that he and his brothers would always provide for the spiritual and material needs of the Sisters. Thus he ackowledged the union of the two Franciscan families, and it always remained Clare's ideal.

To Francis and Clare, from the beginning and always, Poverty was the key-note of their vocation, and Celano relates: "Wishing her order to bear the name of Poverty, Clare made a petition to Pope Innocent III of holy memory begging for this privilege, and he was greatly gladdened at the fervour of this virgin, and said that no one had ever asked the Holy See for such a singular privilege. And in order that no one should scorn this concession, he wrote the first letter with his own hand." This statement has been questioned: there is no record of such a document in the Vatican archives, the first surviving papal letter about the Poor Ladies being the Bull *Litterae Tuae* of Honorius III, written to Cardinal Ugolino in 1218, granting San Damiano exemption from episcopal control. Yet, would Celano have been mistaken about something so important? Clare herself in her Testament — if this is accepted as genuine — repeats that Innocent III, "in whose pontificate we began," granted her the privilege of poverty. That was in 1215 or 1216, and for the rest of her life Clare took her stand upon it.

During those first years the community was not officially enclosed; and the Sisters seem to have gone out on works of charity. Certainly Celano says that St. Clare never left San Damiano during her forty-two years of religious life, but even this statement does not disprove the story of her visit to the Porziuncula which is first told in the *Actus* and *Fioretti*, but not by Celano. It is true that his life of St. Clare is the older by some seventy years, but it is quite likely that the story of this episode may have been among the writings of the first companions of St. Francis which Brother Leo left at San Damiano. The publication of these stories depended largely on the fluctuating opinions in the Order, and the dependence of the Poor Ladies on the Friars Minor quickly became a burning question in which this particular episode was of great importance.

At any rate during the first years of Clare's life in San Damiano there was no reason of enclosure to prevent her absenting herself for a few hours; and during those early spring days of the Fraternity, before the formality of organisation had become necessary, why should Clare not have expressed the wish that the Brothers and Sisters should share a meal as a symbol of their joint vocation in Christ? Francis emphasized the sacramental aspect of the meeting by deciding that it should take place at Santa Maria degli Angeli, the place which of all others held a sacramental meaning in the life of the Fraternity. Celano tells that, soon after the Brothers arrived there, a devout man had a vision of a multitude kneeling round the chapel and everyone was blind. Loudly and pitiably with clasped hands and upturned eyes they besought God for sight; suddenly a wonderful radiance shone from the sky, and all eyes were opened. Some people and places are chosen by God to bring light to others: Francis, Clare, and the Porziuncula are among them.

This is how the story is told in the *Fioretti*:

When Saint Francis was in Assisi he often visited Saint Clare giving her holy counsel. She greatly desired once to eat with him; but though she begged this of him many times he would never grant her this consolation. Seeing this desire of Saint Clare, Saint Francis' companions said to him: "Father, it seems to us that such strictness is not in accord with divine charity, and that thou should'st deny to Sister Clare, so holy a virgin, beloved of God this small favour of eating with thee, all the more since it was through thy preaching that she abandoned riches and the pomp of the world. Is it not true that if she asked of thee a greater favour than this is thou would'st have to grant it to her who is thy spiritual plant?" Then Saint Francis answered: "Does it seem to you that I ought to satisfy her request?" And the companions answered: "Yes Father; it is just that thou should'st give her this consolation."

Then Saint Francis said: "As it appears thus to you, so it appears to me: and in order that she may be the more consoled, I wish this meal to take place at Santa Maria degli Angeli, for she has long been shut up in San Damiano, and it will do her good to see Santa Maria once again, the place where she was shorn and made the bride of Jesus Christ; and there we will eat together in the name of God."

When the appointed day came, Saint Clare set out from the monastery with another sister and accompanied by the companions of Saint Francis they came to Santa Maria degli Angeli. When she had devoutly saluted the Blessed Virgin Mary before that altar where she had been shorn and had received the veil, the brothers took her to see all the place until it came to the hour for dinner. Meanwhile Saint Francis had the table set upon the bare ground even as was his custom to do. When it was dinner time Saint Francis and Saint Clare with one of his companions and with her companion sat down, and then all the other companions sat down too at the table with great humility. And with the first course Saint Francis began to speak of God so sweetly, so sublimely, so wonderfully that the abundance of divine grace descended upon them, and they were all rapt in God. And while they all remained thus in ecstasy with eyes and hands lifted up to Heaven the people of Assisi and Bettona and the surrounding countryside saw that the church at Santa Maria itself and the whole place and the wood all round it were burning fiercely, and the blaze was so great that it enveloped the church and the place and the wood. Then the people of Assisi rushed down in haste to quench the fire fearing that all would be burned. But when they reached the spot and found no fire, they went in and found Saint Francis and Saint Clare and the whole company rapt in God in the ecstasy of contemplation even while they sat round that humble board. Then they understood that that what they had seen was spiritual and not material fire, which God had allowed to appear miraculously in order to make manifest that fire of divine love which burned in the souls of those holy friars and sisters; and these people went home with their hearts filled with great consolation and holy edification. After a long time when Saint Francis and Saint Clare and their companions came to themselves they were so comforted with spiritual food that they cared little for any bodily nourishment.

Then when that blessed meal was ended, Saint Clare, worthily accompanied, returned to San Damiano; and when the other sisters saw her they were full of joy for they had feared that Saint Francis might have sent her to direct some other monastery as he had already sent her blessed sister Agnes to rule the monastery of Monticelli at Florence. Saint Francis had already said several times to Saint Clare: "Hold thyself ready in case it might be necessary for me to send you to another place": and she, the daughter of holy obedience had answered: "Father, I am always ready to go wherever you may send me." Therefore the sisters were very glad to see her back again; and ever after Saint Clare remained with great consolation in her heart. To the glory of Christ. Amen.

I cannot see why the historical foundation of this episode should be categorically denied, though the chief difficulty lies in the implied date of the visit. Agnes went to Florence in 1221, and three years earlier Cardinal Ugolino had compiled the rule for San Damiano which to a certain extent did enclose the nuns. This has to be borne in mind, though it is not conclusive. Psychologically the date rather justifies the story, for, after Francis' return from the East with the increasing pressure of difficulties within the Fraternity, both he and Clare, and she especially, must have wished to express the deep spiritual union between the First and Second Orders. As regards the meeting in itself, it is but one episode in lives full of wonders surpassing ordinary experience. Light plays a great part in the story of these lives; Francis was often seen surrounded by brilliant light, the sky over La Verna was aglow during the night of the Stigmata, often Clare's Sisters saw her in a radiance with light round her head. Why should it have been impossible to God to open the eyes of those folk in Assisi to a light which was beyond that of the sun, and which was the fire of divine love in elected souls?

It has often been said that Clare loved Francis: of course she did; had he not kindled in her soul a twin flame of the love of God from that burning in his own, each flame adding something to the other? On this subject Sabatier wrote: "It is possible to meet souls . . . who are so pure, so little of this world that with one step they enter into the holy of holies, and once there, the thought of any other union would not be so much a fall as an impossibility. Such was the love of Saint Francis and Saint Clare."

There was another aspect of Francis' attitude to Clare, for it was his task to guide the Sisters in the path of evangelical perfection. He directed them in everything, and Celano stresses how strictly he insisted that the visiting friars should behave with the greatest circumspection. Brother Stephen reported: "Brother Francis would not suffer any woman to show him familiarity; blessed Clare was the only one for whom he seemed to have affection, but he never presumed to call even her by name and always spoke of her as "Christian woman." He was her spiritual director and in charge of her monastery, but he never ordered any other monastery to be founded, and when he heard that these were established and that the nuns were called Sisters, he was troubled and said: "The Lord has delivered us from wives, and now the devil has given us sisters." The Lord Ugolino of Ostia who was the Cardinal Protector of the Friars Minor and cherished these Sisters commended them to St. Francis saying: "Brother, I commend these ladies to you," whereas the blessed man smiled and said, "Holy Father, let them no longer be called Sorores Minores, but as you call them Dominae."

Thus Clare and her Sisters acquired the name of Poor Ladies of San Damiano; in this title there is still an echo of Knights of the Round Table.

Francis explained his attitude still more definitely in the following parable: he always insisted that only friars of proved discretion should direct the Sisters: when one day he was reproached for not having gone to them himself, he declared that his affection was unchanged, but that in all things he wished to be an example, and he went on to tell of a king who sent two messengers to his promised bride. The first returned and only told of his mission; the second expatiated at length on the beauty of the queen. The king called back the first messenger and asked, "What of the queen? You have told me nothing about her." "Sire, she listened to me in silence and with great attention." "But what of her beauty?" "Sire, that is for you to judge of; my task was to deliver your message." And Francis commented: "If earthly kings can demand such an attitude from their servants, what can Christ not ask from his servants the Little Brothers when they carry His words to His brides."

Celano describes Clare as "noble by birth, but still more noble by grace, and she was of angelic purity. Though still young, she was mature before her time, fervent in the service of God, endowed with rare prudence and deepest humility, she was one of those great souls whom the human tongue cannot worthily praise."

These extraordinarily balanced qualities were all focused in the following of Christ with Francis along the path of poverty, obedience, and simplicity. She loved poverty as ardently as he did, and with the same vision, "for Poverty was Christ's faithful companion from his birth in a stable to His death and burial. . . . O, who would not love Lady Poverty above all things; of Thee, O Jesus, I ask to be signed with this privilege, I long to be enriched with this treasure, I beseech of Thee, O most poor Jesus, that for Thy sake it may always be the mark of me and mine to possess nothing of our own under the sun." Clare fully shared Francis' feeling in this prayer, and had she but known it the struggle to maintain this poverty was to last till her death.

"He has never perfectly renounced the world who keeps hidden in his heart the treasure of his own will," taught Francis who aspired to share in the Christ-life by sharing in the perfect obedience of our Lord who came not to do His own will, but the will of His Father. It is far harder to renounce self-will than possessions. Francis pursued obedience as others pursue power, and with untiring ingenuity in finding the means of expressing it in action. The Three Companions tell how the Brothers placed themselves in the service of perfect obedience; as soon as an order was given they hastened to obey, not questioning whether it were just or unjust, accepting it as the will of God "and therefore it was sweet to them. The brothers in charity of spirit obey and serve each other, and this is the true obedience of Jesus Christ." Francis went still further, for he said: "Holy obedience makes a man subject to all the men in the world, and not to men alone, but also to all beasts and wild animals so that they may do with him whatsoever they will in so far as it may be granted to them from above by the Lord." This goes far beyond the ordinary human limits, but it was the ideal inculcated by Francis.

The passion for obedience had, as its twin, unbounded trust in God, and in men as the children of God; and all this was as active in Clare as it was in Francis, and formed the foundation of the Sisters' life in San Damiano.

Clare's first recorded miracle was one of trust. They had been there for about two years, dependent on alms for their daily bread and for every necessity; therefore trust was of every day and every hour. There was no oil in the house, and that means much to Italians. Brother Bencivenga prepared to set out and beg; Clare washed out the flask and put it ready for him to take from the window ledge of the refectory. He found it full of oil, and wondered why he had been unnecessarily summoned.

In Francis and in Clare poverty and obedience were warmed with charity and humility, insisted on through never failing example. "Because he was the most humble of all, he was full of consideration for other men, and knew how to adapt himself to each. Among saints he was holier than they, among sinners as one of themselves; he showed himself as subject to all."

There is the famous story of Masseo who, after one of Francis' extraordinarily successful sermons, asked him: "I wonder why the whole world runs after thee more than others, and all men want to see and hear and obey thee? Thou art not fair of body, thou art not deeply learned, thou art not of noble birth; why does the whole world run after thee?"

When St. Francis heard this, he rejoiced in his soul, and turned his eyes to heaven, and stood a long time thus with soul lifted up to God, and when he came to himself, he knelt down and gave thanks and praise to God and turned to Brother Masseo and said with great spiritual power:

You wish to know why this happens to me. I know it from the all-seeing God who sees the good and bad in all the earth. His most holy eyes have nowhere seen a greater, a more miserable, poorer sinner than I. Because in the whole world He found no more wretched being to do the wonderful work He wishes done, therefore He has chosen me, so as to put to shame the noble, and the great, strength and beauty and worldly wisdom, that all may know that power and virtue come from Him alone and not from any creature, and that none can exalt themselves before His Face.

Such humility inevitably leads to a certain kind of fear; and a very illuminating story is told of a much esteemed Brother who left the Fraternity. His companions asked Francis why it had happened, and he replied: "I want to read something, and to ask myself some questions which I will answer; let no one speak to me till I have done." Then he repeated the words, "Chastity, Abstinence, Poverty" several times, asking himself after each, "Do you know that?" And he answered: "Yes, I know that." Finally he repeated the word "Fear. Do you know that? No." Again he cried out, "Fear, fear. Do you know that? NO. Fear, fear, fear," he repeated, and at last whispered, "Yes, I know fear," adding, "it is useless for a man to seek all the virtues and leave out fear; yet few have it and therefore it is hard to teach them. That good brother fell and left the order because he had no fear."

It was fear of his own self-will which, very early in their vocation, made Francis defer the decision concerning his own way of life to Clare and Sylvester. He was immensely attracted to the life of prayer, "the life of angels," he called it, withdrawn from the world in some remote hermitage, but he distrusted his own judgement. So he sent Masseo to the other two, begging for their prayer and advice. When Masseo returned Francis greeted him as a messenger of God, washing his feet and serving him while he ate. Then they went into the wood, and Francis knelt with his arms outstretched crosswise while Masseo told him that independently of each other, after long prayer, Clare and Sylvester had reached the same conclusion that his mission was to preach the Gospel for the salvation of souls.

"Then let us go forth in the name of God," was his unhesitating answer, and he accepted the decision as final.

All the episodes of Francis' life, all his teaching are intensely relevant to the history of Clare; he and she, San Damiano and the Porziuncula, his companions and the Poor Ladies, cannot be separated. Francis' influence was paramount in the formation of the Sisters, and "he lived as though he were alone in the world with God," which Clare too was fast learning to do. Her ideal of an abbess was the same as his of a minister. "Superiors," in the usual sense, there could never be in a Franciscan family, and Francis' own wish was to be the servant of all. His words are very clear; "Let no one ask from another more than he is himself ready to give to God"; and to a minister he said, "Let there be no brother in the world who if he has sinned, no matter how grievously, having seen thy face shall not go away without the assurance of thy mercy. And if he seeks not mercy, ask him if he desires it, and if he should appear before thee a thousand times, love him more than me to the end thou mayest draw him to the Lord . . . those who are set over others must never pride themselves on their office more than if they were set to wash their brothers' feet; woe to any religious who being in a place of authority does not wish to give it up; blessed the superior who in the midst of his subjects comports himself as though they were his masters."

The fruit borne by Francis' teaching and example is clear from the beginning of Clare's religious life. When the lay Sisters returned from their errands Clare always washed their feet herself, and served them in the refectory; and there is another echo of Francis in her injunction that whenever on these errands they happened to see a tree in leaf or flowers, always they were to praise God for His creatures.

When the begging Brothers brought back whole loaves she would only exclaim that the offerings were too generous, "and she did this because she preferred to receive the alms of broken loaves rather than whole ones."

From the first Clare was as unremittingly harsh to herself as Francis. Celano describes her habit as consisting of one tunic of cheap, common, harsh cloth with a very common cloak giving little warmth, an equally common black veil and bare feet. This in the cold and on the stone floors of Assisi! She had two hair-shirts on which she rang the changes, one of boar's hide, the other of knotted horsehair: she slept on vine twigs with a stone as her pillow, perhaps varied by a log: three days a week she ate and drank nothing, and the community kept two Lents in the year which for Clare meant bread and water. Only on Sundays she took a "little wine out of reverence for Holy Communion." No wonder that Francis and the Bishop went together to San Damiano and ordered her by holy obedience to eat at least one and a half ounces of bread a day; no wonder that after a few years she became a chronic invalid, and had to obey Francis' command to sleep on a mattress and a straw-stuffed pillow. There is, however, a great deal to wonder at, that this regime never made her harsh to others: on the contrary the witnesses in the cause of canonization emphasize her great sympathy and compassion, her unfailing gentleness and kindness. It was she who went round to see if anyone were in trouble, who would cover up any sick Sister with warm blankets, who thought of everyone's physical, as well as spiritual, well-being. Like Francis she was always insistent on the care of the sick — when the sick person was not herself.

Sister Beatrice said of Clare: "Her sanctity was in her chastity, her humility, her patience and kindness. When she issued an order, it was with great humility and fear, and often she hastened to do herself what she commanded to others; she made herself the last of all." Here we have Francis' ideal personified; and in her own later rule, Clare enjoins it on every abbess of a community of Poor Ladies. She learnt the lessons of Francis from putting them into practice through forty-two years.

By 1215 the Poor Ladies were recognized as a religious community; and that year saw Francis in Rome for the Fourth Lateran Council. The Pope approved the new orders of Friars, and made a stirring appeal for reform, for a new life in Christ of every believer, and for the Crusade. He quoted the pitiful and heroic venture of the Children's Crusade, which indeed was bound to touch all hearts and bring shame on many.

One result of Innocent's appeal was Francis' "Letter to All Christians," burning with longing to reach the unknown multitudes, imploring them, mostly in the words of the Gospel, to love God and to follow Christ, to learn to know the sweetness of the Lord, and to love light, and not darkness.

He knew that God was not asking everyone to leave their homes and follow him like the First Companions and Clare; yet multitudes of those not called to the fullness of poverty still in Giles' words "wanted to be with him for love of Christ," and these Francis would not turn away. From them he demanded absolutely a right and unselfish use of all God's gifts, free from exploitation, and he called every Christian to a new sense of responsibility, a new respect for the values of justice and charity.

It was a glorious opening out, enabling those living in the world under his motto of *Pax et Bonum* to share in the life of their elder brothers the Friars, and their Sisters the Poor Ladies. Among the first to join this outer circle of followers was the rich Roman lady Jacopa dei Settesoli who became such a friend to the Fraternity that Francis nicknamed her "Brother Jacopa." She carried out his ideal of life in the world as thoroughly as Clare did in the cloister; the two must have known each other well. Thus arose the Order of Penance later known as the Third Order of St. Francis: the crumbs of humanity were always precious to Francis as well as the loaves.

There is no better symbol of the union of the First, Second, and Third Orders than the badge of the Fraternity in which the arm of Christ is crossed with that of Francis. It is the emblem of the fullest, most intimate union of the crucified Christ with the Christian, and therefore of the union in Christ of all who wish to follow Him.

Clare, of course, knew of this widening out of the Franciscan family; and first by prayer, and also in other ways she must have contributed to its increase. Her fame had naturally spread beyond Assisi, and Celano tells how women came to her from all sides: and "because of her example the unmarried determined to preserve their virginity, the married to live more chastely, those who are noble and illustrious learned to despise grand palaces and build humble monasteries wherein they consider it a great honour and glory to live for love of Christ. Many living in the married state separate by mutual consent, the men betaking themselves to hermitages, the women to monasteries. Mothers encourage their daughters, and daughters their mothers, sisters each other in the service of Christ, aunts do likewise with their nieces. On hearing the fame of Clare, many single women who could not take up life in the cloister according to an order and rule, lived religiously in their family homes. Clare's example and virtue brought her so many spiritual children that indeed the words of the prophet seemed fulfilled in her, that many are the children of the desolate, more than of her that hath a husband." The Third Franciscan Order has a tremendous debt towards the Second.

Innocent III died in Perugia in the June of .1216, and soon afterwards while praying in the chapel of the Porziuncula Francis received a command from Christ to go and ask the Pope for a plenary indulgence for all who should visit the Porziuncula with contrite hearts. He set out at once for Perugia with Masseo and presented his petition to the newly elected Pope Honorius III. When asked how many years of indulgence he wished for, he answered; "Holy Father, I do not want years but souls." Honorius demurred, pointing out that it was not customary for the Church to grant such favours, but Francis replied, "What I ask is not from myself, but from Jesus Christ who sent me." He conquered the new Pope as he had done Innocent, "My son, it is my will that you have what you seek"; and when the cardinals objected that this was folly and would prejudice the Crusade indulgence, he still would not alter his decision.

Francis had wanted the indulgence for every day in the year, but the Pope restricted it to two days: as Francis left the room, he called him back. Was he so simple that he did not want a sealed official ratification of his privilege? "Holy Father, your word is sufficient for me. If this is the work of God, it is for

Him to manifest His will. I desire no document, but the Blessed Virgin shall be the charter, Christ the Notary, and the Angels the witnesses." The Porziuncula indulgence has always rested on the Pope's verbal assurance as Francis wished that it should.

The Porziuncula chapel of Our Lady of the Angels was consecrated on August 2 by seven bishops: they wished Francis to preach, and he began "I want to send you all to Heaven . . . all of you who have come here to-day, all who shall come on this day each year with a contrite heart shall have an indulgence for all their sins."

This was another reaching out to the multitudes whom Francis would never see, and whose salvation mattered to him so much; another great light kindled in the Porziuncula, another proof of the mothering presence of our Lady. Francis loved her as a child, a lover, a knight; her name was continually on his lips, her presence always with him, and he turned to her with every tender word and song that came into his head. He was so sure that she, who never failed God in loving, could not fail the children given her by Christ, mothering every virtue, every tiny impulse of love, protecting, sheltering, guiding, for God has put all graces into her hands. "When I say Hail Mary the heavens bow down, angels rejoice, Hell trembles, and the devils flee away," Francis was fond of declaring, and he amplified his words saying: "As wax melts in the fire and dust flies before the wind, so at the invocation of the name of Mary the whole host of evil spirits is dispersed . . . in danger, anguish, difficulty, call on Mary, think on Mary, let her not out of your heart or mouth."

He wished all chapels of the Fraternity to be dedicated first of all to our Lady, and at the centre of all these chapels and churches stands the Porziuncula of Our Lady of the Angels.

Did Clare ever go down to the Porziuncula after the granting of the indulgence? It was a tremendous event in the lives of all Francis' followers, especially in Clare's: and as the stricter enclosure was only given to San Damiano some three years later, there was no particular reason why she should not, especially considering her own strong spiritual ties with St. Mary of the Angels. Certainly one direct result of the consecration of the Porziuncula and the granting of the indulgence was that an upstairs oratory in San Damiano was also solemnly consecrated to our Lady, and the monastery was henceforth known as Our Lady of Saint Damian's (Sanctae Mariae de Sancto Damiano). Like Francis, Clare wished that her name should always come first in the dedication of every convent and church of the Second Order, and this became a general custom. The consecration of the oratory in San Damiano was performed on the eve of St. Laurence by the same seven bishops who had officiated at the Porziuncula, and a special indulgence was attached to it; all this was done at Clare's particular wish, and the chapel was held in great honour by the Assisans.

We catch a glimpse of San Damiano about this time in the writings of Bishop Jacques de Vitry who was at Perugia when Innocent died. He was scandalized by much that he saw; and all the more ready to notice the doings of Francis and the new movement with interest and approval. After commenting on the friars he adds: "The women live in communities in hospices at the gate of the city; they depend for their livelihood on the work of their hands for which they receive no remuneration. They only complain of one thing, that they receive too much honour from the populace."

This is a valuable testimony because it throws light on the relation between the Poor Ladies and the citizens of Assisi. Clare shared Francis' idea of work, and he hated idleness as much as he did money. "I worked with my hands," he said later, and always wished his followers to do likewise. Clare, too, was a worker, but neither she nor her Sisters wanted pay; when they had no food the friars begged for them, and obviously the French Bishop saw no sign of grievance among those who contributed to the upkeep of the monastery. They knew that the title "Poor Ladies" was genuine, and already the Sisters were respected and loved.

Not long after all this, another very important moment came in Francis' and Clare's lives when he met Cardinal Ugolino, bishop of Ostia, who soon became the protector of the whole Fraternity. The friendship between these three is very touching: the Cardinal was nearing seventy and Francis and Clare were more than forty years younger. From the first moment Ugolino had been powerfully attracted to Francis in whom he saw personified many of his own ideals; and besides being a great churchman, he was also a very humble man, and a man of vision with a young heart. He believed that Francis and Clare had really heard the voice of Christ, and he wanted to help them in the practical realisation of a vocation whose difficulties and dangers he well understood.

When Francis stayed in the Cardinal's house in Rome he took Lady Poverty with him, for there as everywhere he insisted on going out to beg, and distributed the bits of bread he received among the other guests. It is easy to imagine the faces and voices. For a moment Ugolino recoiled; "Brother, why have you gone out begging thereby slighting my house which is also yours and that of your brothers?"

"But I have honoured it through paying homage to our great Lord, for God is pleased through poverty and voluntary alms. And for me it is a royal dignity to follow the God who being so rich, for love of us became poor. I find greater delight in a poor table spread only with small alms than in a banquet of countless courses."

Francis' speech gave no offence; the Cardinal turned to him: "My son, do whatever seems good to thee because the Lord is with thee." The understanding of a friend could go no further.

His affection for Clare is shown in the following letter:

To his beloved Mother and Sister in Christ, the Lady Clare, handmaid of Christ, Ugolino, Bishop of Ostia, a miserable man

and a sinner commends his whole being, his present and future state.
Dearest Sister in Christ,

When the necessity of returning home separated me from your
holy conversation and tore me away from the joy of those heavenly
treasures, such bitterness of heart overcame me, such cruel pangs and
floods of tears, that unless I had found at the feet of Jesus His
wonted pity, I think my spirit would have failed me and my soul
melted away. When I celebrated Easter with you and with the other
handmaids of Christ, and we talked together of Christ's most holy
Body, truly I was wrapt in a glorious ecstasy of gladness; and as
Our Lord's disciples were filled with immense sorrow when He was
taken from them and nailed to the cross, so I am now desolate
because deprived of your presence.

I have always felt myself to be a poor sinful man, but now that
I know your pre-eminent merits, and have seen with my own eyes
the austerity of your life, now I say, I know for certain that I am
not in a fit state to die. I am so weighed down by the burden of
guilt, and have so grievously offended the Lord of the whole earth,
that I can never hope to be gathered into the company of the
elect unless you obtain the forgiveness of my sin by your prayers
and tears. Therefore to you I commit my soul, to you I commend
my spirit, and if you have not been solicitous for my salvation, you
will have to answer for me in the day of judgment. Your earnest
devotion, your many tears can certainly obtain whatever you ask
from the Supreme Judge of us all.

The Lord Pope is not going to Assisi at present, but I long to
see you and your sisters, and somehow or other I shall contrive
to visit you.

Salute the virgin Agnes for me, and my sister and all your sisters
in Jesus Christ. Farewell.

Rome.

The lack of a date makes it impossible to know exactly when
this was written, but the mention of Agnes implies that she was
still at San Damiano. She left a few years later for Florence.

Ugolino's affection and enthusiasm did not blind him to the
fact that a time of great difficulty was fast approaching; and
to his lot fell the ungrateful task of directing the organisation
of a divine inspiration which had come into being, as free as
air on the wings of love, but which — the world being what it is

—could not remain so. The first "Rule" which had amply sufficed
for twelve like-minded men was inadequate for twelve thousand
or even twelve hundred, since numbers change circumstances.

It was also clear that the first simple Rule of the Poor Ladies
would have to be revised, for one reason because the Lateran
Council had decreed that any new community must follow one
of the existing rules.

Ugolino must certainly have discussed the whole matter with
Francis, but the latter was in Syria when the Cardinal drafted
the new Rule for San Damiano. He based it on that of the
Benedictines: ascetically it was harsh, which would have been
no drawback to Clare, and dispensation could always be obtained
for those who found the penitential clauses too hard. What
mattered so vitally to her was the omission of any mention of
"sublime poverty." On this subject obviously Ugolino meant
to gain time: his able, legal mind believed in the virtue of
prudence; he may have wanted to leave the Sisters as free as
possible, and he declared that the only object of his Rule was
"to enable them to fulfill their divine vocation." Clare thought
otherwise since, for her, complete poverty was the corner-stone
of the whole building. She may have been slightly comforted
when he obtained a privilege of exemption from episcopal control
for San Damiano, for this reinforced the bond between the Poor
Ladies and the friars, especially as the exemption held good only
so long as the Sisters remained without possessions. He also
obtained from the Holy See the recognition of the Poor Ladies
as the Second Franciscan Order, with the right to own nothing
except their house and chapel; and from Clare's point of view,
although this was insufficient, it was still a gain.

This must have been an extremely hard period for Clare:
the Sisters probably heard the current rumour that Francis had
died in the East; they certainly knew of the confusion and
distress among the Brothers which were largely due to the
mistakes of Brothers Matthew and Gregory who had been
appointed as Francis' vicars during his absence with the charge

that they should "console the Brothers." In this they failed; some of Francis' close friends took refuge in the hermitages; other Brothers wandered about at their own sweet will, and one of them collected a following of male and female lepers who wished to be included in the Fraternity. Clare's duty must have appeared perfectly definite: in the midst of all this trouble she would have wished to stand unflinchingly for Francis' primitive ideal.

Cardinal Ugolino's Rule imposed the enclosure on San Damiano, but several episodes told by Celano suggest a far less rigid *clausura* than that which was later established by Boniface VIII. Apparently the sick were admitted to see Clare, and when she lay dying "a great crowd of secular folk" were also allowed in which would certainly have been impossible later. Francis' ideal for himself and his Brothers was to serve and help all; surely Clare and her Sisters followed his example as far as it was practicable. Clare was obviously in touch with some people living in the world, for Messire Ugolino in giving evidence for the cause of her canonization told how Clare had sent to tell him that God willed his reconciliation with his wife whom he had not seen for twenty-two years. He obeyed out of respect for Clare.

Ugolino took San Damiano under his own jurisdiction, and appointed as "visitor" first a Cistercian, and then Francis' early companion Brother Philip, whom Celano describes as a man "whose tongue the Lord had touched with the pebble of purity so that he spoke sweet words concerning Him, and though he was not learned he could understand and interpret the sacred Scriptures." One day while Brother Philip was preaching, Clare was marvellously consoled during the greater part of the sermon by the vision of "a most beautiful Child," and Celano adds: "she who was deemed worthy to behold this thing concerning her Mother, was filled with ineffable sweetness."

With excessive zeal Brother Philip obtained letters from the Holy See enabling him if necessary to defend the Poor Ladies by excommunicating anyone who troubled them. This too was quite alien to Francis, and on his return from Syria he appealed to the Cardinal to have the letters cancelled.

What boundless joy and relief there must have been at San Damiano when it became known that he was back, and though ill, more himself than ever! That day nothing else can have mattered!

It was never claimed that Francis approved Ugolino's Constitutions, as his Rule for the Sisters was called; only that he sanctioned it. Clare accepted it "with great sorrow" for it was a clear move away from the first inspiration; nevertheless she and her Sisters observed it for nearly thirty years, but during this time she never ceased to press for a ratification of the "Privilege of sublime Poverty" granted by Innocent III.

After his return, Francis took over the guidance of San Damiano; and surely he told Clare and the Sisters of the Holy Places, carrying them into the depths of his own experience, and firing them with his own missionary spirit and longing for martyrdom, a longing always shared by Clare. When Francis heard that five of his Brothers had been martyred in Morocco he exclaimed, "Now I have five real brothers"; and incidentally their deaths brought the young Portuguese, the future St. Anthony of Padua, into the Fraternity. Through him and the friars in Spain Francis and Clare surely heard how our Lady had revealed to Peter Nolasco and Raymond of Penafort her wish for an order dedicated to ransoming Christian slaves from the Moors. What could have appealed more to Francis than the idea of converting the Moors through such an act of Christian charity as that of taking a brother's place at the oars of a Moorish galley?

The second mission to Germany too was gaining many followers, and had opened the Franciscan ideals to Elizabeth of Hungary, the first princess to love poverty as Francis and Clare did. She put on the spirit of Francis long before he sent her his old cloak which she used to wear when praying.

The fame of her holiness must early have reached San Damiano, for Elizabeth had one of those hearts which radiate charity.

Already Francis' followers were carrying their message far and wide: the cry was for missions, missions, and the response came in increasing waves. Here was the answer to his obedience to the call which had come to him in Spoleto and San Damiano; he was being given the whole world as his field. The Franciscan eagerness for missions is more important than any of the dissensions in the Order; and it was being emphasized while Francis was entering the darkest period of his life. His enormous success had inevitably brought new problems, and he realized that a formal spirit, entirely alien to his own, was creeping into the Fraternity. He was harassed by demands which were contrary to all he stood for; discord and discontent among the Brothers made the chapters increasingly difficult.

At San Damiano, however, there was no jarring note: Clare was as disappointed with Ugolino's Rule for the Sisters as Francis was when the Holy See insisted that the missionary Brothers must carry credentials to protect them from being mistaken for heretics. It was a necessary precaution but not Francis' ideal, for he wished the Brothers to set out armed only with the cross and the Gospel: "For myself I wish only this privilege that I may never have any privilege from man save only that I may reverence all and convert mankind through my obedience to our holy rule more by example than by word."

Clare's example was also active: Celano insists upon this point and says how the little spring of heavenly grace which had sprung up in the valley of Spoleto was not allowed to exhaust itself within such narrow limits, but was transformed by divine Providence into a great river. "The news of these things was spread abroad and began to gain many souls for Christ. Although Clare lived enclosed the fame of her virtues caused her name to shine splendidly in all the world. It became known to illustrious ladies; and duchesses and queens talked of her in their palaces. The highest nobility bowed in admiration before her example, and pride was converted into humility. Many ladies worthy to become the wives of the greatest princes, when they heard of Clare, chose the narrow way of penance. Many cities, hills, and plains are adorned with monasteries built with the spiritual stones of Clare's example: and the pattern of her life has increased the cult of chastity also among those who live in the world."

New communities wishing to follow the Rule of San Damiano were constantly springing up. There were Poor Ladies already in Spello, San Severino, Perugia, and Siena, and in 1221 the Benedictines of Monticelli near Florence asked to be transformed into a house with the San Damiano Rule. In this they were encouraged by Cardinal Ugolino, and Monticelli was one of the four convents immune from episcopal control. It was settled that a Poor Lady from San Damiano should go and help these new Sisters in learning the way of poverty, and the choice fell on Clare's Sister Agnes. One of her letters to Clare has survived, evidently written soon after her arrival:

To her venerable Mother and Mistress in the Lord, to her dearly loved Lady Clare and to all her community from Agnes, the humble servant of God, who kneels at her feet.

No created thing is stable; the most splendid lot may suddenly be turned into misery. O Mother, this has happened to me, and it is an intense tribulation. I am suffering more than I can say by being separated from you and my sisters when I hoped to live and die beside you. I can see no end to this misery, only an increasingly dark cloud, a night with no dawn, an unavoidable storm.

We seemed united by so many bonds, by blood, faith, by our vows, and I imagined we were inseparable in life and death, and that one grave would receive us. Alas it was all an illusion, and my heart is filled with sadness!

Dear Sister, have compassion on me, and cry with me, and pray to Our Lord to save you from such torment; you will not find greater unhappiness than mine. I am oppressed with grief, consumed by fire, and I languish without any rest. I am in the midst of a sea of bitterness; O help me, and with your prayers obtain for me the strength to carry this heavy cross.

What can I say or do, Mother, now that I have lost all hope of seeing you and my sisters again in this world? O if I could only tell you all that is in my heart; if only these pages which are wet with tears could tell you all I suffered and suffer! My skin is parched and I am dying of despair at the thought of not seeing you and those I love again: no one can console me.

As compensation for all this, you will rejoice with me concerning the mission you entrusted to me. From the first moment all the nuns of Monticelli welcomed me tenderly with unanimous respect and joy. There was not one discordant note. They all promised to obey and be subject to me, and all unite with me in begging your prayers and those of your community, and implore you to consider them as your most docile daughters, always anxious to obey your orders, and to follow your advice. I must tell you that as regards Poverty, the Lord Pope has consented to my wishes which are yours.

Please remind Brother Elias that he is in duty bound to come often, very often, and see and comfort us. Farewell.

Poor Agnes, and poor Clare! In choir, in the refectory, everywhere each must have seen an empty place! Clare's answer to this letter is lost, and she also sent Agnes various objects, among them her own veil which remained a precious relic for Monticelli. Agnes stayed there for thirty years, content with her lot since it was the wish of Clare, but always homesick for San Damiano. She is also said to have visited the houses of Poor Ladies in Venice and Perugia; she may even have gone to other places and in the end she was called home to San Damiano before her sister's death.

Round Francis the difficulties were thickening; and Clare was involved in everything that happened to him. He had once warned his Brothers that their early days together were easy: "It is like eating apples, sweet and pleasant to the taste; a little later the apples will not be so sweet and pleasant, and in the end some will be so bitter that we shall not be able to eat them, even though outwardly they will look fair and juicy." The bitter fruit came when he saw Lady Poverty being betrayed by her own knights. Clare surely knew how, at the Porziuncula, he was seen standing alone behind the apse with raised arms in great distress imploring mercy on his Fraternity.

In the spring of 1223 he went one day to San Damiano, and as always there must have been a flutter through the house at his coming. He spoke to no one but went straight to the chapel and stood there for some time silent, with uplifted arms while the Sisters waited for a word or sign. At last he turned and asked for ashes, and when they were brought he sprinkled them on his own head and all round him. Then he intoned the *Miserere,* after which he left hastily and in silence.

He was already an ill man, yet fighting for Poverty every step of the way, and those who begged of him to modify his ideas could not see that, to him, change was impossible. The chapter of 1223 was held in an atmosphere of bitter tension — and yet all the Brothers loved him! Could — can — vision such as Francis' be "organized" on a large scale without being tarnished? "Would there were fewer Friars Minor" he exclaimed, "would that seeing them, the world should wonder at their fewness." At last when pressed for new alterations he answered, "Do as you wish, but my permission shall never be a snare to my brothers." His protest was to live the rule, simple, and subject to all.

A new phase was opening in Francis' life to which there is a clue in the words which Celano says were spoken to him by Christ: "O little Poor Man, why are you distressed? Have I set you over My religion and you do not know that I am its chief Protector? I set you, a simple man, over it to the end that those who will may follow you in those things I work in you as an example to others."

He went to the hermitage of Fonte Colombo to rewrite the Rule, still pestered by dissident Brothers who complained to Brother Elias: "We are afraid it will be too hard for us to follow. For he is very strict with himself and might easily command what we cannot observe." He described his ideal for the Friar Minor saying: "The perfect Friar Minor must be as true to Poverty as Bernard, simple and pure as Leo, chaste as Angelo, intelligent and eloquent as Masseo, contemplative as Giles, a man of prayer like Rufino whose mind is with God whether he sleeps or wakes, patient as Juniper, strong as John, loving as Roger, detached like Lucidus who when he found he was beginning to like a place would leave it saying, 'Our home is in Heaven.'"

Francis might have added "as faithful as Clare." Already he was sometimes anxious over the future of San Damiano; could Clare persist in the way of complete poverty? A popular legend tells that Francis and Leo were returning from Siena where they had been harshly received. Francis was discouraged thinking of Clare's sufferings in the fight for poverty: would her spiritual and bodily strength be equal to the strain? He was resting by a well and looked down; after a time he raised his eyes smiling. "Brother Leo, what do you think I have seen here?"

"The moon, Father, which is reflected in the water."

"No, Brother Leo, not our sister Moon, but by the grace of God I have seen the true face of Sister Clare, and it is so pure and shining that all my doubts have vanished."

Finally the Rule which has led thousands to the heights of sanctity was approved by Honorius III in the autumn of 1223, and from Rome Francis went to spend Christmas at the hermitage of Greccio. It had always been the "feast of feasts" for him, the day when Heaven and earth are united, and he wished not only for every poor person to be entertained by someone richer, but that even the walls should be polished with oil, every ox and ass have double rations, and corn be scattered for the birds. In the tiny chapel a crib was prepared according to Francis' wish, and Celano says that "Greccio was transformed almost into a second Bethlehem and that wonderful night seemed like fullest day to both man and beast for the joy at the renewing of the mystery." Francis composed a beautiful canticle for the feast, and probably sang it in the woods of Greccio as well as in the chapel, for Celano says that at such times "he would invite all the elements to the praise of Jesus." The last verse runs: "Bring to the Lord glory unto His name: bring your own bodies and bear His holy cross, and follow His most holy precepts unto the end."

The Passion was present even in those Christmas praises, though Francis cannot have known how prophetic his words were, and that within the next few months his own body would be sealed with the marks of the cross so that men would dare to refer to him as *"alter Christus."*

Probably during that Lent he composed the Office of the Passion which shows clearly how he must almost have known the whole Psalter by heart, and gives us an idea of how intensely he lived in the Liturgy. Clare loved this Office and constantly recited it for she lived in the Passion as he did, not as in some far-away event, but as in a reality that is always happening, and in which she was actively participating. The cross was completely the living centre of their lives: while Francis was still restoring the Porziuncula, a passer-by came on him wandering round it crying, and when asked what was his trouble he answered: "I am weeping over the sufferings of my Lord Jesus Christ, and I will not be ashamed to wander round the whole world and weep for them." The stranger was so moved that they wept together.

The sight of a crucifix sent him into a transport of love and compassion: "Then he would sing so full was his soul of melody. He would begin softly, and then the song would become louder, and French words would pour from his lips as though he were rendering into words other sounds which his ears heard. He would pick up two bits of wood, and sing songs of love to Christ His crucified love, until love so overcame him that he broke into piteous sobs and lamentations, and forgetting his make-believe viol, he would fling himself on the ground in an ecstasy."

What to us is dim, to Francis was clear. Like children begging for safety we pray "within Thy wounds hide us," but Francis knew that in those wounds is hidden our own share of the evil that made the cross a necessity. His love was sufficiently strong to penetrate our Lord's agony of soul and body, and to know the horror of the death through sin of souls created for God. Long and bitterly Francis wept that "Love is not loved," and his one desire was "to die for love of Thy love Who, for love of my love, hast not refused to die."

His two early visions of Christ crucified coloured all his life. Of the first St. Bonaventure wrote: "One day there appeared to him Jesus Christ the Crucified, and at this sight his soul was so filled with love, and the memory of Christ's Passion was so impressed on his heart that henceforth he could not think of Christ and the cross without breaking into tears and sighs." Of the second in San Damiano, Celano tells, "From that hour he was so penetrated with compassion for the Crucified that ever afterwards he carried in his heart those stigmata which later were to appear in the wounds on his own body."

What must it have been to hear Francis speak of the Passion in San Damiano with that same crucifix hanging above his head? He would have transported any audience; how much more Clare and her Sisters! No wonder they knew the Office of the Passion by heart; each time they raised their eyes to that painted cross the flame of love from the soul of Francis must have leaped in theirs. This tremendous love of Christ crucified was the impulse behind all Clare's penance.

When in the August of 1224 news came that Francis with Leo and several other Brothers had gone to La Verna, had she a premonition that he would come back changed? The wonderful story of those weeks was surely told her by Leo: he must have described the extraordinary fissures and chasms of the rocks, and how it had been revealed to Francis that they had been thus rent at the hour of the Crucifixion; and she, who knew how he always needed animal friends would have heard gladly of the falcon that watched over him. Leo certainly repeated Francis' words about the Fraternity, "Lord, I commit to Thee the family Thou hast given me, I cannot lead them any longer"; and how he had prayed, "Permit me to experience in my soul and body the sufferings of Thy Passion, permit to feel in my heart Thy love for mankind." Every detail of the anguish of Francis and of the divine consolations that came to him was precious to Clare: "I did not see the final vision," Leo must have told her, "but when he asked us whether or no it was right for him to speak of the secrets of God, Illuminato reminded him, Brother, thou knowest that the heavenly secrets are not revealed to thee only for thyself." And then, in Francis' own words Leo could describe the coming of the seraph, and how through an inner flame he had been entirely transformed into the likeness of Christ crucified, with the marks of Christ's wounds upon his own body.

Leo may have added how Francis had bidden Rufino to consecrate the stone on which the seraph had stood, and how that night the light over La Verna was so bright that some muleteers got up and saddled their animals thinking the time had come to go on their way into Romagna. And surely he produced the parchment on which he had noted the song composed by Francis at La Verna:

> Thou art the holy God, the God of gods who alone workest marvels.
> Thou art strong, Thou art great, Thou art most high.
> Thou art almighty, the holy Father, King of Heaven and earth.
> Thou art threefold and one, the Lord God of gods.
> Thou art good, every good, the highest good, the Lord God living and true.
> Thou art Love, Charity, Thou art Wisdom, Thou art Humility.
> Thou art Patience, Thou art Fortitude and Prudence.
> Thou art Security, Thou art Rest, Thou art Joy and Gladness.
> Thou art Justice and Temperance, Thou art all our Wealth and Plenty.
> Thou art our Refuge and Strength, Thou art our Faith, Hope and Charity.

Thou art our great Sweetness, Thou art our eternal Life,
Infinite Goodness, great and wonderful Lord God almighty,
Loving and merciful Saviour.

Then he must have turned the parchment over so that Clare
could read the blessing that Francis had written with his own
hand for "Brother little Sheep of God." Kissing it, he put it
back into his habit, "I shall always wear it."

Leo would also have told of Francis' farewell to La Verna,
and of the journey back to Santa Maria degli Angeli, and how
everywhere people had run to meet him waving olive branches
and crying, "Here is the saint," and bringing the sick to be
healed by his touch. But he, who had always been responsive,
was now often so absorbed in prayer that he did not even
notice either people or places. As they neared home it had
seemed to Leo that a cross of light with the figure of Christ
went before them.

Francis was now always in pain, almost blind, unable to walk,
but he wished to start off on another missionary journey. However, Cardinal Ugolino insisted that he should go to Rieti to
consult a specialist about his eyes.

He paused at San Damiano, and Clare had a hut put up for
him in the garden; probably she never knew it was overrun
with mice. One night he was so suffering that he prayed his
courage and patience might not fail, and a voice answered: "Tell
me, Brother, if in return for thy sufferings and infirmities thou
shouldst be offered a treasure so vast and precious that the
whole world by comparison would be as nothing to it, wouldst
thou not greatly rejoice?"

"Great indeed, O Lord, would be this treasure, and very
precious, and exceedingly wonderful and desirable."

"Then, Brother, be glad and make merry in thy infirmities
and sufferings, and for the rest be assured of My Kingdom as
though thou wert already there."

The next day Francis was so exultant that the Canticle of

the Sun burst from him as leaves burst from a tree at the
touch of spring.

>All-highest, omnipotent good Lord,
>To Thee all praises, glory honour
>And every benediction.
>To Thee all-Highest they are due,
>And no man living
>Is worthy to speak of Thee.

>Praised be Thou, my Lord, with all Thy creatures,
>Especially for our Master Brother Sun
>Who is our day; through him Thou shinest on us.
>And he is glorious and radiant
>In his great splendour,
>Thee, All-Highest, he reveals.
>Praised be Thou, my Lord, for Mistress Moon and for the stars
>In Heaven Thou hast formed them, shining,
>And precious and fair.

>Praised be Thou, my Lord, for Brother Wind
>For the air, for clouds, for sunshine and all weathers,
>Through which Thou givest food to all Thy creatures.
>Praised be Thou, my Lord, for Sister Water
>For she is very humble and useful
>And precious and pure.

>Praised be Thou, my Lord, for Brother Fire
>By whom Thou enlightenest our darkness,
>And he is beauteous and merry, boisterous and strong.

>Praised be Thou, my Lord, for our sister Mother Earth,
>Who sustains and nourishes us all,
>And brings forth divers fruits and many coloured grass and
>>flowers.

God makes the stars *"chiarite e belle,"* so Chiara's name is
also in the Canticle, she, who to so many was a shining star.

This is Francis' grace for all creatures, for life itself. He saw
the beauty of every single thing, then he paused, as an artist
may before adding the final touch. How should he sing of man?
To sing of him in his separation from God and his fellows

would be a discordant note; Francis needed to sing of man in his wholeness of whom it could be said, he lives now, not himself, but Christ lives in him.

While he was waiting for that inspiration, word reached San Damiano that a new feud had broken out between the Bishop and the Podestà of Assisi. The Bishop had excommunicated his enemy who retaliated by forbidding the citizens to sell anything to the Bishop or to have any communication with him. Francis was deeply perturbed: "This is a great disgrace for us servants of God that the Bishop and Podestà should be in such enmity and that no one should try and reconcile them." He sent two friars to the City Fathers requesting them to go to the Bishop's house; they consented, probably expecting Francis to step in and arbitrate. He did not go, he would not set himself up as the judge between men, the only solution he would offer was that of charity. In his stead there was a group of friars led by Brother Pacifico, the poet and musician, who had composed the melody for the Canticle. Francis' message was the Canticle which they sang with a new verse he had added for the occasion:

Blessed be Thou, my Lord, for those who forgive for love
     of Thee,
And bear infirmity and tribulation,
Blessed are they who abide in peace
For by Thee they shall be crowned.

"I have confidence in God that He will touch their hearts and bring them back into charity and peace." When the antagonists heard the blessing on peace they may have smiled; Francis had repeated such words so often, yet they knew that even among his own followers there was discord. That day, however, the words went home. Francis' confidence was justified, for when the song ended there were tears in the eyes of the listeners, the Podestà advanced, and his answer broke the silence: "I declare in truth that not only do I ask pardon of the Bishop whom I hold to be my Lord, but I would forgive him had he killed my son or brother. For the love of God and of His servant Francis I am ready to make any reparation he may ask." He was kneeling before the Bishop who raised him with the words: "It were fitting to my office that I should be humble; but since by nature I am irascible, you must treat me indulgently."

What rejoicing there must have been at San Damiano!

Before Francis left, Clare made special shoes for him since he could no longer go barefoot or with ordinary sandals. Those shoes still exist; they are of soft kid, and an ingenious padding in the sole kept the wounds in his feet off the ground. Those weeks of his presence were the most precious gift he could have given Clare and the Sisters, for in his presence they found the essence of all he had taught them. Francis, marked with the stigmata, had become more than ever the "charioteer" of every soul; he had opened before all his followers new horizons of love.

Despite his desire for secrecy, the reports of the stigmata spread, and when he left for Rieti the news that filtered back to San Damiano was of a triumphal progress. Many ill people were healed: perhaps it was during this journey that he cured an ill baby of Bagnorea who would become famous as St. Bonaventure. Clare must have been most pleased with the account of a leper who "abused the brothers till none could bear to listen to him."

But St. Francis approached this abandoned leper and greeted him,

"God give thee peace dear Brother."

"What peace can I have when God has taken everything from me, and has made me all decayed and malodorous? Besides I would not complain of my disease, but the brothers whom thou hast set to wait upon me do not look after me as they should."

"Son," answered Francis, "since thou art not content with the others shall I care for thee?"

"I should like that, but what couldst thou do more than they?"

"I will do all thou wishest."

"Then I want thee to wash me all over, for the stench is such that I cannot stand it."

Thereupon Saint Francis prepared warm water with many aromatic herbs, he undressed the sick man, and began to wash him with his own hands, helped by another brother. And by a miracle of God, wherever Saint Francis touched the sufferer with his blessed hands the leprosy disappeared and the flesh was entirely restored. And as the flesh was healed, so too the soul was restored; for when the leper saw he was well, he was overcome with great sorrow for his sins and began to weep bitterly. . . . But Saint Francis thanked God for so great a miracle and went away because, from humility, he wished to flee from honour, and sought in all things only God's honour and glory and not his own.

All through that journey Francis gave wonderful last lessons of what it meant to be his follower. The stigmata had in no way lessened his humanity, and this in itself was a lesson: he was eager to help all.

At La Foresta the priest who was his host ruefully saw his vineyard stripped by the crowds who had come to meet Francis. "Do not worry," Francis said, "we cannot do anything about it now, but let us have confidence in God who can make good this loss you have suffered for me." The stripped vineyard gave greater yield that autumn than it had ever done before.

At Rieti he was ready to undergo any treatment Brother Elias, the Minister General, wished. While the iron was being heated for the cauterisation of his temples he seems to have been afraid of flinching. "O Brother Fire," he cried, "among all creatures most noble and useful, be courteous to me in this hour, for I have ever loved thee, and will love for love of Him Who made thee." He put all that he taught into action. He said he felt nothing during the operation; it proved useless, but increasing blindness did not prevent him from singing. He composed songs to send to Clare, and spoke much of the service of the lepers exclaiming, "My Brothers let us begin to serve God for hitherto we have done nothing or hardly anything."

One day when he was suffering more than usual he asked

a Brother to play the viol, "to bring comfort to Brother Body who is so full of pain." The punctilious Brother demurred fearing this apparent frivolity.

"Then we will let the thought go," replied Francis, "one must give up much to avoid irritating one's weaker brothers." In the night as he lay awake, the air was suddenly filled with music, and the next morning he said, "I was not allowed to hear the music of men, but I have heard other and far sweeter."

All this must have come to the ears of the Poor Ladies, and how the Rieti doctors had given Francis plenty of good advice pointing out that though he had always impressed on others the need of considering their body, his own practice had been very different. "Has not thy body been a good and willing servant and ally all thy life? How hast thou treated it in return?" And Francis, perhaps a little conscience-stricken, apologized to Brother Ass, "Rejoice, Brother Body, and forgive me; now I am ready to humour you in every wish."

The next news that came of him was from Siena where Cardinal Ugolino had sent him to other doctors who were also useless; and then by slow stages he was brought back to Assisi, and lodged with his old friend Bishop Guido, watched over by guards, for his own city was running no risks with what was by that time her greatest treasure. The guards were surprised to hear perpetual singing; and Brother Elias remonstrated with Francis, fearing that people would be shocked at his saint, so near to death, and always wishing for songs. But Francis then was beyond any such consideration; "Leave me, Brother, to rejoice in the Lord and in His praise, and in my infirmities, for by the grace of the Holy Spirit I am so united to my Lord that in His mercy I can well be merry in the most High."

His wished the doctor, whom he nicknamed "Bembegnato," to tell him the truth, and when he heard that he would only live a few weeks, he knew the time had come to complete the Canticle of the Sun, and he added two final stanzas:

Praised be Thou, my Lord,
For our sister Death of the Body
From whom no living man can flee.

Woe to those who die in mortal sin,
Blessed are they she finds in Thy most holy will
To whom the second death can do no harm.

All praise and bless and glorify my Lord and thank Him
And serve Him with deep humility.

"Sister Death is to me the gate of life." To see God as He is,
to see Christ, and to follow Him is the perfect fulfilment of
life even on this earth. And of Francis it could be said that he
held the whole world in his "magnificent heart," and his heart
was in Christ's, and five words sufficed him, "My God and
my All."

In those weeks he sent messages of comfort to all the friars
commending Lady Poverty to their care. He still had strength
to dictate His Testament insisting that it was not another "rule,"
but "a remembrance, a warning, and an exhortation which I,
Little Brother Francis, make for you my blessed Brothers in
order that we may observe in a more Catholic way the Rule
we have promised to the Lord."

Francis dying in the midst of his Brothers was the symbol of
a unity transcending all divisions. Had he provoked a schism
in the Fraternity when points of view were in contrast, that
unity would have been irremediably lost. The Testament is his
last word; he had abdicated no principle, and he left his
Brothers that most eloquent of all testaments and testimonies
—himself.

Equally he thought of Clare and her Sisters, and sent them
too "sweet words of comfort like a song for their comfort and
edification knowing them to be greatly afflicted by his suffering," Clare, at that moment also gravely ill, may have written,
perhaps begging for a visit, but "because he could not visit

them in person he sent a letter in which he called them anew to praise the Lord to whom man owes his whole love." He reminded them of their calling, of their vow of poverty and obedience, and of the gratitude they should feel for the alms by which they lived. "Should a Sister ask for something which is denied her, let her suffer this patiently for love of the Lord who lacked so many things in this life, and sought in vain for consolation. Every privation a Sister suffers in this life will be counted to her as a martyrdom; and even should her health suffer, let her forgive the injury with all her heart." He again insisted that Brother Body must be spared if he is to stand the burden of the spiritual life; he exhorted them to inner mortification, to gentleness, compassion, and mutual charity, and with this he sent them all his blessing.

At San Damiano there was only one thought; they could not bear to think they would not see him again. They heard of the move from the Bishop's palace to the Porziuncula and of the blessing to Assisi on the way down. Anyhow, Clare seems to have written and he sent her a last message: "I little Brother Francis desire to follow the life and poverty of our most high Lord Jesus Christ, and of His holy Mother, and to persevere therein until the end. And I beseech you my Ladies, and I counsel you that you live also in this most holy life of poverty. And be greatly careful of yourselves lest by the teaching and counsel of anyone you in any way or at any time draw away from it." He also sent her word: "Go and tell Sister Clare to put aside all sorrow and sadness, for though she cannot see me now, yet before her death she and her Sisters shall see me, and have great comfort through me."

During those days at San Damiano there was much anxiety and little consolation; all hearts were at the Porziuncula. The news came of Brother Jacopa's arrival, and the Sisters were glad to know of the little comforts she had brought, glad to know she was there. Messengers reported the happenings of each day and Francis' words and blessings to all his followers. "I have

done what was mine to do; may Christ teach you what is yours."
Divisions and differences of opinion no longer existed; Francis'
crossed arms and pierced hands were the final seal on the union
of his followers, on his and their vocation. Christ in all, and
all in Christ.

Perhaps on the evening of October 3 someone at San
Damiano, like one of the Brothers, saw a marvellous light over
Santa Maria degli Angeli disappear into the sky while the birds
were singing; and even before the messenger arrived the Sisters
will have known that Sister Death had opened the gate. "Francis,
poor and humble, enters rich into Heaven."

The crowds that flocked to the Porziuncula saw Francis' body
with all trace of suffering gone; awestruck they looked on the
wounds of the stigmata, and Celano says that the subsequent
vigil was like "a watch of angels."

The funeral procession up to Assisi was one of triumph with
songs and waving olive branches and lighted candles. When it
reached San Damiano the Brothers paused and "at the grating
through which the handmaids of the Lord were wont to receive
the sacred Host, the brothers lifted the sacred body from the
bier, and held it in their raised arms in front of the window
so long as my Lady Clare and the other sisters wished for
their comfort."

Of all people she and her Sisters knew the triumph of their
Father, yet, "who would not be moved to tears when even the
angels of peace wept so bitterly? . . . Never again shall they
have speech with him who will not now return to visit them
for his feet are turned into another way! Therefore with sobs
and groans and tears they would not be checked in gazing on
him and crying, 'O Father why hast thou abandoned us and
left us desolate? Couldst thou not have allowed us to go daily
before thee to where thou now art? All our joy is gone with
thee. Who will comfort us in our poverty of this world's goods,
and above all in our poverty of spiritual merits? O poor one
among the poor, O lover of poverty, who will help us now

in temptation when thou who understood temptation so wisely art no longer here! Who will comfort us in our tribulations? O how bitter is this separation, how dire thy absence, how cruel thy death!'"

According to Bartholomew of Pisa, Clare tried to take one of the "nails" from Francis' hand, but it was impossible, so she measured the body with a strip of linen and later had a picture of Francis painted in the niche where as a youth he had hidden from his father.

Then the procession went on and when it was out of sight Clare and the Sisters could only look towards the church of San Giorgio which had become the shrine for Francis' body.

I cannot but believe that Brother Jacopa went that day to see Clare, and that, left behind as they both were, their union in Francis increased.

IV

San Damiano (Continued)

AFTER Francis' death the Minister General Elias wrote to all the Provincial Ministers of the Fraternity: "The loss is common to us all for our true light was the presence of our Brother and Father Francis who directed our steps into the way of peace." He signed the letter, "Elias, sinner." That was the Elias who loved Francis and whom he loved; whom Clare trusted, and for whose visits Agnes longed.

During Francis' lifetime all his immediate followers had been in a secondary position; with his death they step into the chief places in the foreground. This is especially true of Clare who became increasingly a witness to, and guardian of, his ideal, and the mother of his brothers. For her Francis' ideal was absolute; it was not even his, but Christ's. She had received this from him as the most wonderful of gifts; and she needed the closest possible human imagery to describe how she felt her complete dependence on him, and union with him. In one vision she saw herself fed by him as a child by its mother, and what she took in her mouth seemed to her to be of such pure and shining gold that she saw her own reflection in it as in a mirror. This throws another ray of light on Clare's extreme fortitude and her amazing carry-through of the original inspiration.

All Francis' followers turned for comfort to the Porziuncula and to San Damiano where every stone recalled some incident or word. It is no long flight of imagination to think of Leo telling Clare of La Verna or reading her the Parable of Perfect Joy which Francis had bidden him write down, or confiding to her the gentleness with which Francis had treated Leo's diffidence and what was perhaps a touch of jealousy in his love. It may have been about this time that Leo began the beautiful Missal and Breviary which he wrote for Clare; and he must have told her of the many times he had recited the Divine Office with Francis, often standing in the open, unheeding of wind or rain, or of the Office of Insults which Francis had demanded of him one day when they had no Breviary. "He wished for insults, but only blessings would come out of my mouth." One can almost hear Leo's voice, see Clare's face. Rufino, Bernard, Giles, Angelo, Masseo, and other Brothers must have told her every precious detail of their long intercourse with Francis, and it had become enormously important for all such details to be remembered. She may well have seen and kissed the cloth, now in the treasure of the Sacro Convento, which Jacopa de' Settesoli had brought to cover his face, and which is said to be her handiwork. In the centre are embroidered the initials A.M.A. which might be read by his friends as expressing his last command. Jacopa would certainly have told her of Francis' visits, of the little human details as well as the spiritual for the two went hand in hand. Jacopa was soon to move permanently to Assisi and Clare would naturally be deeply interested in the increase of the Third Order which meant a spreading of the spirit of Francis.

It seems likely that, about the time of Francis' death, Ortolana joined the community of San Damiano, where she, the great feudal lady, took a vow of obedience to her own daughter. Report says that she had always remained in close touch with Clare whom she often visited, and that Clare assured her: "Mother, if I left thee to embrace the life of religion, I did so to unite myself to thee in a more intimate manner. I assure thee thou wilt have the joy of dying in the arms of thy children." In just about thirty years it must have seemed to Ortolana that the prophecy of Clare's birth had already been fulfilled.

All through that year of 1226 miracles were happening at Francis' tomb, each one a precious sign of his presence to those who loved him. In 1227 Honorius III died, and was succeeded by Cardinal Ugolino as Gregory IX. He at once commissioned Thomas of Celano to write the life of his friend; and when he was driven from Rome through the unrest of the city, he came to Assisi and spent two months with the Bishop, during which time he certainly visited Clare.

In the following year he returned for Francis' canonization, and on that July day friends must have hurried down to San Damiano to tell the Poor Ladies of the triumph of their Father, and how Gregory, with the tears on his cheeks, had spoken. "He shone in his days as a morning star in the midst of cloud, and as the moon when she is full; and as the sun when it shineth, so did he shine in the temple of God." All over Europe those words were repeated, and never was a *Te Deum* more unanimous. No honour could now be too great for Francis, and his own prophecy in the prison of Perugia was also fulfilled!

It was decided to build a church which would be the final tomb of the saint, a house for its guardians, and a papal palace. Gregory put the whole matter into Elias' capable hands and granted an indulgence to all who contributed to the building. Does this seem far from the spirit of Francis? In one sense, yes; but at the time it seemed not only an expression of universal love and homage, but an inevitable practical necessity for the safe preservation of his body, and there is no hint of disapproval on the part of Clare.

In the incredibly short time of two years the lower part of Elias' church was ready to receive the treasure it had been built to guard. Elias directed the translation of Francis' body in such a way as to outwit the relic hunters but which spoilt the official rejoicings. Everyone including the Pope was furious, and yet, perhaps Elias was right! At any rate the millions who have found peace and inspiration in his church owe some gratitude to its builder. A great painted crucifix by Giunta Pisano used to hang in the nave of the upper church bearing the inscription "*Frater Elias fieri fecit. Jesu Christe pie miserere precantis Helie.*"

During Gregory's visit of 1228 there occurred a famous miracle at San Damiano described by Celano and other legends. The Pope accompanied "by many cardinals" had gone to her convent to hear Clare speak of celestial and divine things, and while they discoursed on divine matters St. Clare caused the tables to be set with bread that the Holy Father might bless it. When their spiritual discourse was ended, St. Clare, kneeling before the Pope with great reverence, besought him to bless the bread set on the table. The Holy Father replied, "Clare, thou servant and friend of God, I wish thee to bless it with that sign of the cross to which thou hast dedicated thyself." Then Clare answered: "Holy Father, absolve me from such an act, for surely I should be worthy of harsh correction were I, a most miserable little woman, to dare give such a blessing in the presence of the Vicar of Christ." The Pope, however, continued, "To the end that this may be imputed to the virtue of obedience and not to presumption, I command thee by holy obedience to make the sign of the cross on this bread and to bless it in the name of God." Then St. Clare being a true daughter of obedience devoutly blessed the loaves with the sign of the most holy cross. O wonder! On each of the loaves there immediately appeared impressed the sign of the cross, most fair to see. Then some of the loaves were eaten, and some, for the sake of the miracle, were set aside. "And when the Holy Father saw the miracle, he partook of the bread and departed leaving Saint Clare his blessing."

It was probably during that visit that Clare begged Gregory

to ratify the privilege of poverty accorded by Innocent twelve years before. The Pope pointed out that the times had become more difficult, and he would willingly dispense the Sisters from their vow of poverty. "Holy Father," answered Clare, "absolve me from my sins, but I shall never wish to be dispensed from following our Lord Jesus Christ."

There was little more to be said, and in a letter to Clare dated September 17, 1228, the Pope made a step in the direction she wished.

Gregory, Servant of the servants of God, to Clare our beloved daughter and to the other sisters of the monastery of San Damiano in the diocese of Assisi, health and apostolic benediction.

It is clear that in absolutely renouncing all earthly property you have had no other motive than to serve God. And now that you have sold your goods and given the proceeds to the poor, you propose to persevere in this complete renunciation in order to follow in the steps of Him, Who being the Way, the Truth and the Life for us became poor. You are boldly walking in His steps, and allowing nothing to turn you aside not even the lack of what is necessary because with the help of grace and the ordering of charity you have subordinated the flesh to the law of the spirit.

On His side, He Who gives the birds their daily food, and clothes the lilies will be your eternal sustenance in the glory of the beatific vision. Therefore, since you have besought Us, by Apostolic favour, We confirm your resolution to live in the utmost poverty, and by the authority of this present letter we confirm to you the privilege that no one can coerce you to receive possessions.

Let no man dare to lacerate this page, or to contradict it. Should anyone have the temerity to do so, let him be warned of the indignation of Almighty God, and of the Apostles Peter and Paul.

Given at Perugia in the second year of Our pontificate.

This was not the only time that Clare got the better of the Pope, who to some extent had to keep a middle course even when sympathizing with her. In 1227 he had warmly commended the Poor Ladies to the care of Giovanni Parenti who had succeeded Elias as Minister General: he wrote: "Seeing that the order of the Friars Minor is most pleasing to Almighty

God, I commit the charge of these women to you and to your successors for ever. Take heed that you bestow on them such solicitude and care as a good shepherd does on the lambs of his flock, and We place you under strict obedience to carry out this command to the letter."

This was in the true spirit of Francis, and in her own "Rule" St. Clare records his exact words: "Seeing that by divine inspiration you have become the daughters and hand-maids of the Most High, our Heavenly Father, and have espoused yourselves to the Paraclete by choosing to live according to the perfection of the Gospel, I will and hereby I promise on behalf of myself and my successors for ever to have for you the same diligent care and special solicitude as for the brethren." Celano corroborates Clare's words and says: "When the man of God had tested them, and knew by manifest signs that the Lady Clare and her sisters were ready for Christ's sake to suffer the loss of all things and to work with their hands, inclining always before Christ's holy commandment, to them and to all other women professing poverty in like fashion he promised the help and counsel of himself and his brothers for ever. He carried out this promise faithfully as long as he lived, and when the hand of death was on him he bade his disciples do likewise for, said he, 'we and these poor little women have been led from the world by the same spirit . . . if we had not called them we should have done them no wrong; but were we to neglect them now where would be our charity? . . . It is not my will that any man should visit them at his own choice and pleasure, but I command you, let spiritual men be appointed who by their lives have long proved themselves worthy, and do not desire this kind of service.'"

Given all this, Clare felt she was on firm ground, but in 1230 Gregory issued the Bull *Quo Elongati* which allowed trustees to hold property for Franciscans, and restricted the Brothers' right to visit the Poor Ladies. Both these clauses were very disheartening to Clare and each was beset with difficulties. As regards the visiting, Elias had followed his master's direction, but Giovanni Parenti was not perhaps so close a personal friend of Clare, and his interpretation of the whole situation was more formal. He could allege the clause in the Rule of the friars which strictly forbade the Brothers from visiting any Sisters without explicit permission, and among the Brothers themselves there was great difference of opinion as to their obligation to beg for the Sisters. Obligation! How Francis would have hated the word; for him it was a privilege! The difficulty arose partly from the multiplication of the houses of the Second Order; the same old difficulty which beset the whole increase of the Fraternity.

Probably Gregory never intended the clause regarding trustees and visitors to apply to San Damiano, which was always on a different footing from any other house: and which appeared to be completely protected from any innovation by his letter to Giovanni Parenti. Clare, however, was not satisfied, and Celano says: "When the Lord Pope forbade the friars to visit the houses of the Poor Ladies without his special license the gentle Mother was grieved because she feared that her daughters would be able less frequently to partake of the food of holy doctrine, and groaning a little, she said, 'Now that he has deprived us of our spiritual almoners, let him also take away those that minister to our temporal needs'; and without delay she dismissed every one of the friars attached to her service. When the Pope heard what had happened he at once relaxed his prohibition, and committed the matter to the Minister General." Gregory indeed only had to insist on the observance of his own letter. Certainly Clare's old friends, Leo, Giles, and others of the early companions, were never deterred from visiting San Damiano; we catch sight of them there all through her life.

Other Brothers also came, and neither Gregory nor Giovanni Parenti could really have wished to deprive Clare of the sermons she enjoyed, and a pleasant story is told of an English Brother, probably Haymo of Faversham, who was preaching. He was learned and eloquent, but Brother Giles, who was also present, evidently thought that his words were out of tune with the spirit of the house, for he called out: "Be still, Master, and I will speak." The English doctor stopped, and Giles broke out, "in the heat of the spirit of God," and when he had finished, the English Brother continued, while Clare greatly rejoiced even as though the dead were brought back to life, "for this was our holy Father's wish that a doctor in theology should have sufficient humility to be silent when a lay Brother wished to speak." San Damiano could also be called a school for good manners!

The difficulties regarding poverty were constantly and inevitably increasing, but Gregory obviously wished to help the Poor Ladies to observe their vow, and in 1235 he made an appeal to all Christians to "assist these women who are so weighed down by the burden of penury that it is impossible for them to live unless charitable folk stretch out their hands to relieve their necessities." He added an indulgence of forty days for whosoever did so.

His solicitude had also been shown in another letter written in 1228 which throws light not only on his personal friendship for Clare, but also on his ideal of the Sister's vocation. He writes:

Gregory to his dear daughter in Jesus Christ, the abbess Clare, and to the cloistered religious of the monastery of San Damiano at Assisi health and benediction.

Blessed be for ever the most high God to Whom you have consecrated yourselves as lowly handmaids, and Who by the grace of His holy Spirit has condescended to adopt you as His beloved daughters, to raise you to the sublime dignity of brides of His only Son, and Who will crown you with glory in Heaven. More than all others you are bound to love Jesus Christ with your whole hearts, to serve Him with your whole strength, and to reach out to Him with such ardour that nothing shall be able to separate you from His love. Remember that of your own free will you have followed the divine call, that you have enclosed yourselves in these poor cells to the end that being free from the tumult of the world, and preserved from the snares of earthly vanity, you may unite yourselves by a pure and holy love to the heavenly Bridegroom, Whom you have preferred to all others until He shall introduce you into His eternal dwellings.

Let constant meditations on these holy truths sweeten the bitterness of the trials of life; and change into pleasures the pains you endure for love of Jesus, Who, for our sakes, suffered such shame and torment.

For ourselves, We can say you are our joy and consolation in all the cares and anxieties which continually oppress our heart. We therefore beseech you in our Lord, and if need be, we command you, by this apostolic letter, to be mindful of what we have done for you. Walk in the way of the spirit as we have taught you; endeavour to grow in perfection; forget the things of this world; always desire the better gifts according to the advice of the Apostle; and ever advance from virtue to virtue.

By acting thus you will be giving glory to God, and our own joy will be full, because we love you in Jesus Christ from the depth of our soul as children of predilection and brides of Jesus Christ. Therefore being convinced of your intimate union with God, we entreat you to be always mindful of us in your prayers, and continually to raise your holy hands for us to the Lord, imploring Him to defend us from the countless dangers which surround our pontificate, to aid us in our infirmity, and to strengthen us in virtue, so that by the faithful discharge of our ministry, we may give to God the glory due to Him, joy to the Angels while obtaining grace for ourselves, and for all the children of Holy Church life everlasting. Dear Sister fare you well in the Lord.

Never was an old man more harassed in more directions than this indomitable Pope. There was the ever present problem of the spiritual reform within the Church, of the suppression of heresy, and of the dire dissensions between Eastern and Western Christendom. In all this Gregory had high hope in the friars; hence his preoccupation with all that concerned them: on the deepest and highest levels he was heart and soul with their ideals. Just about the time he was writing these letters to Clare yet another family of friars, the Servites, was springing into life through the action of a group of Florentines.

In every country the difficult relations between Church and State had to be watched; the Latin dominion of Constantinople was visibly crumbling; again the Pope was trying to galvanise the Christian rulers into a Crusade.

There were dangers on every side not lessened by the presence in Italy of the enigmatic and slippery and immensely gifted Frederick. In force of personality he and the Pope were perhaps equally matched, but the young genius lacked the backing of the institution which was behind Gregory. In the words of Brunetto Latini "the heart of Frederick only beat for being lord of all, and sovereign of the whole world." He considered himself to be the living personification of the law on earth, "and with consummate ability he had consolidated his Sicilian dominions into an extremely well-ordered state. Frederick's many-sided ambition inevitably led to incessant friction with the Pope. In 1220 Gregory had crowned Frederick in St. Peter's with magnificent pomp, and the Emperor swore to protect the Church and her possessions and promised to start a Crusade for the liberation of the Holy Sepulchre. Tradition says that he met Francis at Castel del Monte in 1221 on Francis' return from the east. A meeting of two magnets, and who can judge of its effects? Frederick had great appreciative power, and there are episodes in his life that may quite easily have been the result of that interview. He did not keep his promise for an immediate crusade, much to Gregory's disgust; neither was the Pope satisfied when Frederick did start on an independent expedition which in 1228 resulted in a treaty with the Sultan. By this Frederick obtained a ten years' truce during which time pilgrims were free to visit the Holy Places: it was a diplomatic success, but not exactly a victory for Christian arms. Two years later he was reconciled to the Pope, but the tension remained if only because Frederick was an incalculable genius and everything he did was exciting and exhibitionist. He could act simultaneously as the legislator, the reformer—of the Church as well as of everything else—the poet, the centre of the most brilliant, cosmopolitan, and learned court, the ruthless tyrant, and just

about the time of Gregory's letter to Clare he was parading
about Italy with a menagerie of elephants, dromedaries, camels,
panthers, lions, leopards, falcons, and bearded owls. Frederick
was one of Gregory's permanent anxieties: in his harassing life
it is no wonder that he turned to San Damiano which is thus
described by those who knew it:

"On the hill of San Damiano there germinated and flowered
in the light of the sun the most exquisite virtues of adoring love,
self-sacrificing charity, and the spirit of prayer that touches the
heart of God, the patience that bears the hardest things serenely
and joyfully, and that lovely Christian modesty which is the sign
of a soul mistress of itself." All hearts were united, all wills bent
to the same end. Detached from themselves and all else, the
Sisters thought only of imperishable goods. There at least he
found Francis' followers living as he had done, "as though
alone with God."

Outwardly the Sisters' Rule was very rigorous, but they did
not feel it so. The church and choir and refectory, the oratory
and little terrace and dormitory have remained so untouched
that the vase of flowers we see marking Clare's place at the
refectory table might have been put there by one of her own
Sisters, and it is possible, at least superficially to imagine the
daily life of the community. It was very much a growing family,
and besides Agnes and Ortolana, Clare's younger sister Beatrice
had become a Poor Lady, as well as her niece, Amata. She too
seems to have been a beautiful girl, and the day was already
fixed for her marriage to a wealthy noble; but when she went
to see her aunt, she realized her vocation, "I belong to God,"
and she never again left San Damiano. The families stormed and
even threatened to burn down the monastery, but in vain, and
history repeated itself for Amata's sisters, Balvina and Agnese,
also joined the Order. And Clare was not the person to receive
novices easily: even during Francis' lifetime she had shown her
intuition of the real vocation. On one occasion he had suggested

several girls who wished to join the Poor Ladies; Clare doubted the vocation of one of them, but finally accepted her, and within a year the girl had left.

Several of the Sisters followed in the steps of Agnes and left the "beloved nest" to found other houses; for instance another Chiara and Agnese were sent to Barcelona, Lucia to Cortona, Benedetta to Siena and Spello, Cristiana to Campello. According to Wadding a list compiled in 1238 gives the following names; although it does not mention Ortolana there is no evidence that she was already dead. The names are extraordinarily musical: Agnese, Filippa, Giacoma, Illuminata, Cecilia, Egidia, Anastasia, Cristiana, Giacomina, Balvina, Mansueta, Amata, Benvenuta, Benricevuta, Bonaventura, Consolata, Andrea, Aurea, Leonarda, Agata, Francesca, Angeluccia, Felicita, Massariola, Maria, Gregoria, Giovanna, Bennata, Lucia, Elia, Mattia, Stella, Lea, Beatrice, Bartolomea, Prassede, Erminia, Daniella, Chiarella, Pacifica, Vertera, Patrizia. Some of the names are doubled in the list, but the exact number seems uncertain.

These were the Sisters whom Clare taught daily both by example and word: she was a great believer in teaching and always wanted to be taught herself; hence her love of sermons. Celano says that the skill and tender discipline of her teaching were beyond description, and she taught her Sisters "how to drive distractions and noise from the mind, in order that in solitude and quiet they might penetrate into the things of God, and draw near to Him in loving attention. For the devil is even more cunning than men in throwing a noose round the pure and the saints. For this reason she wished that during certain hours they should be occupied with manual work according to the design of their Founder unless they were busy with prayer or some work of charity. At all costs they must avoid idleness "which enables the devil to fill the mind with vain thoughts and causes the love of God to grow cold." She taught them too the inestimable value of silence, "for unbridled talk will always cause the mind to slip and dart hither and thither; silence keeps us close to God; careless speech always weakens our love for Him." She herself was always abstemious in her use of words.

Clare promised these daughters absolute and holy poverty "which alone buys for us the precious pearl of ardent desire for God. No one can possess this who is hampered by temporal things." In frequent exhortations she taught them that their community could only be acceptable to God when, abounding in poverty, they felt the lack of temporal goods. She ever encouraged them to conform themselves to Christ, naked upon the cross; Christ, that Poor One whose poor Mother had placed Him in the manger. This particular thought was to Clare "as a golden breastplate protecting her against the dust of earthly things."

We see these same Sisters seated round the refectory table when, one day, there was only a single loaf for dinner. Sister Cecilia, who had been with Clare since 1213, was on duty as dispenser; her eyes and those of all the community were turned confidently to Clare. "Do, daughter, with trust what I tell thee," was perhaps almost an unnecessary injunction. Clare then "lifted up all their needs to Jesus Christ," after which she gave the order that the loaf should be divided into two halves, one to be taken to the begging Brothers, and the other divided among all the Sisters, "and that half loaf sufficed abundantly for each sister to be fully satisfied."

At this time Clare appears in the full power of her natural and supernatural gifts, and often it is hard to remember that she was also a chronic invalid. Her gifts had been matured by a discipline that controlled and enhanced her spiritual life, without ever making it rigid. Like Francis, habit never dulled her perception of grace either in nature or supernature. As each sunrise was a marvellous new creation, so each Mass, each Holy Communion, each recitation of the Office was a new contact with God. "In God and for God" was the motto of the house, and the Sisters never ceased to wonder at His love for them. The bread on the refectory table was set there by Him, the oil, the wine, the fruit of the orchard were his gifts as were the alms brought in by the begging Brothers from the charity of others. Francis had put the words on the lips of every friar, "Praised and blessed be God the Lord God, give us alms for the love of God." For those who asked and those who received, the accent was on God, not on any human needs.

Clare was leading the contemplative life in its fulness, which means that all the powers of the soul are released and strengthened for the purpose of prayer. We catch glimpses of her through her companions, and Celano says that "because of her ceaseless meditation on the Passion often she appeared unconscious of everything as though she were dead. And often it seemed to her so bitter that Christ should have suffered such pain that it was as though her heart and soul were transfixed by a knife." She loved Him so dearly. At other times she appeared transported with joy at the thought of the redemption of human nature. And ever she besought her Sisters and novices that they should weep for the Passion of Jesus Christ. When she spoke thus her face was bathed in tears and her eyes seemed two water springs. Between the hours of Sext and None she did great bodily penance that she might immolate herself with the Lord, saying that during the time of Christ's Passion no one could weep sufficiently. One day while she was in her cell weeping, the devil came and gave her a blow on the face which made her mouth, nose, and ears bleed, and caused her cheek to swell, but she remained absorbed in the divine love. When praying she always remembered the wounds of Christ and recited daily the Office of the Passion as St. Francis had taught her. Every night she took the discipline with a whip of five knotted cords, and she kept round her waist a cord of thirteen knots as a secret remembrance of the Passion.

In Holy Week she prayed and cried and meditated still more assiduously, and it happened that on Holy Thursday she was in her cell, her mind filled with the thought, "My soul is sorrowful even unto death"; and her soul was so full of pain and sorrow that, sitting on her bed, she was lost in contemplation of the Passion, and all that night she remained unconscious of every bodily sensation, and entirely one with Jesus Christ received many new lights and revelations.

She had a disciple, a girl whom she greatly trusted, and to whom she had repeatedly said, "When you see that I am lost to myself and do not come among you, do not disturb me unless I am dying." At nightfall this Sister, finding her in a state of ecstasy, did not dare to approach and went away without saying a word to anyone of what she had seen for fear of disturbing the work of God. The following morning she returned, and found the abbess in the same position and state, and again left her undisturbed. At last when evening came she remembered with fear the warnings of Francis, and went up to Clare's cell with a lamp in her hand. "Mother, have you forgotten how Blessed Francis ordered you not to let a day pass without eating?" At these words Clare came back to herself. "Why have you brought a lamp? Is it not day?" "Dear Mother, you have not noticed that a day and night have passed, and this is the night of Good Friday." Then the abbess understood, but not wishing to publish the secrets of the Great King, she only said: "O what a blessed sleep I have had when I most needed it. O most blessed dream! O grace! But my daughter, keep this to yourself while I am in this world."

Like Francis, Clare was often "entirely occupied with God"; like him, she knew moments of anguish. "If you cry so much you will lose your sight," the evil spirit suggested to her, to which Clare answered that "no one is blind who contemplates God." "Go on crying then," was the retort, "and you will see what you will suffer." "Love that cannot suffer is not worthy of the name," was Clare's proud reply.

Her realization of the love of Christ in the Passion made her pray: "O Thou who hast so wounded my soul with love, do not ever heal me." Her own love had to find an outlet in penance, and she was as unrelenting to her body as Francis had been to his. Presumably she obeyed his order about eating, given when she first became ill, and he had also insisted that she was to sleep on a mattress and straw-filled pillow instead of on the bare ground with a log under her head, but these mitigations were a sacrifice to her. Sister Agnes — not her own sister — on entering San Damiano in 1220 wanted to try Clare's hair-shirt of boar's hide, but she found it unendurable.

As with Francis some of Clare's penances were visible to her Sisters, but none knew with what relentless observation she pursued self-will and self-love into the hidden crannies of her being, and with what determination she cast them out.

On another point of the spiritual life Clare faithfully followed Francis' example and teaching. St. Bonaventure tells of him that "when he returned from his private devotions, during which he would be transformed into a different man, his chief concern was to behave in the most ordinary manner so that the subtle fragrance of the favours he had been granted should not evaporate by being outwardly displayed. . . . He often said to his familiars: 'When a servant of God experiences a divine consolation in prayer, he must say: "This consolation Thou hast sent to me, an unworthy sinner O Lord, and I commit it to Thy custody, for I feel that I am a thief of Thy treasures. . . . "' Francis never revealed the secrets of divine wisdom unless it was for the good of others, and he used to say: 'It is easy to lose a priceless treasure, and thus cause the Giver to withhold it a second time.'"

Clare had made all this her rule, and her reticence grew with her love. In this love of the Passion the sign of the cross became something life-giving that transported her ever more deeply into the mystery of the love of Christ, and through this sign she received extraordinary graces, especially the power of healing. Celano writes: "The Beloved repaid His lover for her love with outward miraculous signs, for when she signed the sick and infirm with the cross their ills vanished." Sometimes she would touch the sufferer, but more often she made the sign of the cross while praying. "No one ever heard what she said while making the sacred sign," said Sister Pacifica, "for she always spoke very low." This power was of long standing, for already Francis had sent Brother Stephen to her when he was losing his reason, together with a leper to be thus signed and both were healed. Sister Cecilia was cured of a violent cough; Cristiana of deafness; Amata of dropsy; Benvenuta, who for two years had been voiceless, dreamed on the vigil of the Assumption that Clare would cure her next day, as indeed happened; another Benvenuta suffered from ulcers for twelve years and she too was cured. On another occasion, five Sisters in the infirmary were all instantaneously cured when Clare made the sign of the cross. There were many other cases, and the sick, and especially lepers, came from all round the countryside, and Clare shared her power of healing with Ortolana. "Go to my Mother, she will help you," and like her daughter, Ortolana would make the sign of the cross and pray, and her fame as a healer was also widespread.

Clare had, too, a great devotion for holy water because it represented the saving water that flowed from the wounded side of Christ, and therefore communicated the graces of the Passion; and above all for the Blessed Sacrament. In this she was in complete harmony with Francis of whom it was said that "every fibre of his heart was kindled into love for the sacrament of Christ's Body, and greatly wondering he pondered on the condescending love of God." He had considered it an unpardonable negligence not to hear Mass every day when possible. He communicated often and with such devotion that he enkindled the hearts of others. "Because he revered the most holy Sacrament with all his heart . . . whenever he received the sweet and spotless Lamb he surrendered himself to God with that flaming ardour which ever glowed on the altar of his own heart." He constantly exhorted his brothers to let no occasion slip for bringing others to know Christ living in the Blessed Sacrament; and in his Admonitions he says: "Why will

men not recognize the truth and believe in the Son of God?
. . . Daily He descends from the bosom of the Father upon
the altar in the hands of the priests . . . and in this way Our
Lord is ever with His faithful as He Himself says, 'Behold I
am with you always.'"

His intense reverence for priests sprang from this worship
of Christ in the Blessed Sacrament, and he repeated, "I desire
to fear, love and honour all priests as my lords, and I am unwilling to consider sin in them because in them I see the Son
of God. And this because in this world I see nothing corporally
of the most high Son of God except His most holy Body and
Blood which priests receive and alone administer to others."

"Consider your dignity O my brothers who are priests, and
be holy because God is holy. . . . It is a great misfortune and
miserable fault to have Him so near you and be thinking of
anything else in the world. . . . O amazing splendour and
astounding condescension! The Master of the universe, God
Himself, humbles Himself to hide for our salvation under the
feeble appearance of bread. . . . Keep nothing of yourselves
for yourselves, so that He may possess you entirely who has
given Himself wholly for you."

In an age of many abuses Francis declared that were he
confronted with an angel and an unworthy priest, he would
kiss the hand that had touched the Body of Christ before he
saluted the angel. He put this into practice one day when he
was preaching in a Lombard village. Someone in the crowd
pointed to a priest asking, "Tell us, good man, how can he be
a shepherd who is living himself in notorious sin?"

Instantly Francis knelt before the priest, kissing his hands.
"I do not know whether or not these hands are clean, but even
if unclean the power of the sacraments they administer is not
diminished. These hands have touched my Lord, and out of
reverence for Him, I honour His vicar. For himself he may
be bad; for me he is good."

Clare perforce was deeply impressed by this devotion of

Francis; his attitude had been her school. Even before his conversion he sent costly and beautiful gifts to adorn poor churches; nothing was good enough for the dwelling place of Christ. Clare did the same, and even during her long illness she had herself propped up in bed, and made many things of the finest material for churches of Umbria. Sister Francesca told how she had counted some hundred corporals made by Clare, and she had seen a beautiful Child in the Host while It was being brought to Clare in Holy Communion, and on another occasion that same Child was resting on her heart and covering her with luminous wings.

Celano describes how "when Clare came to Holy Communion she wept hot tears of love, and was filled with the utmost awe and reverence towards the Lord of Heaven and earth who thus abased Himself. She cried so much that it seemed as though her heart were being poured out. For her the thought of the consecrated Host was as awe inspiring as that of God the Creator of all things. Even in illness she was always perfectly recollected in Christ, and always thanked Him for all her sufferings and for this the blessed Christ often visited and comforted her, and gave her great joy in Himself." She often said, "This is our honour that we carry God in our heart."

It seems to me that Francis and Clare must be considered as heralds of that increasing devotion to the Blessed Sacrament which rather later was to culminate in the miracle of Bolsena and the feast of Corpus Christi. Already that devotion was beginning in the Low Countries where their contemporary St. Juliana of Liége had seen a vision of a shining sphere in which a section was lacking, and it was revealed to her that the sphere was the Church's liturgical year, and the missing section, a feast in honour of the Blessed Sacrament. A local celebration of such a feast was sanctioned in Liége a year before Clare's death, but she may easily have heard of Juliana's vision through the friars who were already established in Belgium and through her correspondence with Sister Ermentrude. On their side, the

Brothers would certainly have spread the knowledge of Francis' and Clare's intense devotion to the Blessed Sacrament. At any rate this is one of the may-have-been's of history.

There were many outward signs of Clare's rich spirituality, and these were noted by her Sisters who all stress the humility, patience, and kindness of the woman who, as a girl, had asserted herself so vigorously. One Sister told how she would lie prostrate before the altar in the deepest self-abasement, and "when she prostrated herself in this manner it seemed as though she were kissing the feet of Christ." The place where she habitually prayed was often seen so filled with light that the Sisters had the impression of material fire. Often she herself was surrounded with light, and Agnes — who had been in San Damiano almost from childhood — saw the Christ Child near Clare during a sermon of Brother Philip and heard the words: "I am in the midst of them": she saw Clare with stars all round her, and an indescribable sweetness filled Agnes' heart. Another time she saw Clare holding the Christ Child and told how "she held Him joyfully and talked familiarly with Him." All the eyewitnesses lay emphasis on light in their descriptions of Clare: and they agreed in saying that when she "came from prayer her face was more shining and beautiful than the sun and she comforted them with the words of God so that they rejoiced as though she was come from Heaven." It was her habit to remain a long time in the chapel after Compline praying with her Sisters; and often it was she who rang the bell for Matins, the bell that is still preserved in San Damiano.

A very impressive testimony is that of Filippa, who told how "Clare was always gay in the Lord, and was never seen to be disturbed; her life appeared entirely angelic." Yet besides the usual difficulties of community life Clare shared in many of the problems of the whole Fraternity; she had to face the daily question of poverty, she saw this most precious poverty continually in jeopardy. To be always gay and never disturbed meant that her trust in God had reached the point of heroic virtue.

Sister Beatrice — her own younger sister — said "she lived in purity, humility, patience, benignity, correcting when necessary, but admonishing her sisters tenderly, assiduous in prayer and contemplation, in abstinence and fasting, in harshness of bed and clothing, despising herself in the fervour of love of God, in the desire for martyrdom, and in love with the privilege of poverty." The presence of Christ was felt by all the Sisters: "they had only one heart and soul, and spoke one language, that of love."

When Clare was too ill to go down to the chapel she heard Mass through a trap door in the upstairs oratory; and Celano comments on how "wonderfully power had been made perfect in infirmity as is most evident from the fact that during twenty-eight years of continual illness she uttered no word of complaint, but only holy conversation and acts of thanksgiving ever came from her lips." Very rightly this aspect of her spiritual achievement impressed everyone, and she, who had always been so rigorous to her own body, was very careful of her Sisters. If anyone was ill, Clare was the first to see that they were kept warm and well fed. It was during the years of illness, when unable to walk, that she used to be carried to the little terrace overlooking the valley of Spoleto, from which she could see at least the woods round Santa Maria degli Angeli. There she could indulge her love of flowers and the narrow space became a little garden. It is said that she preferred the rose as symbolizing love; the violet, humility; and the lily, purity. San Damiano is full of the poetry of the love of God, and in it Francis, Clare, and the first Sisters have left the breath of their own spirit as gentle as the most serene sky. Every stone tells something of the beginning, the continuing, and the ending of the life of holiness, that is life in union with God.

It is thought that what is now a corner of the dormitory was

Clare's cell, and the process of canonization notices one small episode that must have happened here. "Like Francis, Clare could make herself understood by the creatures, and by means of her innocence she could make them obey her." Sister Francesca told how once when she was suffering too much to move she wanted a certain small cloth, but that at that moment there was no one to bring it so the little cat of the monastery started to drag it towards her. "Then the Lady Clare said to the cat, 'O naughty one, you don't know how to carry it, why do you drag it along the ground?' And the little cat, as though it understood her, began to roll up the cloth and brought it in its mouth so that it did not touch the ground."

So the life of San Damiano flowed on. Clare and her Sisters were putting Gregory's words into practice by keeping the great Christian truths steadily in mind: they were also experiencing the reality of his assurance that in this way the bitterness of life would be transformed into sweetness. It was what Francis taught, and what he promised to all his followers.

V

The Irradiation

CELANO was right when he emphasized the fact of Clare's influence radiating in ever widening circles. This came about partly through the tremendous expansion of the whole Franciscan family during those years. Missions were starting in every direction, in every country of Europe the friars were gaining ground, houses were being opened, churches built, and often these same friars were entrusted with all kinds of delicate and important diplomatic missions by the Holy See. In Italy Giovanni Parenti was used by the Pope as mediator with the rebellious Romans and with the Florentines. The Franciscans were everywhere and the ideals for which they stood attracted into the Fraternity princes, nobles, and scholars just as readily as the poor and unlearned. The order was growing with springlike vitality, with the natural result that the rule was constantly being strained this way and that to meet new situations. The lines, which now appear as hard and fast and clear cut, were then nothing of the kind; the rule was being lived in the daily efforts of the most divergent and strong personalities, and even a surge of resentment against some innovation or regulation was probably balanced by something else which is now lost sight of. News is always something exceptional; the dissensions of the Order were all noticed, but not its underlying unity.

There was a tremendous gust of sanctity in the Order which

expressed itself through the most different men and women. St. Anthony, who had rebuked the tyrant Ezzelino to his face, died in 1231 and was canonized within a year; Gregory's words on that occasion were prophetic, "I will give you to all nations." Elizabeth of Hungary also died in that year, and was canonized shortly afterwards. At the translation of her body in 1236 Frederick II reappears in a new light. He had wanted to marry her but she had refused, and on this occasion he asked for the honour of helping to carry her body. All the German princes were present, with many bishops and archbishops and a host of the faithful. The Emperor walked barefoot with the crown on his head, and during the ceremony he placed it on the coffin with the words: "I could not crown her on earth, but at least I will crown her as an immortal queen in the kingdom of God." He wrote to Elias at the time asking for the prayers of the brothers. St. Elizabeth was the chief of a clan of saints; we need only remember her aunt St. Hedwig of Poland, her cousins St. Louis of France, and his sister Isabelle who having also refused Frederick's offer of marriage became a Poor Clare. There was St. Louis of Toulouse, Elizabeth's great-nephew; St. Elizabeth of Portugal, her great-niece, who likewise became a Poor Clare; there was her niece St. Margaret of Hungary; her cousins St. Ferdinand of Castile and his two daughters; King Wenceslaus of Bohemia and his sister Blessed Agnes, also a Poor Clare. There were the Queens Marguerite of France and Salome of Galicia; Helena, sister of the king of Portugal; Cunegonde, duchess of Poland; St. Casimir of Poland; all in some way or other connected with the Franciscan Orders. Directly or indirectly Clare touched all these lives, and nearly all of them touched hers.

New convents of the Second Order were perpetually being opened; in many places several houses of Poor Ladies existed in the same place. There were convents in Florence, Spello, San Severino, Perugia, Foligno, Lucca, Siena, Arezzo, Narni, Città di Castello, Todi, Tortona, Faenza, Milan, Rome, Padua, Trent,

Verona, Orvieto, Gubbio, Terni, Spoleto, and Rieti. It is worth remembering that Frederick II founded two Poor Clare houses in Messina. All these came into being during Clare's lifetime, as well as others in Spain, Portugal, France, Germany, Belgium, Bohemia, and Poland.

The first idea of a foundation of the Second Order in France apparently originated with the Archbishop of Rheims when he was in Rome for the Lateran Council of 1215. He spoke to St. Francis on the subject, and four years later Maria de Braye was put in charge of a group of Sisters who set out for Rheims taking with them a corporal made by Clare, and a cord and veil she had used. Their first chapel was dedicated to St. Damian, and they were known as the "Poor Women of Saint Damian." Maria de Braye died in 1230, and Clare put the choice of her successor into the hands of Giovanni Parenti which is another indication of the union of the First and Second Orders. Sister Egidia di Porte was chosen, to whom Clare sent a piece of linen marked with blood from the stigmata of St. Francis. When a larger chapel was consecrated it was dedicated to St. Elizabeth of Hungary, who was already the patroness of the Third Order. From Rheims the Order of St. Damian spread to Bordeaux, Beziers, Toulouse, Besancon, and Montpellier. St. Louis greatly favoured the Poor Ladies of Rheims, and his sister Isabelle founded the monastery of Longchamps.

All this points to considerable correspondence between Clare and her scattered daughters and among them there stands out the figure of Blessed Agnes of Prague. She was the daughter of King Primislaus and Queen Constantia who was a Hungarian princess, and Agnes had been promised in marriage to Frederick II by her father. After his death the plan was much favoured by her brother King Wenceslaus; but Agnes' heart was set on the cloister and she appealed to the Pope. The engagement was cancelled, and the Emperor agreed with a good grace saying: "Had she refused me for a man, I would have run my sword through him, but since she prefers the King of Heaven I will stand aside." Elizabeth of Hungary's life and death must have been a powerful influence with her cousin, and she was canonized just about the time that Agnes, after giving all her fortune to endow a hospital, took the veil in the first convent of Poor Ladies in Bohemia founded by her brother the King.

In 1238 the Pope wrote her a most important letter (*Angelis Gaudium*) which includes some details about the primitive rule given by St. Francis to the Poor Ladies; and also describes the rule he had himself recently compiled and his reasons for doing this. He enforced this rule on Blessed Agnes and her Sisters, most of whom no doubt were friends who had followed her from the world to the cloister. It is interesting to know that their spiritual director at first was Brother Giovanni di Pian Carpine who became famous as a missionary in China.

Agnes' letters to Clare have disappeared, but happily we have four of Clare's to her. They are in the *Acta Sanctorum* under the date of March 6; and in 1914 the late Mr. Walter Seton found fourteenth-century copies of them in German in the libraries of Berlin and Bamberg. The first letter to the Bohemian princess was evidently written when the news reached Clare of Agnes' determination not to marry Frederick, and to live in poverty. Here is the text.

To the illustrious and venerable virgin Agnes, daughter of the most excellent and mighty king of Bohemia, Clare the unworthy servant of Jesus Christ, and the useless servant of the enclosed Ladies in the monastery of Saint Damian in Assisi, offers her humble homage, and in all things commends herself to you, while most respectfully wishing you the glory of eternal joy.

I have heard of the sanctity and perfect rectitude of your life; indeed the fame of it is known to almost all the world. For this I greatly rejoice in the Lord, and my heart overflows with gladness; and not only mine, but the heart of all those who serve, and desire to serve Jesus Christ. Truly you could have enjoyed all the highest honours of the world, and have shared the imperial throne with him whom you might lawfully have married even as he wished, and which would have been becoming to his rank and your own.

Instead you have renounced all this to choose in its place with your whole heart and soul the way of most holy poverty and mortification. Thus you receive the noblest of bridegrooms the Lord Jesus Christ, who will preserve the treasure of your virginity always intact and unspotted, for His love will be the sure protection of your chastity, His touch will purify you more and more, and possessing Him you will always remain a virgin. His power surpasses any earthly might; His magnanimity is unequalled, His beauty is incomparable, there is no love like unto His, and in Him is the perfection of grace. You are now bound to Him in love for He has adorned your breast with precious stones and pierced your ears with rings of inestimable value, He has given you a girdle of finest gold, and set on your head a golden crown bearing the arms of sanctity.

Therefore dearest sister, or rather Lady, whom I cannot sufficiently revere since you are the bride, the mother and sister of my Lord Jesus Christ; be proud to walk under the shining banner of inviolable virginity and most holy poverty. Let your heart burn with the desire to follow Christ, poor and crucified, who suffered for us upon the cross to snatch us from the power of the prince of darkness to whom we were bound through original sin, and to reconcile us to God, His Father.

O blessed poverty who givest eternal riches to those who love and embrace her! O holy poverty, it is enough to desire thee and to share in thee for God to promise us the kingdom of Heaven, eternal glory and a life of rest and blessedness! O beloved poverty whom our Lord Jesus Christ found worthy of His love, He to whom heaven and earth and all creation are eternally subject! For the foxes have holes, and the birds have nests, but the Son of man had no place to lay His head; and Christ allowed His head to rest upon His breast only at the moment of His death.

Truly when so great a Lord descended into the womb of a virgin He appeared to the world as one despised and needy and poor, and this He did that men who are so destitute, so indigent, so famished for celestial food might become rich in the kingdom prepared for them above.

Therefore you must exult with spiritual delight, for having preferred the contempt of the world to its honours, and poverty to the riches that perish, in heaven you are gaining an ample recompense, and there treasures are safe from the rust that corrupts, and the moths that devour, and thieves do not break through and steal. In heaven, and even from this very moment you have the right to be called the sister, the bride and the mother of the All Highest Son of God and of His Virgin Mother.

I feel assured that you believe the kingdom of heaven to be reserved for the poor since the love of earthly riches causes us to lose the fruits of divine love. You cannot serve God and mammon, for either you love one and hate the other, serve one and despise the other. A fully clothed man cannot fight with one who is naked for his garments and harness will offer themselves to the grip of his enemy. We cannot expect to live in splendour in this world, and then to reign with Christ in the other; and it is easier for a camel to pass through the eye of a needle than for a rich man to enter into heaven. Because of this you have thrown off the superfluous garments of temporal riches that they should not hamper you in the fight; you have chosen the narrow path to enter the gate of heaven. What a great and happy exchange which consists in abandoning the good things of earth for those of eternity, to relinquish one and to receive an hundred and to possess a joy which can never end.

Therefore I humbly implore you, excellent and holy sister, for the love of Christ fortify yourself in the service of God, always progress unfaltering and unafraid from virtue to virtue that He, whom you will have served with all your heart may deign to give you as you desire. And further I beg you in the Lord to remember in your holy prayers me your useless servant and the sisters of my monastery who are all devoted to you. Pray that by the help of God we may be enabled to call upon the mercy of Jesus Christ and with you to enjoy His blessedness, in the Beatific Vision. Farewell in the Lord: pray for me. Alleluia.

What a human letter it is. Clare was as well aware of the desirability of the good things Agnes was renouncing as she was of the complete worth-whileness of the sacrifice. The jewels of an empress were dim indeed compared with those of a bride of Christ. She knew to the full the desirability of poverty, but she also knew the cost, and therefore she appealed to Agnes' courage and endurance. She was not disappointed, and she and Agnes were sister souls in fortitude.

This first letter was sent with five Sisters who were intended as a nucleus for the formation of the Prague community; they also took a copy of the Rule, an illuminated *Pater*, a veil, a chalice, a wooden drinking bowl and cord all belonging to Clare, and Agnes preserved the veil and chalice in a reliquary studded with precious stones. She took the veil at Pentecost, probably in 1235, and from that time until her death in 1282 she fought for poverty as valiantly as Clare herself.

Clare sent Agnes a second letter not long after the first, aware no doubt of the difficulties of the young community. The theme is indicated in the title, "Health and Perseverance in Most High Poverty."

To Agnes, daughter of the King of kings, virgin among virgins, the bride of Jesus Christ and therefore a queen, I, Clare the useless and unworthy servant of the Poor Ladies send my greetings and my ardent wish to see you live always in the greatest poverty.

I thank the Giver of all grace from whom as we know comes every good and every perfection that He has adorned you with so many virtues, and has brought you to the point of perfection and makes you a faithful follower of our father. He it is who enables you to receive into your soul such perfection that the Eye of God finds in you no fault. This perfection will unite you in the joy of eternity to the King of Heaven who dwells in glory on a throne of stars.

By refusing the hand of an emperor and casting away all the pomps of the world, you have embraced with holy love blessed poverty, and in the spirit of deep humility and fervent love you have set out to walk in the footsteps of Jesus whose bride you are.

Knowing your virtues I will not importune you with long speeches; though I am sure you would find nothing superfluous in any words of spiritual consolation. One only thing seems to me as necessary, and for the love of God I exhort you that as you have offered yourself to Him as an agreeable sacrifice, so always remember your vocation; and like another Rachel never lose sight of this starting point. The fruits of your action are already in your hand; keep them safely; whatever you do, do it well; never be content with the present state; on the contrary hasten willingly and joyfully along the path of the evangelical counsels and never let the dust of this world hinder your feet. Never stop; always move onwards in the way of perfection which you have chosen believing nothing and consenting to nothing that might hinder your course. With glad confidence aim at that perfection to which the Spirit of God has called you so that your vows may be acceptable to God. Keep these uppermost in your thoughts, and if you need advice follow that of Brother Elias our Minister General; be sure and heed his counsels more than those of anyone else, and hold them as the most precious you can receive.

Should anyone try to detach you from your vocation never listen to such suggestions even were you to acquire the highest worldly power and honour. As a poor virgin, hold fast to Christ the Poor One; tell yourself that it was for your sake that He became abject and despised, and follow Him gladly consenting for His love to be yourself despised in the eyes of men.

Your Bridegroom is the most beautiful of the children of men, yet for your salvation He was disfigured beyond recognition, His body was torn by flagellation and He died on the cross amidst the most intense sufferings. Think of all this, O illustrious Queen, and perforce your heart will burn with the desire to suffer with Him and to imitate Him. If you thus suffer, you will be glorified with Him, if you weep with Him, you will also rejoice, if you remain on the cross with Him, you will dwell with Him in Heaven in the light of the saints. Your name will be written in the book of Life for ever and ever; you will have exchanged the perishable goods of this world with those that are eternal, and you will live in unending joy and blessedness.

Farewell dearest sister, virgin blessed through your Beloved. My sisters and I rejoice greatly at the graces which God has bestowed upon you. May your community join with you in praying for us to the Lord our God.

The mention of Elias fixes the date of this letter as being before 1239, in which year he ceased to be Minister General. Like the first, it too shows Clare's power of sympathy, her appreciation of another's difficulties and dangers, her sense of when to encourage and when to say the harder word. She leads Agnes as Francis had led her by the love of Christ crucified which was the heart of her own life, in which she felt Agnes to be a twin sister, as well as a spiritual daughter.

So close were the two in their devotion to poverty that by 1238 Agnes was begging Gregory IX for a Privilege of Poverty which was granted. Evidently, however, from the time of her profession Agnes had been dissatisfied with the existing rule, and set to work to compile one of her own for the Prague convent. She must have applied to Clare for details of the fasting observances at San Damiano, for Clare's third letter seems to be in answer to such inquiries. It is of great historical importance for it contains a passage from the original *Form of Life*.

To the virgin whom in Jesus Christ I honour above all others, and who holds the first place in the human love of my heart, to my sister Agnes, daughter of his serene highness, the King of Bohemia, and now the sister and bride of the King of Heaven, I, Clare, the humble and unworthy servant of God and of the Poor Ladies, send greetings in the Lord Jesus with every good wish for her salvation and all that she wishes for that is best.

The tidings I have received of your health and progress in the path of salvation fill my heart with intense joy in our Lord. I feel that in imitating Jesus Christ, the Poor and Humble One, you indeed make amends for me and for my other sisters when our imperfections prevent us from faithfully following the divine pattern.

I deeply rejoice, and no one can take this joy from me when I see you realizing what is the greatest desire under Heaven, and I see you triumphing over the wiles of the enemy, of pride and vanity which throw folly into men's hearts and bring them to destruction. You owe this to the grace of God which surrounds you, and to your own rare prudence. You have found the treasure spoken of in the Gospels; you have received it from the hands of Him who creates all things out of nothing; and it is given to you as the reward of your humility, your faith, and the poverty you have embraced. To use the words of the Apostle I hold you to be the co-worker with God Himself for the support and comfort of the weak and failing members of the ineffable Body of Christ! O dearest daughter, rejoice unceasingly in the Lord, and let no bitterness trouble your gladness.

In Christ I love you, a virgin who are the joy of angels and the crown of your sisters, and I say to you place your spirit before the mirror of eternity, place your soul before the splendour and glory of God, place your heart before the divine Essence, and may this contemplation of God transform you entirely into His image. Thus you will be drawn to share the experience of the friends of God who taste that hidden sweetness which God the all-powerful has reserved for them from the beginning, and for all those who do not hesitate to abandon this deceitful world however seductive it may appear to those who are so blind as to attach themselves to it.

Love God with all your heart for He has given Himself entirely for love of you without reserve, love Him before whose beauty the sun and moon are pale while there is no limit to His power. Love this most high Son of God who was born of a spotless Virgin, keep close to this gentle Mother who conceived Him whom the vast heavens cannot hold, and bore Him, as a poor little Being within her immaculate body. How could we not rebel against the deceits of our enemy who tempts us through vainglory and fugitive advantages to lose a good that is greater than the heavens!

For my part the grace of God convinces me that among all creatures, the soul of a faithful man is greater than the heavens; for while all other creatures are incapable of containing their Creator, one single faithful soul can be His throne and dwelling; and this is a gift unknown to those who do not believe. God who is the Truth has Himself assured us of it: "He who loves Me shall be loved of My Father; I too will love him; and We will come and make Our abode in him." As the glorious Virgin bore the God-Man within her, so we, if we imitate Mary in her poverty and humility may carry that same Saviour spiritually in our hearts, thus containing in ourselves Him, the Lord who in Himself contains all things.

You and your sisters who despise the riches of this world will be the dwelling place of the Lord in all His plenitude, while earthly kings and queens who in their pride would exalt themselves until their head is lost in the clouds of heaven will perish on the dung heap.

I come now to the explanations you have asked for regarding those feast days when we have complete latitude in the choice of our food. I will transcribe for you the prescriptions which our holy Father Francis gave as to how each of us should celebrate these feasts.

Saint Francis ordered and commanded that any sisters who are delicate and infirm should be treated with the greatest solicitude and be provided with all the food they require. Otherwise no sister who is strong and healthy has the right to follow any regime but that of Lent, no matter whether the day be a feast or a feria. Fasting is perpetual, except for Christmas day when we can eat two meals; likewise those who do not feel able for fasting may eat two meals on Thursdays.

The rest of us who are strong fast every day except Sundays, Christmas Day, and in Paschal tide as we are instructed to do in the rule of our holy father Francis. Neither are we bound to fast on the feasts of Blessed Mary the Virgin, or the holy Apostles unless such feasts should fall on a Friday. Those of us who are strong and well eat any fare that is allowed in Lent.

Seeing, however, that our bodies are not of brass, and that our strength is not that of stone, but on the contrary that we are weak and subject to corporal infirmities, I vehemently beseech of you in the Lord to abstain from that exceeding rigour of fasting in which I know you indulge, so that placing in Christ all your life and hope, you may offer Him in reasonable service and to this end let your holocaust be duly seasoned with the salt of discretion.

In Christ I wish you good health and all you may desire. Commend us, my sisters and me to the prayers of your holy companions.

Clare the contemplative never gave a better description of the secret of her own long hours of solitary prayers. In this self-revealing letter she gives a picture of the inner life of a Poor Clare as a co-worker of God in the sublime task of saving souls. "You have made yourself the support and strength of the weak and failing members of the ineffable Body of Christ." This is the heroic Christ-life of unity in charity of which St. Paul wrote, and which is the life of the Second Franciscan Order.

Clare's remark about the naked and clothed fighters is also revealing for it shows her fighting for poverty with the same common sense sort of arguments as those used by Francis, and which no one could contradict! At the time she wrote those words which she was quoting from St. Gregory's homily in the Office of a Martyr, she did not know that in the Benedetti family of Todi there was a boy of ten who would become first a successful lawyer, and then, as Fra Jacopone, would be one of Poverty's most impassioned knights as well as one of the greatest of spiritual poets.

> Povertà è nulla havere,
> Ed onni cosa possedere
> In spirito di libertate.

The great Lauds of Jacopone would have set the inmost chords of Clare's heart vibrating.

It had taken twenty years of experience to teach Clare that "our bodies are not of brass." She had been forced to allow that Brother Ass cannot be too roughly treated; perhaps like St. Francis she begged his pardon; anyhow she was quite ready to counsel the salt of discretion to others. One wonders whether Agnes profited by the advice!

The text of the Rule compiled by her is lost, but we have the answer in Gregory's Bull, *Angelis Gaudium,* published in May, 1238, and it contained a flat refusal for any sanction. Coming so soon after the concession of the Privilege of Poverty, this must have been a disappointment to Agnes, and the Pope gives as his reason that the Rule and constitutions which he had drawn up for the Poor Ladies with great care in 1219 had been accepted by Blessed Francis, confirmed by the then Pope Honorius III, and was professed by all the convents of Poor Ladies including San Damiano. He stresses the fact that "Clare and her sisters observe it laudably in place of Saint Francis' earlier rule."

The friendship of Clare and Agnes is a lovely episode in both their lives, an example of the intimacy of two human beings who have never seen each other's faces, but who have met in the love of Christ.

Clare's fourth letter to Agnes seems to have been written towards the end of her life perhaps in answer to some complaint of the latter on the gaps in their correspondence. It sounds a note of leave-taking as though new light were streaming in through an opening door, and she seems to be wanting to tell her friend and sister of the glory of the poverty of the incarnate Saviour as she had known it in her own ecstatic prayer. She writes:

To her who is the half of my own soul and a particular sanctuary of divine love, Agnes an illustrious queen, and my beloved mother and dearest of daughters. It is to you that I, Clare the unworthy servant of Christ and the useless servant of the monastery of Saint Damian's send my greeting and my wish that you may take your place with the other wise virgins before the throne of God and of the Lamb, there, where a new song will be sung and His lovers follow the Lamb wherever He goes.

O my mother and daughter, bride of the immortal King, I beg of you do not be surprised if I have not written as often as both our souls desired; and I should be distressed if you could believe that the burning love for you could ever be even slightly lessened. Tell yourself that I love you even as your own mother.

The only reason for the infrequency of our correspondence has been lack of messengers and the dangers of the roads. I am seizing an opportunity of writing to you to-day; and in your charity it seems to me that we are reunited in one joy. O bride of Christ, indeed I rejoice in the Holy Spirit that He has inspired you to follow the example of the first Agnes and united you to the spotless Lamb who takes away the sin of the world.

To you it has been given to enjoy the wonders of this heavenly union which amazes the hosts of Heaven, which is the desire of all hearts so that the thought of it fills us with joy and the excellence of it fills us with an indescribable sweetness. This union can cause the dead to rise, and the glorious vision of it delights all the hosts of Heaven for in it they behold reflected the splendour of the glory of God, the immaculate radiance of eternal light.

O queen and bride of Jesus Christ, look each day into the mirror which reflects this light; more and more you will see the reflection of your own face; adorn your house within and without with every flower of virtue, and put on the garment due to the daughter and bride of the King of Kings.

O my beloved daughter, divine grace will permit you to find your joy in contemplating this mirror. Come, look into it with me! On one side there is Jesus, lying in the manger in the midst of the utmost poverty and wrapped in miserable clothes. O admirable humility! O stupefying poverty! The King of angels, the Saviour of heaven and earth lies in the manger. In the middle of this mirror you will see holy and humble poverty for love of whom the Saviour consented to suffer so grievously for the redemption of mankind. Then look at the other side which shows that ineffable love which flung the Saviour on to the wood of the cross there to die an infamous death. Let us put down our mirror on the cross; and we shall understand those words which fall on each of us:

"O all you who pass by this way, stay and see whether there be any sorrow like to Mine." As far as is in us, united in heart and voice let us together answer Him, who groaning, calls to us, "Yes, Master, I will remember You, and my spirit will share in Your sufferings."

O queen, let your own heart be warmed in the fervour of this Love; be mindful too of the ineffable delights of the King of Heaven, of the eternal honour and riches that He offers you, and panting for desire of Him call to Him from the depths of your heart: "Draw me to Thyself, O Lord, and I will strive unceasingly in Thy fragrance, O celestial Bridegroom, until Thou shalt bring me into Thy house where Thy right hand will be held out to me, and I shall receive Thy kiss."

In the midst of this contemplation remember me your poor mother, for I carry the memory of you graven in the depths of my heart since you are dearer to me than any. What can I say? Human language must be silent, for no words will ever express the love I feel for you my blessed daughter. What I write is all too insufficient, but you must receive it kindly, recognizing at least a reflection of the love of your mother which burns day by day for you and for your spiritual daughters.

O most worthy sister Agnes, commend me urgently with my daughters to all yours. Goodbye, most beloved, to you and your sisters until we meet before the throne of the glory of God. Pray to Him for us.

My messengers to-day are our dear brothers Amato, dear to God and men, and Bonagura whom I commend to you with all my heart.

How welcome those brothers must have been when at last they reached Prague! In this letter, as revealing as the former ones, Agnes surely felt the full power as well as the joy of Clare's presence, and her life reflected most faithfully the same love as Clare's. It was said of her that she "worked like any charwoman or cook not with an angry or sour countenance, but with joy, and by her sweet face showing she was the true servant of Christ." She had special care for any sister who was ill, she insisted that the food for an invalid must be daintily cooked, and wore herself out with untiring energy so that the sick might be freed from pain and restored to health. Her last words to her daughters were, "Love God and trust in Him; He will ever come to your help. Hold fast to poverty, for it is the life, the bone and blood of our order."

Only one other of Clare's correspondents is known to us, and she is very different from Agnes of Bohemia. Ermentrude was a pious girl in Cologne who prayed incessantly for the souls of her dead parents. One day she saw Heaven and Hell open before her, and a voice warned her that she would gain Heaven with other virgins to whom she would be a spiritual mother if she followed the advice of her spiritual director. This priest was a Dominican and after celebrating Mass for her intention he assured her that God wished her to leave her home which she did with a companion named Sapientia. They reached Bruges and spent twelve years near the city in prayer and meditation during which time they were joined by several other young women. Ermentrude felt that her little group needed a more definite rule and she consulted the Friars Minor who had been established in Bruges since 1233. From them she heard of Clare, to whom she wrote and received the following answer.

To my dear sister Ermentrude, I, Clare of Assisi, wish all health and peace.

I have learnt, dear sister, that by the grace of God you have renounced the world. This has filled me with gladness, and I greatly admire the generosity of your resolution, and the great fervour with which you and your excellent companions are setting out along the path of perfection. I pray you to keep faithful to the divine Bridegroom to whom you have consecrated yourselves; and be sure that your efforts will be rewarded with the crown of immortality. The period of trial is short; that of the reward unending. Do not let yourselves be discouraged by the splendour of the world which will pass like a shadow; do not be deceived by appearances that are false. It is true the devil will torment you by horrible suggestions; but be strong, shut your ears and you will put him to flight.

Beware, beloved, that you are not overthrown by adversity, and that your heart does not swell with pride in prosperity, for the sign of faith is to make us humble in success, and unmoved by failure. Give to God what you have vowed to Him, give it with scrupulous care, He will know how to repay your sacrifices. Lift your eyes continually to Heaven, for it is Heaven that calls to you to take up your cross and follow Jesus Christ who precedes you for it is written that only through much tribulation is it given to enter into the kingdom of God.

With the whole strength of your soul love God who is infinitely adorable, and His divine Son who deigned to be crucified for our sins; let the thought of Him be always in your mind. Meditate continually on the mysteries of His Passion, and on the sufferings endured by His holy Mother beneath the cross. Watch and pray unceasingly, and apply all your strength to finish the good work which you have begun so well.

Accomplish your duties by living in complete poverty and in sincere humility. Let no fear deter you from your path, beloved daughter, and you will find that the Lord is faithful in all His words, and holy in all His works. The abundance of His blessings will fall on you and your sisters; He will be your defence, your consolation, your Redeemer, your reward in eternity. Let us pray for each other; and thus by bearing the yoke of charity we shall be enabled more easily to observe the law of Jesus Christ.

According to one tradition Ermentrude went to Rome some twelve years later to beg a favour from the Pope, and on her return she passed by Assisi only to find that Clare was already dead; but another version places the journey in 1250 and Clare is reported to have said to her: "Dear Sister and daughter, be faithful to the work you have undertaken. God has warned you through me that the devil will do his utmost to hinder it, but he will not succeed. Place all the strength of your heart in God; only He will be your help."

We can take the last sentence as Clare's message to all Christians, always!

These letters admit us into the inner sanctuary of Clare's spiritual life which, in varying degrees, was that of all her Sisters. It was a life cultivated in penance and self-discipline, and Clare's teaching to her own community was probably transmitted by the Brothers to others. As the years passed, everything she said and did became more important. The chief points of her spiritual teaching were detachment from all earthly things for "idle thought and enjoyment of our own leisure lessen the fervour of heart and quench the light of divine love." She insisted that this inner life of prayer was to be nourished on the Gospel; she always welcomed sermons for herself and her Sisters "because so great was her desire to hear of the most sweet Lord Jesus Christ."

This deep spiritual life of San Damiano was complete in it-self, yet it was never cut off from the outside world, and per-force Clare had to take account of exterior events, and events were preparing that were to spread her fame still farther afield.

The mention of Elias in one of the letters to Agnes shows Clare's confidence in him which was indeed one of Elias' glories. At that period she must have considered him as a faith-ful follower of Francis, and a sound judge on how to deal with the difficulties of the moment. Other people shared this favour-able opinion: Bernard of Besse said that "he excelled in human wisdom to such a degree that it was difficult to find his equal in Italy"; and even Angelo Clareno admitted that "there shone in him a rare prudence." In 1237 Grosseteste of Lincoln was still his warm admirer which says a good deal, for Elias was a lay-man and supported the lay tradition of the Fraternity. In 1233 he had been re-elected Minister General of the Order, and obviously Clare was satisfied. Indeed he may well have seemed the only person who could handle the divergent currents in the Fraternity. There was the current of the learned Brothers, most of them priests, that of the active missionaries, who were a host in themselves, that of the contemplatives, and in the spirit of Francis there was room for them all; the trouble was that the balance that he had held so delicately was often lost sight of.

Elias was carrying the load of a tremendous activity, still busy with the building of the church, facing the most intricate situations in the many different aspects of the Fraternity's life, and deeply involved in politics. Perhaps the best description of him is "that he realized the expectations of his friends, and the evil forebodings of his enemies." There was a growing disaffection against his rule, especially in the English province and among those Brothers who clung to the hermit contemplative side of the Franciscan vocation; while another storm was approaching with Frederick II as its centre.

Elias had always been a warm admirer of Frederick; perhaps there was in each a spark of the same genius. When Provincial Minister in Syria years before, he had become keenly interested in the healing of the schism of the Eastern Church, as in the fate of the Holy Places; and he was a warm supporter of the Franciscan missions in the near East. All his natural gifts pointed to him as a perfect go-between for the Pope and the Emperor; to his own immense misfortune, in 1238, he was appointed Papal Legate to the imperial court.

Frederick was now back in Italy after a visit to his German possessions; he was at the height of his power, and the old quarrel with the Pope flared up. The very difficulty of his task attracted Elias who grasped very clearly how important for both sides it was that some sort of understanding should be reached.

Elias' very powerful enemies in the Order and the Curia rightly or wrongly profited by the general confusion of the situation to denounce him as unworthy of the trust of Minister General. At first Gregory supported him, but the disaffection of the Brothers became more vocal and at the General Chapter of 1239 the Pope declared that he had nominated Elias originally owing to his friendship with St. Francis, but since the majority of the Order was against him, he would relieve him of his charge; his place was taken by Albert of Pisa, provincial of the English province.

Elias returned to Assisi and his church building, but in a short time he had again to revert to public affairs. The war between the Pope and Emperor was intensified. Frederick denounced Gregory to all the princes of Christendom as a false pope, no shepherd but a robber, even while proclaiming his faith in the mystical supremacy of the Apostolic See. He protested that the Church was his mother, and that his only desire was to bring her back to the Gospel, to protect her from herself, so that free from all earthly cares she might become a pure school for saints. Gregory replied with a vehement encyclical, and almost while the bells were ringing in the newly finished bell-tower of the Assisi basilica, Frederick appealed to Elias again to act as mediator between him and the Pope. Elias was not the man to refuse, especially as he still enjoyed the Pope's confidence; an unequalled opportunity for peacemaking seemed to be opening before him, perhaps the prospect obscured to him his own ambition.

Elias set out for the imperial court, apparently not considering that by so doing he fell under the excommunication which Gregory had launched against anyone having dealings with the Emperor. He still hoped to make peace; apparently he wrote the Pope a long letter explaining his own position, and putting forward new proposals. This letter was entrusted to Albert of Pisa who died on the way, and the letter was never delivered. The Pope waited for it in vain, and at last Brother Elias was excommunicated by name. When Giles heard of it he threw himself on the ground exclaiming, "I want to get as low as possible since so great a man has fallen into such an abyss." Clare must have felt the same.

It was a terrible position for Gregory, who by this time was 98; with war ravaging his dominions he must have turned more and more in spirit to Clare and San Damiano. Outwardly at least his fortitude never left him: the friars were sent out through Syria to acquaint Christians with the excommunication of the Emperor and his followers, who retorted by expelling them from his territory. When the Emperor marched on Rome, Gregory, undaunted, exposed the great relics, harangued the people, proclaimed a Crusade against his enemy, declared the throne vacant and Frederick deposed. Rome was saved, but once again all the papal dominions in Italy were exposed to the horror of marauding bands of imperial troops who were mostly recruited among the Emperor's Saracen subjects in Sicily. The valley of Spoleto came in for its full share, and though Elias had obtained from the Emperor a letter of protection for the Poor Ladies of Valle Gloria at Spello, he had not done anything of the kind for San Damiano. It is best to turn to Celano to hear what happened.

During that tempest by which the Church was buffeted at different times and in different places during the days of the Emperor Frederick, the valley of Spoleto was forced frequently to drink the chalice of affliction. Bands of soldiers and of Saracen archers like swarms of bees were stationed there by his command so that they might lay waste the fields and harass the cities and villages. At one time they had it in mind to vent their fury on Assisi, a city beloved of God, and the army was already approaching the gates when the Saracens — a most evil breed of men athirst for Christian blood who shamelessly perpetrate every kind of wrong — would willingly have violated Saint Damian's. They therefore rushed to that cloister of Christ's holy virgins whose hearts melted like wax at the sight of them, so that they ran to their mother. Blessed Clare was not afraid, and though at that time she was grievously ill, she bade her daughters conduct her to the door of the monastery there to confront those men of Belial. Before her was carried in a silver box encased in ivory the Body of the Holy of Holies, and prostrating herself before Him she prayed: "Doth it please Thee, O my God, to deliver these defenceless children whom I have nourished with Thy love into the hands of these beasts? Protect them, good Lord, I beseech Thee, whom at this hour I am powerless to protect." And a voice, like that of a little child was heard saying: "I will always have them in My keeping." Then the Lady Clare continued: "May it please Thee, dear Lord, to deliver likewise the city which nourishes us for love of Thee." And the same voice answered: "The people of Assisi shall be assailed, but through My grace their enemies shall not prevail against them." Then Clare turned to her weeping daughters saying: "Fear not, little daughters; have confidence in Jesus"; and at the same moment the courage of the Saracen dogs turned to terror, and they scrambled speedily down the walls they had already scaled, routed by the might of a valiant woman's prayer.

Clare ordered Sister Illuminata and Sister Francesca who had been supporting her, and those standing round never to speak of the voice they had heard during her lifetime.

If, as seems probable, this happened in 1240 when Gregory was still alive, how proud he must have been of his friend, she, who had always been so full of faith and courage. He died in August, 1241, just a hundred years old, and with him went another of Francis' close friends.

The threat to Assisi was renewed; again we turn to Celano.

Vitale d'Aversa, a fierce, pugnacious fighter, a man greedy for fame, was captain of the imperial forces, and again he turned his soldiers against Assisi. Having cut down all the trees of the valley and laid waste the countryside he encamped his troops round the walls, swearing that he would continue the siege until the city surrendered. Things had come to such a pass that not only the danger was obvious to all, but the surrender seemed imminent. When the handmaid of Christ heard this, she was grieved, and calling together her sisters, she spoke to them thus: "Dearest daughters, every day we receive many gifts from this city, therefore we shall be guilty of great cruelty and ingratitude if, in the time of need, we do not do our utmost to help it." Thereupon she asked for ashes, and unveiling first of all her own head, she covered it with them, after which she did likewise to all the sisters saying: "Go to our Lord, and with all the love of your hearts beg of Him the liberation of the city." There is no need for me to try and tell how those virgins wept, or how urgent and powerful were their prayers. The following morning God in His mercy caused such trouble in the army that Vitale d'Aversa, that proud man, seeing that he could not succeed in his plan, turned away and no longer molested that part of the country. Shortly afterwards he died miserably.

During the interrogation of the witnesses in the cause of canonization the nuns stress the fact that the Saracens had surmounted the wall, and were already in the cloister of the monastery. This still further explains their panic and adds lustre to Clare's calm courage and confidence.

Since that day the people of Assisi have always kept June 22 as a festa, the Festa del Voto, when they celebrate the liberation of their city through the prayers of St. Clare and her Sisters, and pay their homage at her tomb in Santa Chiara, and to the memory of that day in San Damiano.

After this tremendous achievement Clare and her Sisters can only have turned again to their penances, their unceasing prayer and charity with increased faith and thanksgiving, knowing that the glory was not theirs.

VI

The Later Years

CLARE was nearing fifty, and her health had greatly deteriorated; as one by one Francis' friends passed away — Jacopa de' Settesoli had died in 1239 and been buried in Elias' basilica — everything connected with him became a precious relic for the future.

It was of capital importance to collect and preserve all the sayings of Francis, and Brother Leo confided to Clare's keeping the rolls of parchment in which he and other of the early companions had recorded many of Francis' words. Besides these there were the "many written words" of which Clare spoke in her testament; everything connected with their joint ideal was a sacred trust.

As far as increasing infirmity allowed, Clare led the community life, she healed the sick, cared for all, she did needlework, and almost certainly she wrote many other letters, now lost. She had to keep in touch with the exterior developments of the whole Fraternity with which the Second Order was so bound up. Certainly for some time she must have been preoccupied with the Rule of the Poor Ladies. Gregory had used the argument of her obedience to his own Rule of 1218 to urge it upon Agnes, but there were clauses in it which could never satisfy Clare. Agnes was doing her best to get it changed for the Prague house, and Gregory himself had tinkered at it

through dispensations though he insisted on its nominal observance, partly perhaps for sentimental reasons, partly because of
the difficulty of satisfying the demands of the many houses of
Poor Ladies. After all he could say that Francis had accepted
his Rule, and Clare observed it; and perhaps she felt that
Gregory was too old, too harassed by Frederick and his many
enormous difficulties, to be expected to make substantial con-
cessions to Agnes or anyone else. Only a short time before his
death he had had to cope with and denounce the wandering
women calling themselves Minoresses who posed as belonging
to the Second Order: worries of all kinds pressed him hard on
every side.

The new Pope only lived sixteen days, and no further con-
clave was held until 1243 when Innocent IV was elected. He
had a notable disciple of St. Francis, Brother Niccolò di Carbio,
as his chaplain and confessor, with five other Franciscans in
his household, and he was a staunch protector of the Poor
Ladies among whom was his own niece.

During the early years of his reign, however, he had no personal contact with Clare, for the dire feud with the Emperor
drove the papal court to Lyons. Innocent needed a very strong
fighting spirit to face the situation, since Frederick was by no
means the only trouble. The death of Genghis Khan had not
perturbed his successors in their tremendous onslaught on the
Western World. The Tartars were magnificent soldiers, and
utterly regardless of life they ravaged everything they met, and
their empire sprawled over the far and near East, even threatening Vienna. If ever there was a time when Europe needed unity
it was at that moment, and it must have been extremely irritating and afflicting to Innocent that a good part of the energy
which was essential for repulsing the Tartars was being frittered
away in trying to control Frederick's mercurial ambition, and
in dealing with European quarrels.

The gulf between the Pope and Emperor steadily widened
and deepened; in vain King Louis of France tried to act as

peacemaker, realizing what an enormous advantage it would be to both sides. Perhaps Innocent feared Frederick too much and distrusted him too completely; perhaps he had no choice; anyhow two years later he summoned a General Council which deposed the Emperor though no ruler in Christendom would accept the Pope's offer and step into Frederick's shoes. Louis IX refused the imperial dominions in Italy on behalf of his brother, and again he attempted to mediate when the Pope proclaimed a Crusade against the Emperor, an enterprise which incidentally could only prejudice the Crusade that Louis was preparing against the infidels who held the Holy Places.

At such a juncture Elias' imperial partisanship was undoubtedly an extra thorn in Innocent's side. He summoned him to Lyons to justify his conduct; but even a messenger sent by Giovanni da Parma, the Minister General, who was only too anxious to bring the friend of Francis and Clare back into the communion of the Church and Order, failed to move Elias. He remained in Cortona, and Innocent renewed the excommunication.

During all these tremendous and harassing vicissitudes the Pope was pursued by the difficulties in the Franciscan family, since there was no reason to save him what affection had perhaps withheld from Gregory. His letters show clearly that the friars were only too anxious to be relieved of the material care of the Poor Ladies, who on their side were determined to preserve all the ties connecting the First and Second Orders. It was not a simple matter for the friars, for convents of Poor Ladies were arising all over Europe in all sorts of conditions, and repeatedly the Pope had to urge the faithful to support these houses with generosity for which he offered indulgences. However, in 1245 he decided in favour of the Poor Ladies, and this ruling applied to Italy, France, and Germany. On this point, at least, their minds were at rest, but all these controversies and uncertainties involving the fundamental question of poverty must have been intensely painful to Clare, and the early days of her vocation must have seemed very far away.

The Poor Ladies also complained to the Pope that Ugolino's "Rule" bound them too strictly to the Benedictine observance, but even this feeling was not shared by those houses that had sprung from a Benedictine origin. Anyhow Innocent confirmed Ugolino's Rule for the Poor Ladies in November, 1245, and he stated explicitly that he did so at their own request.

Perhaps the request was not unanimous, for barely two years later, again at their special request, Innocent confirmed a new Rule for them, this time of his own making, and then in 1250 we find him writing to Cardinal Rainaldo, bishop of Ostia, that though he had given the Sisters of the Order of Saint Damian a new Rule of life, he did not wish it to be forced on any community unwilling to profess it.

Innocent's Rule was more or less founded on that of the friars, and it is symptomatic that he uses the word "Sister" and not "Lady." He recommends the Sisters to follow the "use" of the friars in their recitation of the Divine Office, a use which had been compiled by Gregory not long before his death with the help of Haymo of Faversham. But especially Innocent formally committed the Sisters in all things to the care and government of his beloved sons the Minister General and the provincial ministers of the Friars Minor; he stipulated that no new convent was to be founded without the authorization of the General Chapter of the friars; the Sisters were permitted though not forced to hold property in common.

This Rule was distasteful to the friars, who did not want, in a moment of great expansion in their own activities, to have to shoulder the burden of the Sisters; but it was also distasteful to a number of the Sisters. Some houses of Poor Ladies still clung to their old Benedictine tradition and did not favour its efface-ment; among the Sisters, too, as among the friars there was a sharp division of opinion on the rigid or mitigated observance of poverty; neither did they fancy the Pope's hint that this new Rule would abolish dispensations and ensure uniformity. It did not please any of the extremists, and Clare, for all her attachment to poverty, yet at different times had shown herself ready to accept presents, and to allow the same to her Sisters. Francis, too, had accepted extensive presents; one has only to think of La Verna! The general opinion among Franciscan scholars is that Clare did not accept this Rule; the property clause and the general mitigation of the idea of penance would have seemed to her a betrayal of her whole life.

Circumstances combined to urge Clare to compile a Rule which should express and give form to her and Francis' ideal of the life of the Poor Ladies, and probably she actually wrote her Rule about this time; she and her Sisters had lived it for years, and every page is eloquent of personal experience, even though in many places she quotes from the Rules both of Ugolino and Innocent and repeats important clauses from the original Rule given by Francis. It is entitled *Forma Vitae Ordinis Sororum Pauperum* and throughout it shines with Clare's inspiration and with her admirable common sense. She describes herself in the opening words, "Clare, the unprofitable servant of Christ, and the little plant of the most blessed father Francis": like him she wanted to be "humble and subject to all," and it was truly said that "the Lady Clare was as intent upon caring for her Sisters and observing the Rule as any man could be in guarding his treasure." Her solicitude for the suffering was born of her own long experience of illness, just as long experience of community life had taught her that temper and perturbation can never lead to peace between Sisters; the remedy for disagreement is not worry and self-assertion, but prayer. She asks for a friar as chaplain and two honest lay Brothers of holy life "to help us in our poverty even as we have always had through the courtesy of the said brothers." The word *courtesy* is again an echo of Francis, and Clare cared for it as much as he did. Clare's own life as well as her ideal for the order is summed up in the last words when she wishes that "ever stable in the Catholic faith, ever submissive and subject at the feet of

Holy Church we may always imitate the poverty and humility of our Lord Jesus Christ and His blessed Mother, and may always faithfully carry out the words of the Gospel even as we have promised."

About this time Clare must have written her Testament. Many Franciscan scholars deny that it is genuine, and yet it has something of the flavour of her other writings. If it is a forgery, it must have been compiled from traditional sayings. It runs:

Among the many graces we have received, and do receive from the Lord the Father of mercies there is one for which we must show Him most special gratitude, which is the grace of our vocation. Inasmuch as it is the most perfect, so much the more does it claim our gratitude. We should always bear in mind the words of Saint Paul, "Know thy vocation." The Son of God has called us to Himself, and the acts and words of Blessed Francis His true lover have brought us by the narrowest path to this day. Therefore, dear sisters, let us never forget the gifts our Lord has granted us especially this grace of our vocation which He gave us through His servant Blessed Francis.

Soon after his conversion when as yet he had neither companions nor sisters, while he was repairing the church of Saint Damian, through the Holy Spirit he foretold to poor men all that has come to pass. Speaking to them in a high voice in the French tongue he said, "Come brothers and help me, for here there will dwell ladies through whose piety our heavenly Father will be glorified throughout the Church."

Our blessed father foretold this not only for us, but for all who, by their holy lives, should share our lot. Therefore, my sisters, with what fervour, with what faith and perseverance should we keep the commandments of God, and the rule of our holy father that we may appear before our Judge on the last day having multiplied the talents entrusted to us. We have been chosen by Him to be a mirror of the faith together with those sisters who will be called with our vocation that they too may give an example of virtuous life. For all these mercies we are bound to bless the Lord, to praise and follow Him, asking His divine help in all things.

Not long after the conversion of Blessed Francis, I, with a few companions, promised voluntary obedience, and this was manifested to me through the grace in him. Our blessed father Francis gave thanks to the Lord, and was moved with compassion for me and my sisters, knowing well that although we were weak, yet we had not refused to endure poverty and humiliations, and so he promised us his care and protection together with that of his brothers. Thus by the will of the most high God, and of Blessed Francis we came to dwell in the monastery of Saint Damian where soon the Lord of His mercy and grace multiplied us in order that what had been foretold by His holy one might be fulfilled. For we had sojourned in another place, but only for a short time.

About this time Blessed Francis gave us in writing our rule of life which especially exhorts us to persevere in holy Poverty. He was not content during his lifetime to exhort us by frequent discourses and by his own deeds to love and observe holy poverty, but he also sent us many written words, so that after his death we should follow the path he had marked out for us. And we have faithfully observed our promises following in the steps of the Son of God, and of our blessed father Francis, who chose for his inheritance to renounce all earthly possessions.

I, Clare, unworthy handmaid of Jesus Christ, and of the poor servants of Saint Damian's, have twice voluntarily bound myself to the observation of holy Poverty so that after my death the sisters may not depart from it. And to make sure that this might not be altered I procured its confirmation by our holy father Pope Innocent III under whose pontificate our order began.

I commend my sisters present and future to the successors of blessed Francis our father and founder, and to all his religious, that by their example and teaching they may help us to serve God in holy poverty, and humbly I pray them to see to it, that we, frail plants as we are, may not swerve from our sacred purpose. If it should happen that my sisters leave this monastery and go elsewhere, I fervently desire that they keep this rule in strict integrity.

I also exhort all my sisters in the name of Jesus Christ to walk always in the path of holy simplicity, humility, and poverty, and in all intercourse to observe the discretion taught us by blessed Francis. Only by means of these virtues, and through the mercy of Him who has chosen us can we spread abroad the odour of a good reputation. Love one another in Jesus Christ, and let this charity show itself outwardly in good works; thus other sisters, incited by your good example, will grow in love of God and their neighbour. I pray for her who has to govern that she may raise herself more by modesty and virtues than by dignity of office, causing her sisters to obey her through love more than through duty. Let her also watch over her spiritual daughters with the tenderness that a good mother has for her children; in manner let her be kindly, humble, and accessible so that they may never fear to open their hearts to her on all occasions. And the sisters should remember that for love of God they have renounced their own will, and have promised willing and unreserved obedience to their mother, so that she, finding love, humility, and concord among her sisters, may feel the burden of her charge lightened, and her office less troublesome.

Let us take care, O my sisters, that having embraced the life of strict and holy living we may never depart from it through carelessness or ignorance and in doing so cause harm to our Lord, to Blessed Francis, and holy Church whose eyes are fixed upon our conduct. For it is written: Accursed are those who abandon Thy commandment. Humbly kneeling I pray our Lord to grant us the grace of final perseverance through the merits of His holy Mother, blessed Francis, and all the saints.

Dearly loved sisters present and future, I leave these things in writing that they may be better remembered by each of you. And I remain your mother and your servant.

In this, in her letters, in her Rule, Clare had said her last word; but she was still the immensely eloquent living example of what she taught.

Clare's Sisters were often desperately anxious, partly on account of her visibly declining strength, and also because they knew how she longed for a definite papal reassurance that the Privilege of Poverty would be maintained. Encouragement came from her old friends the Benedictines of San Paolo for it was revealed to one of the nuns that Clare would live until she had been visited by the Pope. At that moment nothing could have seemed more unlikely; then suddenly the news spread that the Emperor Frederick *Stupor Mundi* had died at Ferentino in Apulia. Even since his final excommunication one disaster after another had overtaken him in Germany as in Italy: nevertheless when news came in the spring of 1250 of the defeat of the Christian forces in the East, of Louis IX a prisoner of the Sultan with the flower of French chivalry, Frederick wrote to the other

Christian rulers calling for a joint effort in aid of the King of France; he sent an embassy to the Sultan demanding his release and went himself to Sicily to prepare an expedition. He got no further, and at the last his son, Manfred, wrote to Conrad his half-brother, "on his deathbed our Father, full of contrition submitted himself as a good Catholic to his mother the sacrosanct Church of Rome." Who knows perhaps he thought of Elizabeth, Agnes, Isabelle, Francis, and Clare?

This was in December, 1250, and although imperial mercenaries still harassed the papal territory in Umbria the news must have raised Guelph hopes and everywhere have stimulated conjecture as to the consequences since no successor could inherit Frederick's personal ascendancy. Surely Clare's thoughts must have turned to Elias.

The way was opened for the Pope's return to Italy, and in the following spring Innocent began his southward journey, and in 1252 took up his residence in Perugia.

In September of that year Cardinal Rainaldo visited San Damiano and gave Clare Holy Communion, and she begged him to sponsor her wish for a full and categorical recognition of the rule of poverty. Rainaldo himself authorized Clare's own Rule for use in San Damiano, and certainly advocated her cause with the Pope. It would have been strange had he not done so, for Clare had the matured will of a lifetime behind her with the power of sanctity, and in all eyes she was the impersonation of the ideal of Francis.

That Christmas there came to her a beautiful echo of the festival Francis had once kept at Greccio. Celano tells how the Sisters being in choir for the recitation of Matins, Clare was alone in her cell, far too ill to move. "And as she thought on the Child Jesus, she was sad that on this night she could not join with the Sisters in singing His praise, and sighing she said: 'O Lord God, here I am alone with Thee in this place.' As soon as she had so said, suddenly she heard the beautiful music and the singing in the church of Saint Francis. She heard the joyful psalmody of the friars and the sound of the organ; and that church was so far away that truly she could not have heard anything had God not willed that the sweet music of the festival should reach her, or that her hearing should be miraculously increased and strengthened. Surely she who excelled all others had deserved to see what is so excellent, that is the church of Saint Francis, and in it the Crib of the Lord. When her daughters came to her the following morning she said to them, 'Blessed be my Lord Jesus Christ for when you had left me, He would not leave me, and thanks to His grace I heard all the solemn festival that was celebrated in the church this night.' "

Incidentally this mention of the crib seems to indicate that the friars were in the habit of recalling the Greccio Christmas by setting up a crib with the essential figures, manger and Child and ox and ass, "to stir people's hearts to devotion," as Francis had wished. There seems no reason to interpret Celano's words in any other sense.

That spring was to be momentous for Clare, and in April she saw her prayers for Brother Elias answered. After Frederick's death he continued to live in Cortona building his great church there to which he gave the relic of the cross he had brought from Jerusalem. His mind had at last turned from politics; he recognized his own fault to the Church and the Order, and admitted his sin in having supported the Emperor, and begged to be absolved. "Lord have mercy upon me a sinner; forgive my vanity and pride. Miserere mei Domine." On Easter Eve the archpriest of Cortona absolved him, on Easter Monday he received Holy Communion and died the following day. Elias' reconciliation must have been one of Clare's last great earthly joys.

The Pope arrived in Assisi about that same time, and on May 25 he consecrated the upper church of Elias' basilica, to the building of which he had substantially contributed. It was on this occasion that he canonized St. Stanislaus of Poland. He also went to San Damiano to see Clare, and Celano tells:

"Blessed Clare's holy body, worn out by long sickness was attacked by a fresh affliction which betokened that Christ was preparing to call her to Himself into eternal joy. Then the Lord Pope hastened to visit her with his cardinals for he deemed it fitting thus to honour the death of her whose life was universally praised and honoured.

"Having entered the monastery he went at once to where she was lying, and gave her his hand to kiss which she did with much devotion, humbly begging him to suffer her to kiss his foot. Wishing to content her, he mounted a little stool, and having extended his foot she kissed it right reverently on the instep and on the sole. Then, her face shining with seraphic joy, she begged him to absolve her from her sins.

"'Would to God I had as little need of shriving as thou,' said the Pope, 'but for thy greater consolation I absolve thee with all the blessings and indulgences that are in my power to give.' When the Pope and cardinals were departed, Blessed Clare received Holy Communion from the hands of the Provincial Minister of the Friars Minor, and afterwards, her hands crossed, she looked up and said to the sisters, who were beside her, 'Praise the Lord with me to-day, for Christ has given me such a gift that all Heaven and earth could not sufficiently thank Him for I have received Him the All-Highest, and I have received absolution from His Vicar.'" Sister Francesca told later how when the priest brought Clare Holy Communion she saw the Host vanish from his hands and the divine Child appeared radiating light which shone all round the bed.

The Sisters could not bear to leave Clare alone for a moment; they thought neither of food nor drink, says Celano, and wept bitterly, so great was their distress. As for Agnes who had just returned to San Damiano from Monticelli, she was more dead than alive with grief and nothing would comfort her. "O holy Sister," she cried, "don't leave me without you," to which Clare answered, "My dearest, above all, if God wills that I should go, do not cry, for you will follow me very soon and have great consolations before you die." She also comforted some lay Sisters from Monticelli with "divine words," and ordered her veil to be sent to that monastery.

As the summer drew on and Clare became weaker the devotion and faith of the people increased, and "many times cardinals and prelates and people in twos and threes and fours would come to visit her, for all were convinced that she was a great saint. For seventeen days she was unable to eat, but the Lord comforted her with such fortitude that all who beheld her were strengthened and consoled." Brother Rainaldo was often with her, and when he would have consoled her for all her suffering she answered: "Since I experienced the grace of our Lord Jesus Christ through the merits and teaching of our Father Francis no suffering has been hard for me, no exertion or penance or illness painful."

The account of Clare's last days is clearly given by Celano and the Sisters who never left her and were witnesses in the Cause of canonization, especially Filippa, Angeluccia, Benvenuta, Anastasia, and Agnese of Oportulo.

On Friday evening three days before the death of Madonna Chiara of blessed memory the sisters were gathered round their mother weeping sadly; one sister sat close beside her and no one spoke. Then Madonna Chiara began to commend herself to God saying: "Go in peace for thou wilt be escorted since He who created thee provided for thy sanctification, and when He had created thee, He infused into thee His Holy Spirit, and He has ever watched over thee as a mother watches over her little child."

The Sisters could not understand her wonderful familiarity with divine grace, and Sister Anastasia asked her to whom she spoke such words. Whereupon the saint answered: "I am speaking to my blessed soul. . . . Blessed be Thou, O Lord, who hast created me." She spoke also of the Blessed Trinity, but "with such subtlety" that the Sisters could not well understand her meaning. "Then the sister who was watching beside her said to another who was there, 'You who have such a good memory, remember all that our Lady is saying.'" Madonna Clare heard this and said to all present, "You will remember what I say as long as He wishes who is causing me to speak."

Sister Benvenuta was so impressed with the words spoken by her mother to her own soul that she sat there meditating "on the great and marvellous sanctity of the Lady Clare, and it seemed to her that the whole court of Heaven was preparing to honour this saint. Especially our glorious Lady the blessed virgin Mary was preparing the garments in which to clothe this new saint. Then she saw with her bodily eyes a great multitude of virgins dressed in white with crowns on their heads coming in by the door of the cell where the said mother Saint Clare was lying. Among these virgins there was one far more beautiful than the others, and she wore a more splendid crown than any. And above the crown there was a vessel from which shone such splendour that the whole house seemed illuminated.

"The virgins gathered round the bed of the Lady Clare, and she who was the greatest among them covered the bed with a transparent cloth which was so fine that though it covered the Lady Clare, yet she was still clearly visible. Then that greatest among the virgins bent down and her face was quite close to the face of the Lady Clare, above her breast, so that she who saw it could not distinguish one from the other. After this all disappeared."

Sister Benvenuta, who was the witness, went on to assure the judges of the Cause that she was wide awake at the time. On that same Friday evening Clare repeatedly asked Sister Amata, her niece, "Do you see the King of Glory as I do?"

She blessed all her Sisters and daughters and spoke to them gentle words of comfort; and when she made her confession she could say that she had never knowingly transgressed her baptismal vows or those of her Order.

There was, however, still a shadow on Clare's mind, for though Cardinal Rainaldo had assured her that her Rule would be fully approved by the Pope, no document had arrived, and

Sister Filippa testified that Clare's only wish was to see the Pope's letter, to kiss it before she died. At last, on August 9 Innocent issued the Bull, *Solet Annuere,* and a friar brought it to San Damiano next day, "and although she was not far from death the Lady Clare took it reverently into her hands and kissed it. . . . "

She wished the Passion to be read and sent for the Brothers who were priests and the other Brothers among whom was Brother Juniper, that worthy minstrel of the Lord who often spoke to her of Jesus Christ in words burning with love. When he approached she was filled with new happiness and spiritual joy, and asked him what news he had of Christ, whereupon Brother Juniper opened his mouth and "the burning fire of his heart's love sent forth flaming sparks of words."

Brother Angelo the courteous was there, crying himself even when he tried "to comfort the Sisters with gentle words," Brother Giles, too, and Brother Leo who could only repeatedly kiss the bed on which Clare lay. She asked Sister Agnes to recite her favourite prayer to the Five Wounds, and the whispers that the Sisters could catch were all of the Passion; constantly "she repeated the name of our Lord Jesus Christ." The last word that Sister Agnes heard was *"Pretiosa in conspectu Domini mors sanctorum ejus."* Thus "the Lady Clare who truly shone in untarnished purity entered the brightness of eternal light." It was Monday, August 11, the feast of San Rufino, the patron of Assisi.

All Assisi and many people far beyond it had been waiting for the news. Twenty-seven years had passed since Francis' death, forty-two since Clare and Agnes had entered San Damiano: the old folk of the city could still remember them as children. All the citizens streamed down the path to the monastery to pay homage to her who had saved them, who was beloved by all, revered by all, Assisi's greatest daughter. "Alas, alas, good lady, friend of God, truly she was a saint." For once opinion was unanimous!

The Podestà at once set guards round the monastery, for it seemed only too likely that relic hunters would try to rob Assisi of its second great treasure. The next day the Pope came from Perugia accompanied by the cardinals, by the Bishop of Assisi and other bishops, and a multitude of friends. The friars began the Office of the Dead when the Pope remarked that it would have been more suitable to sing the Office of Virgins; and indeed he would have wished to canonize her on the spot. But Cardinal Rainaldo observed that the Church's ritual should be followed and so the Office of the Dead was continued.

It had been decided to bury Clare in San Giorgio as had been done with Francis, and for the same reason of safety. The Pope with the pontifical court and a vast concourse accompanied the body from San Damiano up to the city; and that funeral procession, too, was one of triumph. But how empty the monastery must have been when all was over!

Clare kept her promise to Agnes who followed her sister and mother on November 16 of that same year and was later beatified, and St. Juliana of Liége also died in 1253.

About two months later Innocent delegated the archbishop of Spoleto to record Clare's virtues and miracles; and with the archdeacon of Spoleto, the Bishop of Assisi, the Archpriest of Trevi, and Brothers Leo, Angelo, and Marco, and Ser Martino the notary, he went to interview the Sisters at San Damiano and to collect evidence for the Cause of canonization.

Miracles abounded at Clare's tomb. Two children were liberated from evil spirits, a raving lunatic was cured, Valentino of Spello felt his stiff and deformed limbs suddenly acquire strength and flexibility. Jacobello of Spoleto was twelve and had lost his sight: twice he dreamed that a beautiful lady called him, "Jacobello, why don't you come to me in Assisi and be cured?" When he reached Assisi the crowd in the church was so dense that he lay down outside the door. His dream was repeated, and sight returned as he touched Clare's tomb. Buona di Monte Galliano had lost one child carried off by a wolf, and the same disaster happened to another: with all her strength she invoked the help of St. Clare, and the baby was found in the forest with a dog licking its wounds. Another girl carried off by a wolf cried to Clare for help, and the wolf set her down and ran off. Clare seemed to help all who turned to her.

Innocent died in 1254, and it fell to his successor Cardinal Rainaldo, then Alexander IV, to preside at the canonization in the cathedral of Anagni on August 12, 1255. His Bull of canonization is in itself a poem — "Her feet stood upon earth while her soul was already in Heaven." It was a true description of her who had passed through this world as a living witness to the beatitudes, "Blessed are the poor in spirit for theirs is the kingdom of Heaven, blessed are the clean of heart for they shall see God."

Very soon after Clare's death the Poor Ladies opened proceedings to have the monastery transferred to San Giorgio; they were too desolate at San Damiano without Clare, they longed to carry on her — their — life in the place where she lay; they felt their right to be as great as that of Brothers who guarded the tomb of St. Francis. The continued raids of the Ghibellines in Spoleto — in the year after Clare's death several hundred people were massacred — would also have inclined the City Fathers to moving the nuns within the walls. Eventually an agreement was reached between the nuns, the chapter of San Rufino and the civil authorities, and the exchange of San Damiano for San Giorgio was ratified by a Bull of Alexander IV in 1259: but even before that date the Sisters seem to have moved, headed by the abbess, Benedetta, Clare's first successor.

They took with them the crucifix which had spoken to Francis, the ivory and silver pyx with which Clare had faced the Saracens, the grating through which the Sisters had been in the habit of receiving Holy Communion, and had looked their last on Francis, and a number of other relics. They could not take Francis' and Clare's presence from San Damiano; nor have the centuries taken it, and there it remains, one of the most precious of all relics.

Very soon after Clare's death it had been decided to build a basilica in her honour and to hold her body, into which the older church of San Giorgio could be incorporated. The work was entrusted to Philip of Campello; and like that of Elias' basilica it was carried through with amazing speed. In 1260 Clare's body was translated from its temporary resting place and enclosed in a sarcophagus of travertine bound with iron bars, and it was buried in a small chamber in the depths of the masonry below the high altar. The ceremony took place in the presence of a number of prelates, of Friars Minor including St. Bonaventure, and the civil authorities of Assisi. Five years later Pope Clement IV consecrated the high altar, and in the Bull issued for the occasion he declared that Clare's body lay beneath it.

Already Thomas of Celano's "life" of St. Clare, which had been commissioned by the Pope at the time of her canonization, was being read; and one cannot read that life without being conscious of how acutely the author felt his own words that Clare "was one of those great souls beyond all human praise." To the few remaining Franciscans of the first generation she was the one who had never faltered; to the younger Brothers and Sisters she was a tremendous inspiration; all felt they had a new friend in heaven.

The church of San Giorgio, rebuilt and enlarged, was rededicated to St. Clare, and was probably frescoed by artists who worked in San Francesco, while pictures of her were painted based on detailed contemporary descriptions. For a century after her death she was always represented holding a lily or the book of the Rule, sometimes surrounded by the chief scenes of her life. Then came a change and she began to be depicted with a pyx in her hands or even a vase, and in a picture by Giovanni di Paolo flames are coming from the vase and in the midst of them a Host is discernible. From this the artists passed to the monstrance, and an early example is in the beautiful Flemish tapestry given by the Franciscan Pope Sixtus IV to the Sacro Convento. Therefore in the iconography of Clare the first accent is on her purity of soul and body, on her wisdom as a foundress; but after the institution of the feast of Corpus Christi and the consequent increase in public devotion to the Blessed Sacrament, she was set in her rightful place as one of the great worshippers and lovers of our Lord in the Sacrament of the Altar.

Clare's body remained hidden for six hundred years, but after the discovery of St. Francis' body in 1818, it was only natural that there should have been a general wish to find that of St. Clare. In 1850 permission was obtained from Cardinal Pecci, then archbishop of Perugia and later Pope Leo XIII, to begin excavating in the basilica beneath the high altar. On September 3 the workmen came upon the chamber containing the sarcophagus which was in the same condition as when it had been buried. Those present noticed a very sweet scent emanating from Clare's body which lay with the head turned to the right, one hand on her breast, the other stretched beside her. Thus after six centuries her daughters saw their Mother.

She was reburied in a sarcophagus of plate glass and modern gilding.

A most precious discovery was made some fifty years ago by the Abbess Matilde Rossi who came upon the original of the Rule of St. Clare wrapped in a cloak which is thought to have belonged to her, and had somehow survived the various suppressions and depredations which the monastery had suffered from time to time. It is now preserved in the basilica, and we can see the whole text of the Bull, *Solet Annuere,* of Innocent IV which contains the confirmation of Clare's Rule. The complete Rule is contained in the Pope's letter, and on the reverse of the parchment are the words in a thirteenth-century hand: "Blessed Clare held this, and in her devotion kissed it many, many times."

The present ornate crypt of the Church dates from the

nineteenth century, and round Clare lie Ortolana, Agnese, and others of the first Sisters. All over the world the life of the Second Franciscan Order continues; and though the Sisters are unseen, they are not isolated from their fellow men, for their mission is through prayer to carry the whole world into the will, which is the love, of God. This was the heritage left by Clare to her daughters, and in many ways her light radiates outwards from the cloister to those who are living beyond it. What she taught is valid for all.

Francis holding the cross, and Clare holding the monstrance stand before us, two eloquent living beings whose wish is to convince us that the way to God, to peace, to unity, is found only through Christ and through love. What does their insistence on poverty mean for us who have not thrown away everything? It may not be a reproach, but it is a warning. Everything in creation belongs to God; whatever we have individually is lent us. Every form of selfishness leads to stagnation, slows down and prevents the vital sap of charity from flowing, separates us from God, and therefore from each other.

In this life, Francis and Clare had such great and warm human hearts, and such God-enlightened souls that even reading their story makes us feel near them. Now, in their closeness to God, they are still nearer to all who need them, and they can light the love of Christ in other hearts. There are no barriers left for them, and they can help us to break down those that are the cause of so much of our misery. As Clare said to Agnes, so we can say to her: "Pray that by the help of God we may be enabled to call upon the mercy of Jesus Christ, and with you to enjoy His blessedness in the Beatific Vision."

THE OFFICE OF THE PASSION

In his "legend" of St. Clare, Celano says that "she learned and frequently recited with attachment the Office of the Cross which Francis, the lover of the Cross had instituted." The text of the Office from the Quaracchi edition, was published in English, in 1906, by Father, later Archbishop, Paschal Robinson, O.F.M. We give his text in a somewhat modified form:

"Here begin the Psalms arranged to reverence and recall and praise the Passion of Our Lord. They begin from Compline of Maundy Thursday because on that night Our Lord Jesus Christ was betrayed and taken prisoner. Blessed Francis was wont to say the office in this manner: first he said the prayer taught us by Our Lord and Master, Our Father most holy who art in Heaven, etc., with the Praises as follows: Holy, holy, holy, Lord God Almighty, who is, and was and is to come. Let us praise and exalt Him above all for ever.

"Worthy art Thou, O Lord our God, to receive praise, honour, glory and benediction. Let us praise and exalt Him above all for ever.

"The Lamb that was slain is worthy to receive power and divinity, and wisdom and strength and honour and benediction. Let us praise and exalt Him above all for ever. . . .

"All ye works of the Lord, bless ye the Lord. Let us praise and exalt Him above all for ever.

"Give praise to God all you His servants, and you that fear Him, little and great. Let us praise and exalt Him above all for ever.

"Let the Heavens and earth praise Him, the glorious One, and every creature which is in Heaven and on earth, and under the earth, in the seas and all that are in them. Let us praise and exalt Him above all for ever.

"Glory be to the Father, and to the Son, and to the Holy Ghost. Let us praise and exalt Him above all for ever.

"As it was in the beginning, is now and ever shall be world without end. Let us praise and exalt Him above all for ever.

"Almighty, most holy, most high and supreme God, highest good, all good, wholly good, who alone art good. To Thee we render all praise, all glory, all thanks, all honour, all blessing, and we shall always refer all good to Thee. Amen.

"When he had finished the Praises he began this antiphon, Holy Mary. First he said the psalms of the holy Virgin; besides which he said other psalms which he selected, and at the end of all the psalms he said the psalms of the Passion, at the end he said the antiphon Holy Virgin Mary.

"This completes the Office."

1. At Compline

Antiphon: Holy Virgin Mary:

Psalm 55:9.   O God I have declared to thee my life; thou hast set my tears in thy sight.

Psalm 40:8.   All my enemies devised evils against me.

Psalm 70:10.   They have consulted together.

Psalm 108:5.   And they repaid me evil for good, and hatred for my love.

Psalm 108:4.   Instead of making me a return of love they detracted me; but I gave myself to prayer.

Psalm 21:12.   My holy Father, King of Heaven and earth, depart not from me; for tribulation is near and there is none to help.

Psalm 55:10.   When I cry unto thee, then shall mine enemies be turned back; behold I know that thou art my God.

Psalm 37:12.   My friends and my neighbours have drawn near and stood against me; and they that were near me stood afar off.

Psalm 87:9.   Thou hast put away my acquaintance far from me; they have set me an abomination to them; I was delivered up and came not forth.

Psalm 21:20.   Holy Father, remove not thy help far from me; my God look towards my help.

Psalm 37:23. Attend unto my help, O Lord, the God of my
salvation. Glory be, etc.:

Antiphon: Holy Virgin Mary, there is none like unto thee born
in the world among women, daughter and handmaid of
the most high King, the heavenly Father. Mother of our
most holy Lord Jesus Christ, spouse of the Holy Ghost;
pray for us with Saint Michael Archangel, and all the
Virtues of Heaven, and all the saints, to thy most holy
and beloved Son our Lord and Master. Glory be, etc. Amen.

*The foregoing antiphon is said at all the hours, for antiphon,
chapter, hymn, versicle, and prayer, likewise at Matins. He said
nothing else in them except this antiphon with its psalms. At the
completion of the Office blessed Francis always said: "Let us bless
the Lord God, living and true; let us refer praise, glory, honour,
blessing and all praise to Him always. Amen; Amen; Fiat; Fiat."*

2. At Matins

Antiphon: Holy Virgin Mary:

Psalm 87:2. O Lord God of my salvation, I have cried in the day
and night before thee.

Psalm 87:3. Let my prayer come in before thee; incline thy ear
to my petition.

Psalm 68:19. Attend to my soul and deliver it: save me because
of my enemies.

Psalm 21:10. For thou art he that has drawn me out of the
womb; my hope from the breasts of my mother;

Psalm 21:11. I was cast upon thee from the womb. From my
mother's womb thou art my God.

Psalm 21:12. Depart not from me.

Psalm 68:20. Thou knowest my reproach, and my confusion and
my shame.

Psalm 68:21. In thy sight are all they that afflict me; my heart
hath expected reproach and misery.
And I looked for one that would grieve together with me,
but there was none, and for one that would comfort me
and I found none.

Psalm 85:14. O God, the wicked are risen up against me, and

the assembly of the mighty hath sought for my soul; and they have not set thee before their eyes.

Psalm 87:5. I am counted among them that go down to the pit; I am become as a man without help,

Psalm 87:6. free among the dead. Thou art my Father, most holy, my King and my God.

Psalm 37:23. Attend unto my help, O Lord God of my salvation.

Antiphon: Holy Virgin Mary, etc.

3. *At Prime*

Antiphon: Holy Virgin Mary:

PSALM

Psalm 56:1. Have mercy on me O God, have mercy on me; for my soul trusteth in thee.

Psalm 56:2. And in the shadow of thy wings will I hope, until iniquity pass away.

Psalm 56:3. I will cry to my most holy Father, the most High; to God who hath done good to me.

Psalm 56:4. He hath sent from Heaven and hath delivered me; he hath made them a reproach that trod upon me. God hath sent his power and his truth.

Psalm 17:18. He delivered me from my strongest enemies and from them that hated me; for they were too strong for me.

Psalm 56:7. They prepared a snare for my feet, and they bowed down my soul; they dug a pit before my face, and they are fallen into it.

Psalm 56:8. My heart is ready, O God, my heart is ready; I will sing and rehearse a psalm.

Psalm 56:9. Arise O my glory, arise psaltery and harp. I will arise early.

Psalm 56:10. I will give praise to thee, O Lord, among the people; I will sing a psalm to thee among the nations.

Psalm 56:11. For thy mercy is magnified even to the heavens; and thy truth unto the clouds.

Psalm 56:12. Be thou exalted, O God, above the heavens; and thy glory above all the earth.

Antiphon: Holy Virgin Mary, etc.

4. *At Tierce*

Antiphon: Holy Virgin Mary:

PSALM

Psalm 55:2.   Have mercy on me, O God, for man hath trodden me under foot; all the day long he hath afflicted me, fighting against me;

Psalm 55:3.   My enemies have trodden on me all the day long; for they are many that make war against me.

Psalm 40:8.   All my enemies devised evil against me.

Psalm 40:9.   They have made a wicked plan against me.

Psalm 70:10.   They lay in wait for my soul.

Psalm 40:7.   They went out and spoke to the same purpose.

Psalm 21:8.   All they that saw me have laughed me to scorn; they have spoken with the lips and wagged the head.

Psalm 21:7.   But I am a worm and no man, a reproach of men and outcast of the people.

Psalm 30:12.   I have become a reproach among all my enemies, and very much to my neighbours; and a fear to my acquaintance.

Psalm 21:20.   Holy Father, remove not thy help far from me; my God, look toward my defence.

Psalm 37:23.   Attend unto my help, O Lord God of my salvation. Glory be, etc.

Antiphon: Holy Virgin Mary, etc.

5. *At Sext*

Antiphon: Holy Virgin Mary:

PSALM

Psalm 141:2.   I cried to the Lord with my voice; with my voice I made my supplication to the Lord.

Psalm 141:3.   I pour out my prayer in his sight; and before him I declare my trouble.

Psalm 141:4.   When my spirit failed me, then thou knewest my paths. In this way wherein I walked, they have hidden a snare for me.

Psalm 141:5.   I looked on my right hand, and behold, and there was no one that would know me. Flight hath failed me; and there is no one that hath regard to my soul.

Psalm 68:8. Because for thy sake I have borne reproach; shame hath covered my face.

Psalm 68:9. I am become a stranger to my brethren; and an alien to the sons of my mother.

Psalm 68:10. Holy Father, the zeal of thy house hath eaten me up; and the reproaches of them that reproached thee are fallen upon me.

Psalm 34:15. And they rejoiced against me and gathered together; scourges were gathered together upon me, and I knew not.

Psalm 68:5. They are multiplied above the hairs of my head who hate me without cause: my enemies have grown strong who have wrongfully persecuted me; then did I pay that which I took not away.

Psalm 34:11. Unjust witnesses rising up, have asked me things I knew not.

Psalm 34:12. They repaid me evil for good and

Psalm 37:21. detracted me; because I followed goodness. Thou art my father most holy; my king and my God.

Psalm 37:23. Attend unto my help, O Lord God of my salvation.

Antiphon: Holy Virgin Mary, etc.

6. At None

Antiphon: Holy Virgin Mary:

PSALM

Lam: 1:12. O all ye that pass by, attend and see if there be any sorrow like unto my sorrow.

Psalm 21:17. For many dogs have encompassed me; the council of the malignant hath besieged me.

Psalm 21:18. They looked and stared upon me;

Psalm 21:19. they parted my garments among them and upon my vesture they cast lots.

Psalm 21:17. They have dug my hands and feet;

Psalm 21:18. they have numbered all my bones.

Psalm 21:14. They have opened their mouth against me; as a lion ravening and roaring.

Psalm 21:15. I am poured out like water and all my bones are scattered. And my heart is become like melting wax in the midst of my bowels.

Psalm 21:16. My strength is dried up like a potsherd; and my tongue hath cleaved to my jaws.

Psalm 68:22. And they gave me gall for my food: and in my thirst they gave me vinegar to drink.

Psalm 21:16. And they have brought me into the dust of death:

Psalm 68:27. and they have added to the grief of my wounds. I slept and I rose up again; and my most holy father received me with glory.

Psalm 72:24. Holy father, thou hast held my right hand; and by thy will thou hast conducted me, and hast received me with glory.

Psalm 72:25. For what have I in heaven; and besides thee what do I desire upon earth?

Psalm 45:11. Be still and know that I am God, saith the Lord; I will be exalted among the nations and I will be exalted in the earth. Blessed is the Lord God of Israel,

Psalm 33:23. who hast redeemed the souls of his servants with his own most holy blood; and none of them that trust in him shall offend.

Psalm 95:13. And we know that he cometh; for he will come to judge justice.

Antiphon: Holy Virgin Mary, etc.

7. At Vespers

Antiphon: Holy Virgin Mary:

PSALM

Psalm 46:2. O clap your hands all ye nations, shout unto God with the voice of joy.

Psalm 46:3. For the Lord is high, terrible; he is a great king over all the earth. For the most holy father of heaven, our king before all ages, sent his beloved son from on high

Psalm 73:12. and hath wrought salvation in the midst of the earth.

Psalm 95:11. Let the heavens rejoice and let the earth be glad, let the sea be moved and the fullness thereof:

Psalm 95:12. the fields and all that are in them shall be joyful.

Psalm 95:1. Sing unto him a new canticle; sing unto the Lord all the earth.

Psalm 95:4. For the Lord is great and exceedingly to be praised; He is to be feared above all gods.

Psalm 95:7. Bring to the Lord, O ye kindreds of the Gentiles, bring to the Lord glory and honour.

Psalm 95:8. Bring to the Lord glory unto his name. Bring your own bodies and bear his holy cross; and follow his most holy precepts even unto the end.

Psalm 95:9. Let all the earth be moved at His presence.

Psalm 95:10. Say among the Gentiles that the Lord hath reigned.

Antiphon: Holy Virgin Mary, etc.

Thus is the Office said daily from Good Friday until the feast of the Ascension; on which feast however these versicles are added.

And he ascended into heaven and sitteth on the right hand of the most holy Father in heaven.

Psalm 56:12. Be thou exalted, O God, above the heavens; and thy glory above all the earth.

Psalm 95:13. And we know that he cometh; for he will come to judge justice.

From the Ascension until the Lord's Advent this psalm is said daily in the same manner, namely "O clap your hands" with the foregoing versicle, and the Gloria being added where the psalm ends.

The foregoing psalms are said from Good Friday until Easter Sunday: they are said in the same manner from the octave of Pentecost until Advent, and from the octave of the Epiphany until Maundy Thursday, except on Sundays and the principal feasts when they are not said; on the other days however they are said daily.

Holy Saturday at Compline

Antiphon: Holy Virgin Mary:

PSALM

Psalm 69.   *As in the Psalter.*

This is said daily at Compline until the octave of Pentecost.

Easter Sunday at Matins

Antiphon: Holy Virgin Mary:

PSALM

Psalm 97:1.   Sing ye to the Lord a new canticle: for he hath done wonderful things. His right hand hath sanctified his Son; and his arm is holy.

Psalm 97:2.   The Lord hath made known his salvation; he hath revealed his justice in the sight of the Gentiles.

Psalm 41:9.   In the day time the Lord hath commanded his mercy; and a canticle to him in the night.

Psalm 117:24.   This is the day which the Lord hath made; let us rejoice and be glad in it.

Psalm 117:26.   Blessed be he that cometh in the name of the Lord.

Psalm 117:27.   The Lord is God and he hath shone upon us.

Psalm 95:11.   Let the heavens rejoice and let the earth be glad: let the sea be moved and the fulness thereof.

Psalm 95:12.   The fields shall rejoice and all that are in them.

Psalm 95:7.   Bring to the Lord, O ye kindreds of the Gentiles, bring to the Lord glory and honour:

Psalm 95:8.   bring to the Lord glory unto his name.

It is said thus far daily from Easter Sunday to the feast of the Ascension at all the hours except Vespers, Compline, and Prime. On the night of the Ascension these verses are added.

Psalm 67:33.   Sing ye to God ye kingdom of the earth: sing ye to the Lord: sing ye to God,

Psalm 67:34.   who mounteth above the heaven of heavens to the east. Behold He will give to his voice, the voice of power:

Psalm 67:35.   give ye glory to God for Israel: his magnificence and his power are in the clouds.

Psalm 67:36. God is wonderful in his saints: the God of Israel is he who will give power and strength to his people. Blessed be God.

Antiphon: Holy Virgin Mary, etc.

This psalm is said daily from the Ascension until the octave of Pentecost with the foregoing versicles at Matins, Tierce, Sext, and None. The Gloria is said where "Blessed be God" is said, and not elsewhere. It is said in the same manner only at the Matins of Sundays and the principal feasts from the octave of Pentecost until Maundy Thursday because on that day the Lord ate the Pasch with His disciples. Or when one wishes, the other psalm may be said at Matins or at Vespers namely, "I will extol Thee, O Lord," as it is in the Psalter, but this only from Easter Sunday to the Ascension.

At Prime

Antiphon: Holy Virgin Mary:

PSALM

As above. Have mercy on me, etc.:

At Tierce, Sext, and None

As above. Psalm: Sing ye to the Lord.

At Vespers

As above. Psalm: O clap your hands.

Here begin the other psalms which our most blessed Father Francis likewise arranged to be said in place of the foregoing psalms of the Passion of the Lord on Sunday and the principal festivals from the octave of Pentecost until Advent, and from the octave of the Epiphany until Maundy Thursday.

At Compline

Antiphon: Holy Virgin Mary:
Psalm 69. *As in the Psalter.* O God, etc.

At Matins

Antiphon: Holy Virgin Mary:
Psalm: Sing ye to the Lord, *as above.*

At Prime

Antiphon: Holy Virgin Mary:
Psalm: Have mercy on me, etc.: *as above.*

At Tierce

Antiphon: Holy Virgin Mary:

Psalm 65:1.   Shout with joy to God all the earth.

Psalm 65:2.   Sing ye a psalm to his name: give glory to his praise.

Psalm 65:3.   Say unto God how terrible are thy works, O Lord: in the multitude of thy strength thy enemies shall lie to thee.

Psalm 65:4.   Let all the earth adore thee and sing to thee: let it sing a psalm to thy name.

Psalm 65:16.   Come and hear all ye that fear God, and I will tell you what great things he hath done for my soul.

Psalm 65:17.   I cried to him with my mouth: and I extolled him with my tongue.

Psalm 17:7.   And he heard my voice from his holy temple; and my cry came before him.

Psalm 65:8.   O bless our God, ye Gentiles; and make the voice of his praise to be heard.

Psalm 71:17.   And in him shall all the tribes of the earth be blessed: all nations shall magnify him.

Psalm 71:18.   Blessed be the Lord God of Israel who only doth wonderful things.

Psalm 71:19.   And blessed be the name of his majesty for ever; and the whole earth shall be filled with his majesty.   Amen.

At Sext

Antiphon: Holy Virgin Mary:

Psalm 19:2.   May the Lord hear thee in the day of tribulation; may the name of the God of Jacob protect thee; may he

Psalm 19:3.   send thee help from the sanctuary and defend thee out of Zion:

Psalm 19:4.   be mindful of all thy sacrifices, and may thy whole burnt offering be made fat;

Psalm 19:5.   give thee according to thine own heart, and confirm all thy counsels.

Psalm 19:6. We will rejoice in thy salvation; and in the name of our God we shall be exalted.

Psalm 19:7. The Lord fulfill all thy petitions: now I know that the Lord hath sent Jesus Christ his son,

Psalm 9:9. and will judge the people with justice.

Psalm 9:10. And the Lord is become a refuge for the poor: a helper in due time of tribulation.

Psalm 9:11. And let them trust in thee who know thy name.

Psalm 143:1. Blessed be the Lord my God:

Psalm 58:17. for Thou art become my support and refuge in the day of my trouble.

Psalm 58:18. Unto thee, O my helper, will I sing: for God is my defence, my God, my mercy.

Antiphon: Holy Virgin Mary, etc.

At None

Antiphon: Holy Virgin Mary:

PSALM

Psalm 70:1. In thee, O Lord, have I hoped, let me never be put to confusion.

Psalm 70:2. Deliver me in thy justice and rescue me; incline thine ear unto me and save me.

Psalm 70:3. Be thou unto me, O God, a protector and a place of strength; that thou mayest make me safe.

Psalm 70:5. For thou art my patience, O Lord; my hope, O Lord, from my youth.

Psalm 70:6. By thee have I been confirmed from the womb; from my mother's womb thou art my protector: of thee will I continually sing.

Psalm 70:8. Let my mouth be filled with praise, that I may sing thy glory; thy greatness all the day long.

Psalm 68:17. Hear me, O Lord, for thy mercy is kind; look upon me according to the multitude of thy tender mercies.

Psalm 68:18. And turn not away thy face from thy servant; for I am in trouble, hear me speedily.

Psalm 143:1. Blessed be the Lord my God.

Psalm 58:17. For thou art become my support and refuge in the day of my trouble.

Psalm 58:18. Unto thee, O my helper, will I sing; for God is my defence, my God, my mercy.

Antiphon: Holy Virgin Mary, etc.

At Vespers

Antiphon: Holy Virgin Mary:

Psalm: O clap your hands, *as above.*

Antiphon: Holy Virgin Mary:

Here begin other psalms which our most blessed Father Francis likewise arranged; which are to be said in place of the foregoing psalms of the Passion from the Advent of our Lord until Christmas Eve, and no longer.

At Compline

Antiphon: Holy Virgin Mary:

Psalm: How long O Lord, *Psalm 12 in the Psalter.*

Antiphon: Holy Virgin Mary, etc.

At Matins

Antiphon: Holy Virgin Mary:

Psalm

Psalm 85:12. I will praise Thee O Lord most holy Father, King of heaven and earth; because

Psalm 85:17. Thou hast comforted me.

Psalm 24:5. Thou art God my Saviour.

Isaias 12:2. I will deal confidently and will not fear.

Psalm 117:14. The Lord is my strength and my praise; and is become my salvation.

Exodus 15:6. Thy right hand, O Lord, is magnified in strength; thy right hand, O Lord, hath slain the enemy.

Exodus 15:7. And in the multitude of thy glory thou hast put down my adversaries.

Psalm 68:33. Let the poor see and rejoice: seek ye God and your soul shall live.

Psalm 68:35. Let the heavens and the earth praise Him; the sea and everything that creepeth therein.

Psalm 68:36.   For God will save Sion and the cities of Juda shall
    be built up. And they shall dwell there; and acquire it
    by inheritance.

Psalm 68:37.   And the seed of His servants shall possess it: and
    they that love his name shall dwell therein.

Antiphon: Holy Virgin Mary, etc.

At Prime

Antiphon: Holy Virgin Mary:
Psalm: Have mercy on me, etc.
Antiphon: Holy Virgin Mary, etc.

At Tierce

Antiphon: Holy Virgin Mary:
Psalm: Shout with joy, etc.
Antiphon: Holy Virgin Mary, etc.

At Sext

Antiphon: Holy Virgin Mary:
Psalm: May the Lord hear thee, etc.
Antiphon: Holy Virgin Mary, etc.

At None

Antiphon: Holy Virgin Mary:
Psalm: In thee, O Lord, have I hoped, etc.
Antiphon: Holy Virgin Mary, etc.

At Vespers

Antiphon: Holy Virgin Mary:
Psalm: O clap your hands, etc.
Antiphon: Holy Virgin Mary, etc.

*The whole psalm is not said, but up to the verse, "Let all the
earth be moved": however, the whole verse, "Bring your own bodies,"
must be said. Thus Vespers are said daily from Advent until
Christmas Eve.*

Christmas Day at Vespers

Antiphon: Holy Virgin Mary:

Psalm

Psalm 80:2.   Rejoice to God: our helper.

Psalm 46:2. Shout unto God living and true, with the voice of triumph.

Psalm 46:3. For the Lord is high, terrible; a great king over all the earth. For the most holy Father of heaven our king before ages, sent his beloved son from on high, and he was born of the Blessed Virgin holy Mary.

Psalm 88:27. He shall cry out to me: thou art my father.

Psalm 88:28. And I will make him my firstborn, high above the kings of the earth.

Psalm 41:9. In the daytime the Lord hath commanded his mercy; and a canticle to him in the night.

Psalm 117:24. This is the day which the Lord hath made: let us be glad and rejoice in it. For the beloved and most holy Child has been given to us and born for us by the wayside.

Luke 2:7. And laid in a manger because he had no room in the inn.

Luke 2:14. Glory to God in the highest; and on earth peace to men of good will.

Psalm 95:11. Let the heavens rejoice and the earth be glad, and the sea be moved and the fulness thereof.

Psalm 95:12. The fields shall rejoice and all that are in them.

Psalm 95:1. Sing to Him a new canticle; sing to the Lord all the earth.

Psalm 95:4. For the Lord is great and exceedingly to be praised; He is to be feared above all gods.

Psalm 95:7. Bring to the Lord, O ye kindreds of the Gentiles; bring to the Lord glory and honour.

Psalm 95:8. Bring to the Lord glory unto his name. Bring your own bodies and bear his holy cross and follow His most holy precepts even unto the end.

Antiphon: Holy Virgin Mary, etc.

This psalm is said from Christmas until the octave of Epiphany at all the hours.

THE PRAYER TO THE FIVE WOUNDS
BELOVED BY ST. CLARE

To the Wound of the Right Hand of Christ

O my Lord Jesus Christ, be Thou ever blessed and praised for the most holy wound in Thy right hand. Because of this most sacred wound grant me the pardon of all the sins I have committed by thought, word, and deed, and by omission. Give me the grace worthily to venerate Thy most precious death and these Thy sacred wounds; and grant that by Thy help I may mortify my body, and may be able to render thanks for this great gift to Thee who with the Father and Holy Spirit liveth, etc. *Pater, Ave, Gloria.*

To the Wound in the Left Hand of Christ

Be Thou ever blessed and praised, O most sweet Lord Jesus Christ, for the most sacred wound in Thy left hand. Because of it have mercy upon me, and deign to take from me all that is not in conformity with Thy most holy will. Grant me the grace to be victorious over Thy most cruel enemies and to repulse all their assaults: by Thy most holy death free me from all the dangers of this life and from the eternal pains of Hell; and by Thy grace may I be worthy to enter the kingdom of the blessed there to enjoy Thy glory for ever. Amen. *Pater, Ave, Gloria.*

To the Wound in the Right Foot of Christ

Be Thou ever blessed and praised, O most sweet Lord Jesus Christ, for the most sacred wound in Thy right foot. Because of it give me the grace to do penance for my sins: and by Thy most precious death I humbly beg Thee not to permit that I, Thy servant, should ever turn away from Thy most holy will, and save both my soul and body. Receive my soul when I come to die into Thy most holy arms and bring me into Thy blessed kingdom there to share in Thy eternal joy for ever. Amen. *Pater, Ave, Gloria.*

To the Wound in the Left Foot of Christ

Be Thou ever blessed and praised, O most merciful Lord Jesus Christ, for the most sacred wound in Thy left foot. Because of it pardon me all my sins, and by Thy holy grace save me from the pains of Hell. Most kind Lord Jesus Christ, I pray Thee by Thy most holy death to grant that before I pass to another life, I may have perfect contrition for my sins and the grace to be able to make a good confession of them, that purified in soul and body I may be able to receive Thee in holy Viaticum; grant me also to receive Extreme Unction that thus I may be comforted in my passage into eternity. Amen. *Pater, Ave, Gloria.*

To the Wound in the Side of Our Redeemer

Be Thou ever blessed and praised, O most kind Lord Jesus Christ, for the sacred wound in Thy most holy side. Because of it, and because of Thy infinite mercy shown to Longinus when he tore open Thy breast, which Thou ever holdest open as our only refuge, I pray Thee, O most pitiful Jesus, that as through Baptism Thou hast cleansed me from original sin, so, by Thy most precious blood, and by the merit of all the Masses offered today throughout Thy whole Church, to free me from every evil, past, present, and to come. Through Thy most bitter death grant me firm faith, constant hope, and perfect charity to love Thee with my whole heart and soul, and with all my strength. Confirm me in good works, give me perseverance in Thy holy service that in everything and always I may be able to please until the end of my life. Amen. *Pater, Ave, Gloria.*

To Jesus Crucified

My most merciful Jesus, who art full of kindness and love for men, I look to Thee with all the poor love of my heart, and pray to Thee through the immense suffering of Thy most holy soul when, for love of us on the cross, Thou wast oppressed by the weight of that most mysterious abandonment of Thee by Thy heavenly Father to whom Thou didst turn with the words: "My God, my God, why hast Thou forsaken Me?" Because of this Thy dereliction I beseech Thee save me from the terrible effects of Thy just indignation at my sins. Most kind Redeemer, hearken not to Thy divine justice but to Thy infinite mercy, and grant that though all unworthy as I am I may still experience Thy goodness to those who trust in the infinite merits of Thy most holy Passion, and in the bitter sufferings and martyrdom of Thy most holy soul. *Pater, Ave, Gloria.*

PRAYER TO THE CRUCIFIX
WHICH SPOKE TO ST. FRANCIS IN SAN DAMIANO

I. O most benign and crucified Lord, who deigned to hear the ardent prayer of St. Francis, Thy poor one, and to repay his trusting love of Thee by speaking to him from this Crucifix bidding him repair the mystical temple of the Church Thy bride, grant that each one of us may turn to Thee with love and confidence. From this Crucifix Thine eyes still speak to us; O may Thy look urge us to run in the way of perfection, having Thee always before our eyes, Thou our goal and our reward. Illuminate our minds to know Thee always better; fortify our wills that we may steadfastly accomplish all that Thou teachest from this throne of Thy love, this altar of Thy mercy. Let Thy divine will be fulfilled in us, let us contemplate and love Thy cross that we may share in Thy glory. *Pater, Ave, Gloria.*

II. O most sweet crucified Lord, who from this throne of infinite loving kindness didst shower divine graces upon afflicted humanity through the intercession of our holy Mother Clare, look in pity upon all our weaknesses, and by the merits of Thy beloved bride and mindful of the tears of love which she poured out before Thee, grant us, we pray, the grace to weep bitterly for our sins which have crucified Thee with infinite suffering upon this hard wood. May Thy five most holy wounds be the continual object of our loving meditation; and grant that from them, as from miraculous springs, heavenly blessings may be poured into our souls with all Thy divine consolations and graces which may render us worthy of Thee, and draw us into ever closer union with Thy divine love, and bring us to eternal salvation. *Pater, Ave, Gloria.*

III. Most loving Jesus, prostrated before Thee, we beseech Thee from Thy cross to speak words of mercy and kindness to our souls. We well know that we are unworthy of such grace, but Thou, in Thy loving kindness hast said to us, "Ask and you shall receive, knock and it shall be opened to you." Therefore trusting in Thine own promises we pray for all those who suffer, begging of Thee to hear them. May Thy restoring grace descend into their souls and console them, and into their bodies that they may be fortified to love and serve Thee better. And if our unworthiness is an obstacle to these graces, ah, do not deny them to the saints, Francis and Clare, whom we place before Thee as our intercessors. O good Jesus, deign to conform every single will to Thy most holy will, and to all give resignation in the sufferings of this earthly life. And grant that we, illuminated by Thy grace, may consider our small sufferings as an example of Thy infinite sufferings for us, and also as a proof of Thy special love for us; thus we will consider them as a token of Thy mercy, and of our eternal happiness. Three *Paters, Aves, Glorias.*

The following steps of the Passion are then recited:

Most sweet Jesus, Who in the agony in the garden didst pray to Thy Father and didst suffer the sweat of blood, have mercy on us.

Most sweet Jesus, stripped of Thy garments, and most cruelly flagellated at the pillar, have mercy on us.

Most sweet Jesus, crowned with thorns, mocked and struck, blindfolded and beaten with reeds, overwhelmed with derision and opprobrium, have mercy on us.

Most sweet Jesus, burdened with the wood of the cross and led to the place of execution as a lamb is led to the slaughter, have mercy on us.

Most sweet Jesus, dying on the cross, in the presence of Thy Mother, Thy side opened by the lance, and sending forth blood and water, have mercy on us.

Most sweet Jesus, taken down from the cross with Thy body full of wounds, watered by the tears of Thy Virgin Mother, have mercy on us.

Most sweet Jesus, with Thy wounded body wrapped in linen with many spices, have mercy on us.

They pierced My hands and feet. They numbered all My bones.

Let us pray.

O Lord Jesus Christ, Who didst descend to earth from the bosom of the Father, and didst pour out Thy precious Blood for the remission of our sins; we humbly beseech Thee that in the day of Judgment we may be found worthy to hear Thy words, "Come ye blessed." Who with the Father and Holy Ghost livest and reignest God for everlasting. Amen.

APPENDIX 2

THE RULE OF ST. CLARE

The Bull, *Solet Annuere*, which is Innocent IV's confirmation of the Rule of St. Clare, contains the text of Cardinal Rainaldo's previous letter to Clare giving her his approval, and then goes on to give the text of the Rule itself. It is dated August 9, 1253.

"Innocent, bishop, servant of the servants of God, to his beloved daughter in Christ, Clare, abbess, and the other sisters in the monastery of Saint Damian in Assisi; health and apostolic Benediction.

"It is the custom of the Apostolic See to welcome devout aspirations, and to give benevolent hearing to the godly requests of petitioners. You, dear children in Jesus Christ, have presented to Us a humble petition concerning the form of life given you by Blessed Francis, and accepted by you of your own free will, and according to which you are bound to lead a life in common, in unity of spirit and in the bond of sublime poverty. Our venerable Brother the Bishop of Ostia and Velletri has seen fit to sanction this form of life, as he himself declares in a letter addressed to you; and it is now your wish that We should consent to confirm the same with Apostolic authority.

"Consenting therefore beloved daughters to the prayer of your devotion We ratify what has been done in this matter by the above named Bishop, and on his letter of approbation We set the seal of Apostolic authority, and fortify and confirm it by virtue of these presents, inscribing therein at length the literal text of the same letter as he wrote it:

"Rainaldo, by Divine compassion Bishop of Ostia and Velletri, to his very dear Mother and Daughter in Christ, the Lady Clare, abbess of Saint Damian's in the diocese of Assisi, and likewise to her sisters, present and future, health and paternal benediction.

"Since you, beloved children in God, have despised the world

159

with its pomps and vanities, and following in the footsteps of Jesus Christ and His most holy Mother have elected to serve the All-Highest in abject poverty, and enclosed, in order that your souls being free, you may be the better able for this service, we confirm and ratify for you all, and for all who shall succeed you in the monastery of Saint Damian's for ever, the Form of Life, and the manner of observing holy unity and sublime poverty taught to you by your blessed Father Saint Francis in his writing and by word of mouth. It runs thus:

"'This is the form of life of the order founded by Blessed Francis, called the Order of Poor Sisters, which form is to observe the Holy Gospel of Our Lord Jesus Christ by living under obedience and without property and in chastity.

"'Clare, the unprofitable servant of Jesus Christ, and the little plant of the most blessed Father Francis, promises obedience and worship to the Lord Pope Innocent and his successors canonically elected, and to the Roman Church. And as, in the beginning of her religious life, she with her sisters promised obedience to Blessed Francis, so now she most faithfully promises to obey his successors. Also the other sisters shall always be bound to obey the successors of Blessed Francis, and they must likewise give obedience to Sister Clare and to the other abbesses canonically elected who shall succeed her.

"'Should anyone by divine inspiration wish to embrace this form of life the abbess is bound to consult the wishes of each sister, and if most of the sisters be willing, the applicant may be received, provided that the necessary licence has been accorded by our Protector the Lord Cardinal. First, however, the abbess shall examine the postulant, or cause her to be examined with diligent care concerning the Catholic faith and the sacraments of the Church: if she believes all these things, and is willing faithfully to confess them, and is steadfastly determined to practice them to the end of her life; and if she is unmarried, or even if she has a husband who has already entered religion and vowed himself to continence with the licence of his bishop; and if she unimpeded by old age or mental or physical weakness to observe this form of life, then let it be carefully expounded to her, and if she is deemed worthy let these words of the holy Gospel be spoken to her: "Go, sell what thou hast and give to the poor." If she is not able to do this, then her good will shall be held sufficient.

"'The abbess and sisters shall take care not to concern themselves in her temporal affairs, so that the postulant may be entirely free to dispose of her property as the Lord shall inspire her. If she asks for advice, they can send her to discreet and God-fearing men, and according to their counsel she may give her goods to the poor. After this her hair shall be cut off all round her head, she shall be stripped of her secular garments, and three tunics and a cloak shall be given to her. Thenceforth she may not go outside the monastery save for some useful, reasonable, manifest and praiseworthy purpose: and after a year of probation she shall be received to obedience, and promise to observe our rule of life and form of poverty. In no circumstances shall a novice receive the veil until she has completed her year of novitiate. If the sisters please, they may wear scapulars to save their clothes in their service and labour, and as regards their other garments the abbess shall discreetly provide for each one of them what necessity demands according to the varying seasons of the year, and the climate of the place where the monastery is situated.

"'If children are received before they have reached the canonical age for profession, they can be tonsured like the sisters, and shall put aside their worldly clothes and be clad in whatever religious habit the abbess may think fitting. When they have reached the canonical age, they can be dressed in the habit of the Order, and may then make their profession. The abbess shall take heed to choose a suitable mistress from among the wisest women in the monastery to instruct these children and likewise the novices in good manners and holy conversation as befit our form of life.

"'This same form shall be observed in the examination and reception of sisters who serve outside the monastery, and these may wear shoes. No woman shall take up her abode in the monastery unless she has previously been received according to the form of our profession. I exhort, I beseech, I implore you all my sisters always to clothe yourselves in common garments, and this for love of that most holy and adorable Child Who was wrapped in mean swaddling clothes and laid in a manger, and for love of His most holy Mother.

" 'The sisters who can read shall recite the Divine Office, but without music; as soon as they can obtain Breviaries they shall follow the use of the Friars Minor. Those sisters who are illiterate shall say twenty-four Paters for Matins, five for Lauds, seven for each of the following hours, Prime, Tierce, Sext and None, twelve for Vespers, and seven for Compline. Instead of the Office of the Dead they shall say seven Paters for Vespers with Requiem aeternam, and in like manner twelve for Matins; at the death of every sister they shall say fifty Paters for the repose of her soul. If any of the literate sisters are hindered by a reasonable cause from saying the Hours, then they shall say the Paters instead as do the illiterate sisters.

" 'All the sisters shall always fast save on the feast of Our Lord's Nativity when they may eat two meals no matter what the day of the week. However the young, the feeble, and those that serve outside shall be mercifully dispensed from observing this discipline, either wholly or partially as may seem advisable to the abbess; and in time of obvious necessity none of the sisters shall be compelled to fast.

" 'At least twelve times a year with the abbess' permission the sisters shall make their confession, and in doing so they shall be very careful only to speak of their sins or their soul's salvation. Seven times a year, on Christmas Day, Maundy Thursday, Easter Sunday, on the feast of the Assumption, on that of Saint Francis, and on All Saints' day they shall approach the Lord's table. It is lawful for the chaplain to celebrate Mass within the monastery precincts for the purpose of giving Holy Communion to the healthy, and when necessary to the sick.

" 'In the election of the abbess the sisters must observe the form prescribed by Canon Law, and as soon as possible before the election, they shall summon the Minister General of the Order of the Friars Minor, or the Provincial Minister of the place where they dwell in order that by the word of God he may dispose them to peace and to the choice of a superior who may be profitable to the good of all. Only a professed sister is eligible for the office of superior, and if it should ever happen that a non-professed sister should be elected or otherwise appointed to this office, then the sisters shall not obey her until she has pledged herself to observe our form of poverty. At her death they shall be careful to elect her successor from among the professed sisters. If all the sisters are at any time agreed that the non-professed abbess is insufficient in her service and unprofitable to the community, with all speed let them elect another abbess and mother, and be very careful to comply with the above regulations.

"'Let the elected sister carefully consider the burden of her charge, and to Whom she will have to render account for the flock committed to her keeping: she shall strive to rule her sheep by the veneration inspired in them by her own virtuous life rather than by their awe of the dignity of her office; thus moved by her holy example they will give her their obedience from love rather than from fear. She shall keep herself free from particular friendships, lest by lavishing too much affection on one she may give scandal to all. She shall console the afflicted; and let her be the last refuge of any who may be in disgrace; for if she neglects to dispense the medicine of consolation the weak may easily be swallowed up by the sickness of despair. Always and in all things, in clothing, in choir, at table, in the dormitory and in the infirmary she shall observe the common life, and let her vicar do likewise.

"'At least once a week the abbess shall assemble her sisters in chapter that she and they may humble themselves by making public confession of their faults and negligencies, and since the Lord often reveals what is best to the least, the abbess shall confer with all her sisters in what concerns the good fame and business of the monastery. No heavy debt shall be incurred without the consent of all the sisters, and then only for some urgent necessity, in which case let the business be arranged by a procurator. The abbess and sisters shall beware of allowing anything to be deposited in their monastery, for such condescension can often occasion scandal and strife. In order to preserve the bond of peace and mutual charity let all those holding office in the house be chosen by the common consent of all the sisters, and in like manner at least eight sisters shall be appointed from among the most discreet with whom the abbess shall take counsel touching all those things required by our form of life. From time to time or whenever they may consider it expedient the sisters may remove these officials and members of the abbess' council and appoint others in their place.

"'Except for the sisters serving outside, all the other sisters shall keep silence from Compline until Tierce, and they shall always refrain from unnecessary conversation in the dormitory, in church, in the refectory; but if they happen to take their meals in the infirmary they may always speak with discretion for the recreation and encouragement of those who are sick, and in all places they may say what is necessary provided they do so briefly, and in a low voice.

"'It is unlawful for any sister to speak with anyone in the parlour or at the grille without the special permission of the abbess or her vicar, and even so, the sister shall not presume to speak to anyone in the parlour except in the presence and hearing of two other sisters, nor shall she approach the grille unless she is accompanied by at least three sisters chosen by the abbess or her vicar from among the wise sisters of her council.

"'The abbess herself, and her vicar shall conform to these rules concerning conversation. Very seldom shall anyone speak at the grille, never at the door.

"'A curtain shall be hung inside the grille to be raised only when the word of God is being preached, or when a sister has permission to speak with someone without. There shall also be wooden shutters well fortified with bars and bolts, and with two different iron locks to be locked, especially at night, with two keys, one to be kept by the abbess, one by the sacristan. These shutters shall remain closed except during Divine Service when they may be opened for the above mentioned purpose. No sister may speak at the grille before sunrise or after sunset. A curtain shall also be hung in the parlour, never to be raised; and during the Lent of Saint Martin or in the Greater Lent no sister shall speak here except to a priest in confession, or for some matter which the abbess or her vicar considers an urgent necessity.

"'When the most high Heavenly Father deigned to enlighten my heart by His grace to do penance according to the example and teaching of our most blessed Father Saint Francis shortly after his own conversion, my sisters and I voluntarily bound ourselves to obey him. And when Our blessed Father had seen that we had no fear of want or toil, sorrow or ignominy or the world's scorn, indeed that we rather rejoiced in these things, he was moved with compassion towards us, and he wrote a form of life for us which begins thus:

" 'By Divine inspiration you have made yourselves the daughters and handmaids of the most High Sovereign King our Father Who dwells in Heaven, and have become the brides of the Paraclete by electing to live according to the perfection of the Holy Gospel; therefore I will, and I promise in my own name, and in that of my successors, always to have for you the same diligent care and special solicitude that I have for the Brothers.

" 'Most loyally he fulfilled that promise to the day of his death, and it was his wish that the brothers should keep it for ever. In order that neither we nor our successors should in any way ever abandon that most holy poverty in which we began he sent us also another letter not long before he died in which he made known to us his last wishes:

" 'I, Brother Francis, the least of men, desire to imitate the life and poverty of the most high Lord Jesus Christ and of His most holy Mother. And my Ladies, I counsel and entreat you, that you too should always live in this most holy life and poverty, and that you keep watch over yourselves lest by the advice and teaching of any man you might ever in any way depart from it.

" 'My sisters and I have always been solicitous to observe that holy poverty which we promised to the Lord God and to Blessed Francis; therefore the abbesses my successors, and their sisters shall be equally solicitous to observe it to the end, that is to say, they shall neither receive nor hold possessions, nor have any rights of property, or what might reasonably be considered such in anything whatsoever, either they themselves directly, or indirectly by means of a third person. It is however permissible to hold as much land as is necessary for the decency and seclusion of the monastery; but this land shall only be cultivated as a garden for the sisters' own use.

" 'Those sisters to whom the Lord gives the grace to work shall faithfully and devotedly busy themselves with some honest handicraft of profit to the common good, after the hour of Tierce; they shall do this in a way that banishes indolence that enemy of the soul but yet does not quench that spirit of holy prayer to which all temporal things must be subservient. The abbess or her vicar shall assign their several tasks to these sisters in the presence of the community in chapter. Then too let assignment be made of all the gifts received to relieve the sisters' needs, so that prayer may be offered in common for the benefactors. The abbess or her vicar shall distribute these gifts for the common good, acting according to the advice of the council of wise women.

" 'The sisters shall not appropriate anything to themselves, but as strangers and pilgrims on the face of the earth, they shall gather alms with confidence, and be content to serve the Lord in poverty and humility. Nor should they be ashamed to live thus, since for our sake Jesus Christ made Himself poor in this world. Beloved Sisters, this is the height of that sublime poverty which has purchased for you a royal inheritance, even the kingdom of heaven, and which, while rendering you poor in material things, has enriched you with spiritual treasures.

" 'Let that be your portion on earth which leads to the land of the living; cleave to it, dear sisters, with your whole strength, and never wish to possess anything else under the sun, for the love of Our Lord Jesus Christ and of His holy Mother.

" 'No sister shall presume to receive letters or anything else, or to send anything out of the monastery without the permission of the abbess, or to hold anything beyond what the abbess has given her, or has authorized her to hold.

" 'The abbess is bound to deliver to a sister any present in kind sent her by her kinsfolk or friends, and let the sister keep it if she needs it; and if not then, in her charity she can transfer it to some more needy sister; but if the gift be in money the abbess shall not deliver it to her, but according to the advice of her wise women she shall buy with it something which the sister may require.

" 'Concerning sisters who are ill, the abbess, by personal observation and also by questioning the other sisters, shall carefully and diligently try to learn what is most necessary for the relief of their infirmities; whether medicine, nourishing food, or anything else; for which, as far as her resources permit, she is bound in conscience charitably and compassionately to make provision. Indeed all the sisters are bound to cherish and serve those that are sick among them, even as they themselves would wish to be cherished were any infirmity to befall them. Therefore, make your necessities known confidently one to another. If an earthly mother cherishes her children according to the flesh, how much more should a spiritual sister cherish her sisters in religion!

" 'The sick shall lie on mattresses stuffed with straw, and have feather pillows under their heads, and those that need them may likewise have woollen blankets over their feet and quilted counterpanes to cover them.

" 'The sick sisters are always free to answer briefly any good words that may be spoken to them by a friend or by friends who may have entered the monastery to visit them; but the sisters shall in no wise presume to speak with these people unless they have first obtained the necessary permission, and then only in the presence and hearing of two discreet sisters appointed to listen by the abbess or her vicar. The abbess herself and her vicar shall also observe this rule.

" 'If, at the instigation of the enemy, any sister commit a grievous sin against the form of our profession, and if, having been twice or thrice admonished by the abbess or the other sisters, she still refuses to make amendment, then her diet shall be bread and water for as long as she continues obdurate, and she shall be made to eat it on the floor of refectory in the presence of all the sisters, and if it seems well to the abbess, she shall suffer still more grievous punishment. But all the sisters shall beseech the Lord to enlighten her heart to do penance.

" 'The abbess and sisters shall be careful not to be angry or anxious on account of the sin of the offending sister; for anger and perturbation of spirit will not promote charity either in themselves or her.

" 'God forbid that at any time scandal or strife should arise between sister and sister on account of saucy speech or act or any other thing; and should it arise, then let the offending sister at once, before she offers the sacrifice of prayer, not only, prone at the other's feet, humbly ask for forgiveness, but likewise in all simplicity beg that sister to intercede with the Lord for her, that He too may show her mercy. Then the offended sister shall remember Our Lord's saying, "If you from your hearts forgive not every one his brother their trespasses, neither will your heavenly Father forgive you your trespasses," and she shall freely forgive the other all the wrong she may have done her.

" 'The extern sisters shall not remain long outside the monastery without some cause of manifest necessity. Their gait shall be sober, and their words few; and let them be a source of edification to those whom they meet by the way. They shall beware of all encounters and talk with men lest people should wag their tongues, and they shall never consent to act as sponsors to children of either sex since this might lead to gossip or troubles. Moreover they are firmly bound not to repeat inside the monastery the tittle-tattle of the world, and not to whisper outside anything said or done within, that might be likely to generate scandal. If any sister should fail to observe either of these prohibitions, and her fault be the outcome of folly, the abbess shall impose on her such penance tempered with mildness as her own prudence shall dictate; but if this fault proceeds from vicious habit, then with the aid of her council, the abbess shall devise some chastisement equal to the heinousness of the sin.

" 'The abbess shall admonish and visit her sisters, and correct them with meekness and charity, not ordering them to act against their own consciences or to do anything contrary to the form of our profession. The sisters subject to her must recollect that for God's sake they have renounced their own will: and therefore they are strictly bound to submit themselves to their superiors regarding all those things which they have vowed to the Lord to observe, and in all things not contrary to the soul and our rule of life. The abbess shall always have such familiarity with her sisters that they may not be afraid to speak to her, and to act towards her as mistresses to a servant; for the abbess should be the servant of all the sisters.

" 'O my sisters, I admonish and exhort you in the Lord Jesus Christ to beware of all pride, vainglory, envy, covetousness, care and solicitude for earthly things; eschew utterly all backbiting, enmity, murmuring and strife, always striving to preserve among yourselves that unity of spirit which is the bond of peace. Let not the unlettered be anxious to learn, but rather let them consider that, above all else, they should desire to possess the Spirit of the Lord which worketh all wisdom. Be humble, prayerful, pure in heart, patient in time of sickness and adversity. Love them that hate you, and pray for them that despitefully use you, for the Lord says: "Blessed are they that suffer persecution for righteousness' sake; for theirs is the kingdom of Heaven; and again You shall be hated of all men for My name's sake; but he that shall persevere unto the end, he shall be saved."

" 'The portress must be a wise woman of mature age and suitable manners. In the daytime she shall stay in a lodge having no door, set close to the entrance, and a worthy companion shall be given her to replace her in time of need. The monastery door shall be furnished with bars and bolts and two iron locks of different pattern in order that it may be locked, especially at night with two keys of which the abbess shall hold one, and the doorkeeper the other. In the daytime the door shall always be guarded and securely fastened with one key. The portress and her companion shall be very careful never to open the door more widely than is necessary, and only to open it entirely for those who have obtained permission to enter from the Supreme Pontiff or from our Lord Cardinal. The sisters shall not allow anyone to enter the monastery before sunrise or to remain inside after sunset, unless this is required for some manifest, reasonable, and inevitable cause.

" 'If any Bishop should obtain permission to celebrate Mass inside the monastery for the purpose of blessing an abbess, or consecrating a sister or some such reason, he shall be content to enter with as small a retinue as possible, very carefully chosen from among his most virtuous attendants.

" 'When the services of workman are required for some necessary labour, the abbess shall be careful to place a suitable sister at the door, in case some unauthorized person should presume to enter with them; upon such an occasion the sisters shall take care not to be seen by these workmen.

" 'Let our Visitor be always of the Order of the Friars Minor, appointed by our Cardinal. He must be a man of such irreproachable fame, that his virtue and integrity can never be questioned. His office shall be to correct any excesses committed against our form of living either by the abbess who is the head of the community, or the sisters who are its members. In exercising this office he shall stand in a public place so that he can be seen by all, and let him address his observations to all the sisters collectively, or to any one of them individually as it may seem good to him.

" 'For the love of God and blessed Francis we beg the Brothers of the Order of Friars Minor to give us of their grace a chaplain with one companion, a clerk of good fame and proved discretion, and two honest lay brothers of holy life to help us in our poverty; even as the courtesy of the Brothers has provided hitherto.

"'The chaplain may only enter the monastery accompanied by his companion and when once they have entered it, they shall remain in public together so that they may be continually seen of each other, and by all.

"'It shall also be lawful for them to enter the monastery to hear the confessions of the sick and of those who are too feeble to go to the parlour; and when their services are required the chaplain and his companion may also bring Holy Communion to the sick and feeble, and may enter to administer Extreme Unction or for the Commendation of a departing soul.

"'The abbess may always admit as many outsiders as she considers necessary for funerals, for solemn Masses for the dead, for the digging of graves, or the opening and preparing of vaults, provided these outsiders be honest and capable.

"'Lastly let the sisters always have as governor, protector, and director that Cardinal of the Holy Roman Church whom the Lord Pope shall have deputed to act in like capacity for the Order of the Friars Minor. And this to the end that, ever stable in the Catholic faith, ever submissive and subject at the feet of Holy Church, we may always imitate the poverty and humility of Our Lord Jesus Christ and His blessed Mother, and may always faithfully carry out the words of His Holy Gospel, even as we have promised. Amen.'

"Given at Perugia on the sixteenth day from the calends of October in the tenth year of the pontificate of the Lord Pope Innocent IV.

"Let no man therefore infringe this letter of confirmation, or with rash audacity venture to contravene it, and if any attempt of this kind be made, let them that make it know that they will incur the indignation of Almighty God and His blessed Apostles Peter and Paul.

"Given at Assisi on the fifth day from the Ides of August in the eleventh year of our pontificate."

This precious autograph is preserved in the monastery of Santa Chiara in Assisi. On the reverse side a contemporary hand has noted: "Bulla confirmationis regule Sancte Clare per Dominum Innocentium IIII. Hanc beata Clara tetigit et obsculata est pro devotionis pluribus et pluribus vicibus."

On the face in very small characters in the left-hand upper corner are the words, "Ad instar fiat S. Ex causis manifestis michi et protectori monasterii fiat ad instar." Father Oliger says: "These words were written by Pope Innocent IV himself."

APPENDIX 3

THE TESTAMENT OF ST. CLARE

The text of this Testament appears both in Wadding and the Acta Sanctorum, *and it is published in the* Seraphicae Legislationis Textus Originalis, *1897:*

In the Name of Our Lord. Amen.

1. Among all the benefits that we have received, and receive each day from the liberality of the Father of all mercies, and for which we must offer Him incessant praise, the chief is the benefit of our vocation. We are the more indebted to Him for it in that it is the greatest and most perfect of benefits. As the Apostle says to us, "Consider your vocation."

2. The Son of God has made Himself our Way; that way which our blessed Father Francis showed and taught us by his word and example.

3. Dear Sisters, we must therefore consider the immense benefits which God has showered upon us, especially those which He has given through His beloved servant our blessed Father Francis, and all those benefits which we have received, not only after our conversion, but also while we were living among the vanities of the world.

4. Before Saint Francis had either Brothers or Companions, immediately after his conversion he was working on the Church of Saint Damian's, and there he was made conscious of the Lord, and filled with consolations so that he was impelled to leave the world completely. It was at that time that in a transport of holy joy and by the light of the Holy Spirit, he made the prophecy concerning us that the Lord subsequently fulfilled. Standing on the wall of that church and addressing himself to some poor folk

of the neighbourhood he spoke to them in French saying loudly: "Come and help me with this monastery of Saint Damian, for here there will be an order of ladies whose fame and holy life will glorify the heavenly Father in His whole Church."

5. In this we recognize the immense goodness of God towards us, since out of the superabundance of His mercy and charity He caused His Saint to speak thus of our election and vocation. Our blessed Father did not prophecy these things regarding us alone, but of all those others who should follow us in the holy vocation to which the Lord has called us.

6. What solicitude, what dedication of body and soul we must have in obeying the commandments of God our Father, in order that we may return the talent we have received from Him with increase!

The Lord has placed us as patterns and mirrors not only for all the faithful, but also for those other sisters who are called to our vocation; and this in order that they in their turn, should be patterns and mirrors for those who live in the world.

The Lord, therefore, has called us to such great things that our sanctity must serve as the pattern and mirror, not only of all the faithful, but in which all those sisters may see themselves who are called to be the pattern and mirror again for others. Therefore we are under an extreme obligation to bless and praise the Lord, and to fortify ourselves increasingly in Him in order to do good.

Therefore by living the preceding rule we shall be enabled to leave a noble example to others, and by a brief period of trial we shall gain the prize of eternal happiness.

7. After the most high heavenly Father had deigned in his mercy and grace to illuminate my heart and inspire me to do penance according to the example and teaching of our blessed Father Francis, who was himself but recently converted; then, together with those few sisters whom God gave me almost immediately after my conversion, I made a voluntary vow of obedience to him according to the light and grace which the Lord had given us through the holy life and teaching of His servant.

8. Blessed Francis saw that though we were feeble and fragile

in body, neither privation nor poverty, neither travail, tribulation, ignominy, nor the contempt of the world, that none of all this had any power to make us turn back; on the contrary, following the example of his Brothers and all the saints, all these things seemed to us ineffably delightful. And this has often been remarked on by our Father and his Brothers, and because of it they greatly rejoiced in the Lord.

For this reason our Father was moved with paternal affection for us and promised for himself and his Order that he would care for us with the same attentive and special solicitude as he had for his Brothers.

9. Thus by the will of God and our blessed Father Francis, we came to dwell in the church of Saint Damian; and here in a short time, the Lord in His grace and mercy multiplied us in order that what he had prophesied by His holy servant should be fulfilled. Before this we had sojourned in another place, but only for a short time.

10. Saint Francis wrote for us a form of life, above all to make us always persevere in holy poverty.

He was not satisfied during his life to exhort us frequently by his own words and example to love and observe holy poverty; besides this he left us several documents in order that after his death we should never leave it in any way. And this because in like manner the Son of God while He lived in this world would never desert this same holy poverty.

Our blessed Father Francis following in the steps of Our Lord, and having chosen holy poverty for himself and his Brothers, would never depart from her in any way whatsoever, whether in his teaching or in his actions.

11. And I, Clare, the unworthy servant of Christ and of the Poor Sisters of the monastery of Saint Damian, and the little plant of the holy Patriarch have considered with my sisters our most high profession, and the command of such a Father; we have also considered the fragility of others fearing it too for ourselves after the death of our Father Saint Francis who was our support, our only consolation, our helper after God Himself.

In consequence of all this we have voluntarily renewed our pledge to our Lady holy Poverty; and we have done this so that after my death the remaining sisters, and those who will follow later, can in no way depart from it.

12. I myself have always been careful and solicitous too in the observation of holy poverty, and I have caused the others likewise to observe holy poverty which we have promised to the Lord and to our Father Saint Francis; therefore the other abbesses who will follow me are bound to observe it themselves, and to cause their sisters to observe it until the end.

In order to ensure this with greater certainty, I hastened to address myself to Pope Innocent under whose pontificate our institute began, and after him to his successors and thus I was able to obtain that their pontifical privilege should confirm and fortify our profession of holy poverty.

13. Therefore on bended knees and prostrated in body and soul before our Mother the holy Roman Church, before the Sovereign Pontiff, and especially before the Lord Cardinal who has been assigned to the Order of the Friars Minor and to ourselves I enjoin these things on all my sisters whether present or to come; that for the love of Jesus, poor in the manger, poor during His life, naked on the cross: for love of Him I pray the Cardinal to protect the little flock which the All-Highest has brought forth in His Church through the word and example of the blessed Father Francis, who was the imitator of the poverty and humility of the Son of God and of the glorious Virgin Mary His Mother; I beseech the Cardinal always to protect and encourage this flock and to ensure that it should observe that holy poverty which we have promised to God and to our blessed Father Francis.

14. Since the Lord gave us our blessed Father Francis to be our founder, our Father, and our support in the service of Christ, and in those things we have promised to God and to this blessed Father who by his teaching and example was so careful to cultivate the growth of us, his little plantation; now in my turn, I enjoin on all my sisters whether present or to come; and I commend them to the successor of our blessed Father Francis, and

to all the Brothers of his order, that they may always help us
to advance in good, to serve God better, and above all to observe
holy poverty more completely.

15. If it should ever happen that the sisters leave this place
and are transferred elsewhere; nevertheless after my death, wherever
they may be they are bound to observe the same form of poverty
that we promised to God and to our blessed Father Francis.

16. She who fills my office and the other sisters must always
have care and foresight never to buy or accept land round their
house beyond what is strictly necessary for a vegetable garden.
If at any time the privacy and decorum of the monastery demand
that there should be a further stretch of land outside the limit
of the garden; then they must not acquire more than is demanded
by strict necessity; and that land must not be tilled, but always
remain wild and uncultivated.

17. I warn my sisters present and future, and warn them in
Our Lord Jesus Christ, that they should always study to follow
the way of holy simplicity, of humility and poverty, and that
religious honesty which is apparent in holy conversation; and this
in conformity with that way of life in which our blessed Father
Francis formed us from the earliest days of our conversion. Not
by our own merits, but only through the mercy and grace of the
Father of all mercies, through such virtues the sisters will cause
the fragrance of their good name to spread abroad for all other
sisters whether they be near or far removed.

18. Love one another in the charity of Christ; and let the love
you have inwardly be manifested outwardly by your works, that
by such an example the sisters may be incited always to grow
in the love of God, and in mutual charity.

19. I pray that sister who has the charge of leading the
sisters, to see to it that she precedes them more by the sanctity
of her virtues and life than because of any dignity; thus the
sisters, encouraged by her example will obey her not only as a
duty, but in love.
Besides she who leads the sisters must have for them that

prudence and foresight which a good mother has for her daughters: and with those alms that are sent by the Lord she shall provide for all the sisters according to their individual need.

Besides this she must have such kindliness, and be so accessible to all the sisters that they can safely tell her of their necessities, and turn to her at any hour as may seem best to them, either for themselves or for their sisters.

20. But on their side let the sisters who are subject to her remember that for the Lord they have renounced their own will.

Therefore I wish that they should obey their Mother as they have spontaneously promised the Lord to do; that this Mother seeing the charity, humility and unity which exists among the sisters, shall find the burden of her charge lightened; and that their holy life may change what is hard and painful for her into sweetness.

21. How narrow, however, is the path that leads into life! And the door which leads to it is equally narrow! And we must add that only a few walk in this path, and enter by this door! And even among those who follow this way for a moment, O how few are those who persevere therein!

Happy, however, are those to whom it is given to walk in it, and to persevere until the end!

22. We who have entered into the way of the Lord, let us take heed never to depart from it by ignorance or negligence or in any way by our own fault; for this would be to inflict a great injury upon so great a Lord, upon His Virgin Mother, upon our blessed Father Francis, upon all the Church triumphant, and finally upon the Church Militant.

For it is written: "Cursed be they who depart from Thy commandments."

23. Therefore I bend my knees before the Father of Our Lord Jesus Christ, that by the prayers and merits of the glorious Virgin Mary His Mother, of our blessed Father Francis, and of all the saints, the Lord Himself Who gave us the gift to begin this work, will also increase and enrich us and give us always perseverance until the end. Amen.

24. To you my dearly beloved sisters present and future I leave this writing, in order that you may better observe what I say; and that it may be to you a sign of the blessing of the Lord, of our blessed Father Francis, and of the benediction which I give you, who am your Mother and your servant.

THE BENEDICTION OF ST. CLARE

This text is not contained either in Wadding or the Acta Sanctorum, *though both mention the fact that before she died St. Clare blessed all her present and future daughters.*

In the Name of the most blessed Trinity. Amen.

Dear Sisters, may the Lord bless and keep you! May the Lord show you His face and have mercy on you. May the Lord turn His eyes to you and give you peace.

This blessing is for all those who shall enter our community and persevere therein; and for all those others of the whole Order, for those who shall persevere to the end in holy poverty.

I, Clare, the servant of Jesus Christ, and the little plant of our Father Saint Francis, your sister and your mother, however unworthy, pray our Redeemer, that by the intercession of His most holy Mother, by that of Saint Michael the Archangel, and of the Holy Angels, and of all the saints, I beseech Him to give you and confirm to you this holy blessing in heaven and on earth: on earth by increasing in you His grace and strength, in heaven by raising you to be among His saints.

While still living I give you my benediction, as far as I can, and beyond what I can. Amen.

Appendix 4

THE CAUSE OF CANONIZATION

Two months after the death of St. Clare on October 18, 1253, Innocent IV issued a Bull from the Lateran entrusting Bishop Bartolomeo of Spoleto with the charge of promoting the Cause of her canonization. He took as his associates the archdeacon, Leonard of Spoleto, Jacopo the archpriest of Trevi, Brothers Leo and Angelo of the Friars Minor, Brother Marco the chaplain of San Damiano, and a notary. On November 24 they went in person to San Damiano and interrogated thirteen of the Sisters, all of them under oath. Two other Sisters, one in the infirmary, were interrogated on the 28th, and the abbess, Benedetta, in the name of the community, declared the willingness of all to witness to the sanctity of Clare.

On the same day the postulators of the Cause held another meeting in the Assisi church of San Paolo at which the Bishop was also present, during which they interrogated an elderly knight, Ugolino di Pietro Giraldone, the lady Bona Guelfuccio, Ranieri di Bernardo, and Pietro di Damiani, all of whom were connected with Clare's family and had known her intimately from childhood. The following day Giovanni di Ventura was interrogated and he bore witness to one of the miracles which had followed Clare's death.

The text from which the following translation is made is in the Umbrian Italian of the fifteenth century: the manuscript was found by Father Zefferino Lazzeri, O.F.M., in the library of the late Monsieur de Landau in Florence, and the text was published by him in *Archivum Franciscanum Historicum*, Vol. XIII, Quaracchi, 1920. It was certainly used by Wadding in his history of St. Clare and her order.

The Text of the Cause

In the name of our Lord Jesus Christ. Amen. I, Bartolomeo, Bishop of Spoleto, have received the following letter from our holy Father the Lord Pope Innocent IV.

"Innocent, Bishop, Servant of the servants of God to our venerable brother Bartolomeo, bishop of Spoleto, health and apostolic benediction.

"The glorious Lord God Who alone creates and works great and marvellous things shows to His faithful the many wonderful ways and means and signs by which He brings His saints throughout their earthly life to the rewards and blessedness of eternal glory and celestial beatitude. He does this in order that the manifestation of so many signs and wonders, which are only possible through the power of the most blessed Trinity in Unity, should declare this power of the All-Highest God, so that His great and marvellous Name should be ever more reverently adored on earth, for His rule is eternal, and the Heavens declare His majesty.

"These considerations suffuse the blessed memory of the holy virgin Clare, formerly abbess of the Poor Ladies enclosed in the monastery of San Damiano in Assisi. She had heard the words of the prophet, 'O daughter see, and hear and incline thy ear, and forget thy people and thy father's house for the King has desired thy beauty,' and she turned her back upon all passing and transitory things, forgetting what lay behind, looking forward to what lay before her, and willingly and promptly she listened to holy advice. She did not hesitate in the speedy fulfillment of what she had heard gladly; very quickly she gave up herself, her family and all that belonged to her, and already proficient in the things of the heavenly kingdom, she chose to become the bride of Jesus Christ the Poor One, who is the King of Kings and having vowed herself wholly to Him in body and soul in the spirit of humility, she brought Him as her dowry two gifts, the gift of poverty and the vow of chastity. Thus this humble virgin was united to the Virgin Bridegroom, and taken into His arms, and from this most chaste marriage there has come forth a numerous and pure family admired by all. This family lives in the fragrance of her holy conversation and salutary love of perfection, and has spread over almost all the world, like a heavenly plant watered and increased by God.

"This is the bride who, even while she lived in this world was dead to it, and who greatly pleased the most high God through her desires, her virtues, her works and her study for perfection; and after her holy death, and even before, the omnipotent God, Who rewards all good and exceeds in goodness all the merits and desires of those who pray to Him, has allowed that His Name should be glorified in the world through the shining merits of the virgin Clare, and through her intercession has granted great benefits to those who pray. Thus God condescends to work many miracles on this earth through her and through her prayers.

"It is therefore right and just that she should be honoured throughout the Church Militant, and the divine mercy renders her venerable to all the faithful through the gifts of grace and the dignity of miracles; and by this apostolic letter We command you, Our Brother, to enquire speedily and diligently into her life, conversion, and conversation, and also into all the circumstances of the aforesaid miracles according to the questions we address to you and which are included under this Our seal. You shall study to send Us your findings on these points under your own seal written faithfully and openly in order that the soul of her whom We believe to be participating in the joy of heaven in the immortal glory may in this world receive the honour and praise of all the just.

"Given from Saint John Lateran on the XV calend of November (October 18) in the eleventh year of Our pontificate."

After this I, Bartolomeo, went personally to the monastery of San Damiano, and received evidence regarding the life, conversion, conversation, and miracles of the Lady Clare of holy memory formerly the abbess of the monastery of San Damiano in Assisi, and the names and evidence of the witnesses are recorded as follows.

On the 23rd of November in the cloister of San Damiano the ladies: 1, Pacifica de Guelfuccio of Assisi, 2, Benvenuta de Peroscia, 3, Philippa of Messer Leonardo di Ghislerio, 4, Amata of Messer Martino of Corozano, 5, Christiana of Messer Christiano of Parisse, 6, Christiana of Bernardo of Suppo, 7, Benvenuta of Oportulo of Alexandro, 8, Francesca of Messer Capitaneo of Col de Mezzo, 9, Beatrice of Messer Favorone of Assisi, the sister of

Saint Clare, 10, Cecilia of Spello, 11, Balvina of Messer Martino of Corozano, 12, Agnese of Messer Oportulo, 13, Lucia of Rome, all of the monastery of San Damiano took an oath that they would speak truthfully of the life, the conversion, the conversation, and miracles of the aforesaid Saint Clare. This they did in the presence of the witnesses, Leonardo, archdeacon of Spoleto, Jacopo, archpriest of Trevi, Brothers Leo, Angelo, and Marco of the Friars Minor, and the notary Ser Martino in the presence of the venerable father the Lord Bartolomeo, Bishop of Spoleto.

Witness 1

1. Sister Pacifica of Guelfuccio of Assisi, nun in the monastery of San Damiano, swore that she had known Saint Clare while she was still living in her father's house; and that she was considered by everyone to lead a most honest and virtuous life, entirely occupied with pious works.

2. Of her conversion. Sister Pacifica said that following the admonitions of Saint Francis, Saint Clare founded the order which now exists in San Damiano; she entered it as a virgin and always remained one. When asked how she knew these things, the witness answered that she was related to the virgin Clare and their houses were only divided by the piazza, and that they often held conversation together.

3. She told how the Lady Clare greatly loved the poor, and that because of her behaviour and conversation she was venerated by all. When asked how long it was since the Lady Clare had left the world, she answered about forty-two years. When asked how she knew this, she replied that they had entered religion together, and that for the most part she served the Lady Clare day and night.

4. She also told how the Lady Clare was born of a noble family, of a virtuous father and mother, and that her father was a knight named Favorone whom, however, she had never seen, but she had known her mother whose name was Ortolana, and this Lady Ortolana had crossed the sea for reasons of prayer and devotion. She, the witness, for the same reason had accompanied Madonna Ortolana overseas, and they also went together to the sanctuary of

Saint Michael the archangel and to Rome. She said that Clare willingly visited the poor, and when asked how she knew this, she replied that they were neighbours and that she often accompanied Clare.

5. She also told how the Lady Ortolana later came into religion with her daughter blessed Clare, and lived with the other sisters in great humility, and after living very piously and holily she passed out of this life.

6. She also testified that after the Lady Clare had been three years in religion the instant prayers of Saint Francis prevailed on her to accept the ordering and government of the sisters. When asked how she knew this, she said she too was present at that time.

7. Of Clare's conversation in the monastery.
This same witness asserted that often the blessed Mother passed the nights in vigil and prayer, and her fasting was such that the sisters were made sad and lamented over it, and that she herself had shed tears over it several times. When asked how she knew this, she said because she had seen how the Lady Clare lay on the bare ground with a stone from the river bed under her head, and that she heard her while she was praying.

8. She further said that Clare was so sparing of her food that the sisters were amazed that her body could continue to live. For a long time Blessed Clare never ate on three days of the week, namely Monday, Wednesday, and Friday. Even on the other days her abstinence was so great that she became ill, for which reason Saint Francis with the Bishop of Assisi commanded her to eat half a roll on those days when she was wont to fast entirely, the which half roll weighed about one and a half ounces.

9. She told how the blessed Mother was assiduous in prayer, and would lie for a long time most humbly prostrated on the earth. And when she came from prayer she admonished and comforted the sisters, and always spoke with the words of God which were indeed always on her lips for of vanities she would neither hear nor speak. And when she came from prayer the sisters rejoiced as

though she had come from Heaven. When asked how she knew this she replied, "Because I was with her."

10. She also told that when the Lady Clare gave any command to the sisters, she did so with much fear and humility, and nearly always she hastened to do herself what she ordered to others.

11. She told how Clare was very often so ill that she could not get up, but then she caused herself to be raised in bed with a support behind her back so that she could spin, and then with the linen she made corporals which she sent to nearly all the churches of the valley and hills round Assisi. Asked how she knew this, she answered that she often saw the Lady Clare when she span, and that the other sisters helped to sew the linen cloth, and that the corporals they made were then given to the priests who came to the monastery for them to distribute to the different churches.

12. She said that the blessed Mother was most humble, benign, and loving towards her sisters, and while she was well she served them, and washed their feet and gave them water for their hands, and she washed the seats used by the sick. Asked how she knew this, she answered that she herself had seen it many times.

13. She also told of the blessed Mother's love of poverty which was so great that she could never be induced to own anything of her own; she never wished for any possession either for herself or for her monastery. Asked how she knew this, she answered that she had both seen and heard Pope Gregory of blessed memory when he wished to give the Lady Clare many things, and to buy property for the monastery, to which however she would never consent.

14. She also said that the same Lady Clare was as anxious concerning the observance of her order and the government of her sisters as any man might be regarding the custody of his worldly treasure. And she said that she knew all these things from having been always with the blessed Mother for more than forty years except for one year during which time the Mother had sent her to the monastery of Valle Gloria in Spello to instruct the sisters there.

15. The miracle of the oil.

This same witness testified how the life of Blessed Clare was full of miracles. One day when there was no oil in the monastery the blessed Mother called a certain lay Brother of the Friars Minor, by name Bentevenga, whose office it was to beg for alms for the sisters, and she told him to go in search of oil whereupon he bade her prepare a vessel. Then the Lady Clare took a jug which she washed with her own hands, and placed it on a little wall near the entrance to the monastery from which place the Brother might take it. And after it had been there for a short time, Brother Bentevenga went to fetch it and found it already full of oil; but after diligent search it could not be discovered who had filled it. Asked how she knew this, Sister Pacifica said that being in the house at that time she saw the Lady Clare take the jar out empty and bring it in full, but she had never known by whom or how it had been filled, and Brother Bentevenga said the same. Asked in what year this had happened, she said it was about two years after the sisters had gone to live in San Damiano: asked in what month it had happened, she answered that she did not remember: asked whether in the spring or summer, she answered in the summer: asked what sisters were present, she said Sister Agnes, the sister of Saint Clare who was but recently dead, Sister Balvina the abbess of the monastery of Valle Gloria and was also dead, and Sister Benvenuta of Peroscia who was still alive. And Sister Pacifica swore that these things were true, and that she could never find words to describe the miracles and virtues that the Lord had manifested through Blessed Clare.

16. How Saint Clare cured five ill Sisters with the sign of the cross.

This witness also testified how once when five sisters were ill, Saint Clare healed them all instantly by making the sign of the cross over them with her own hand. And very often when any sister had pain in her head or in any other part of her body, the blessed Mother would cure her with the sign of the cross. Asked how she knew this, she replied that she was present when it happened. Asked who were the five sisters, she said that she was one, while two others were dead and two still lived, but she did not remember which they were. When asked how long ago it was since this illness, she answered that it was a very long time, and asked the nature of the illness she said that it had caused her to cry aloud with great shivering and cold. When asked how long it had been that the others were ill before their cure, she answered that she could not remember, and that she had also forgotten the length of her own illness. Asked at what period these sisters had been cured she answered, "before the illness of the Lady Clare."

17. Asked how long Saint Clare had been ill she answered that she thought it must be twenty-nine years.

18. She also said that her chief medicine and that of the other sisters when they were ill was the sign of the cross made over them by their Mother. Asked what words she used when she made the sign of the cross, Sister Pacifica said that she had never been able to hear because the Lady Clare spoke very softly.

19. Asked the date and month when she and the other sisters were healed, she said she could not remember, and neither could she recall the names of the other sisters who had been present at that time.

Witness 2

1. Sister Benvenuta of Peroscia, nun in the monastery of San Damiano, testified under oath to the marvellous humility of the Lady Clare formerly abbess of the same monastery, and so greatly did she despise herself that she always wished to perform the lowest work of the house. Many times she washed the seats used by the infirm sisters. Asked how she knew this, she said that she had entered religion in the same year as the Lady Clare whose religious life had begun on Easter Monday while her own had begun in the following September.

2. Asked how old Saint Clare was when she entered religion, Sister Benvenuta answered that she was always considered to have been about eighteen, a virgin in soul and body, held in veneration by all who knew her even before she left the world, and this on account of her great honesty, benignity, and humility. Asked how she knew this she answered that she knew her before they entered

religion, having dwelt together in the same house. And after her entry into religion she had never left the Lady Clare, but had been with her always for forty-two years except for those months from Easter Monday till September.

3. Of Saint Clare's conversation in the monastery.

This witness declared that since the Mother Saint Clare had entered into religion she was filled with such humility that often she washed the sisters' feet, and so it happened that once she bowed her head wishing to kiss the sister's foot, and that sister while incautiously withdrawing her foot, hit the blessed Mother on the mouth. Besides this blessed Clare brought the sisters water to wash their hands, and at night covered them against the cold.

4. She treated her own body with such asperity that she was content with one habit of "lazzo,"* and one cloak. And if it ever seemed to her that any sister had a habit that was shabbier than hers, then the Mother took it for her own, giving hers to the sister in exchange.

5. Once blessed Clare caused a hair shirt to be made of boar's hide, and this she wore with the bristles next her skin hidden under her woollen habit. Another time she had one made of horse hair knotted with string which she also wore round her body, and thus she tormented her tender flesh. And the witness said that one of these hair shirts still remained in the monastery.

6. She also said that though Blessed Clare afflicted her own body with these hair shirts, she was most merciful with the sisters, for whom she would not hear of such penances, and most willingly gave them every consolation.

7. Asked how she knew of these garments Sister Benvenuta said that she had seen them, and that the Lady Clare would sometimes lend one of them to certain sisters; however, she had never seen the shirt of boar's hide but heard of it from the Mother's own sister who had seen it. The Mother wore it in most hidden fashion in order that the sisters should not reprove her for doing so.

* "Lazzo" was the common home-woven material among Umbrian peasants partly of wool.

When, however, she became ill the sisters took from her this harsh garment.

8. Sister Benvenuta also declared that before the blessed Mother Clare became ill that during the Greater Lent and that of Saint Martin, she always fasted on bread and water except on Sundays when she drank a little wine if there happened to be any. And on Monday, Wednesday, and Friday of every week she ate nothing, until Saint Francis ordered her to eat something every day, after which she obediently took a little bread and water. Asked how she knew this, the witness said that she had seen it, and was present when Saint Francis issued this order.

9. She also told how the Mother Saint Clare was assiduous in prayer by day and by night; and about midnight she would silently awaken the sisters by signs that they should rise to praise God. She lit the lamp in the chapel, and often rang the bell for Matins. And those sisters who did not get up at the sound of the bell, she called by other signs.

10. She also told how the Lady Clare always spoke of the things of God and would not speak of secular matters, neither did she wish the sisters to remember them. And when any person in the world was known to have committed some action against God, she grieved with many tears and exhorted this person to penance. Asked how she knew this, Sister Benvenuta replied that being with the Lady Clare she saw these things happen.

11. She told how the blessed Mother went often to confession, and with great devotion and awe often received the Body of Our Lord Jesus Christ, and when she received This, she trembled all over.

12. Of the corporals spun and made by blessed Clare this sister said the same as Sister Pacifica, the first witness, but she added that blessed Clare kept them in cases lined with silk which she caused to be blessed by the Bishop.

13. How a Sister was cured from loss of voice.
Sister Benvenuta told how having lost her voice so that she could hardly speak, she was told by the Blessed Virgin in a vision

that she would be cured by the Lady Clare the following day through the sign of the cross. And thus it happened after this infirmity had lasted for two years. Asked how long it was since this sister was cured, Benvenuta replied that she could not remember; asked who was present she answered that Sister Pacifica was there with several other sisters now dead.

14. As regards the miracle of the oil, Sister Benvenuta told the same story as the above mentioned Sister Pacifica, except that she could not remember whether Saint Clare had washed the jar herself or caused it to be washed by someone else.

15. How a Brother was freed from insanity.

This same witness told how Brother Stephano of the Friars Minor being afflicted with madness, Saint Francis sent him to the monastery of San Damiano in order that Saint Clare might sign him with the cross; the which being done, the Brother slept for a while in the place where the blessed Mother used to pray, and when he awoke he ate a little and departed cured.

Asked who was present on this occasion, Sister Benvenuta replied that the sisters of the monastery were there, of whom some were still alive, and some already dead. Asked whether she had known the Brother previously, and how long before she had seen him mad, and for how long a time he had suffered from madness, and for how long a time afterwards he was seen sane and well, and what was the name of his native place, she replied to all these questions saying that she did not know the answers as she had lived enclosed and the Brother who was cured went his own way.

16. How a Sister was healed of a sore and a fistula.

The same witness also told how a sister of the monastery, by name Sister Benvenuta of Madonna Diambra, was very ill and suffered grievously from a sore under her arm. Knowing this the compassionate mother Saint Clare took pity on her and prayed for her, after which she made the sign of the cross over her and the sister was instantly healed. Asked how she knew this, she answered that she had seen the sore, and then seen the same place after the sister had been healed. Asked whether she was actually present when the blessed Mother signed the sister with the cross, she answered no, but that she had been told what had taken place. Asked when the sister had been thus healed, she answered that she could not remember the day or month, or how long ago it was, but she had seen her healed and well immediately after Saint Clare had signed her with the cross.

17. Sister Benvenuta also told that in the place where the Lady Clare was wont to pray she had seen so great a splendour of light that she thought it came from material fire. Asked who else had seen this light she replied that on that occasion she was the only one to see it. Asked when this had happened she answered, before the Lady Clare fell ill.

18. How a child was healed of a stone in his nose.

The same witness told how a small boy named Mathiolo of Spoleto, three or four years old, had put a little stone up one of his nostrils, and no one could remove it and the child seemed in peril. He was brought to the Lady Clare and after she had signed him with the cross, the stone immediately fell out of his nose, and he was healed. Asked who was present, she replied that several of the sisters were there, now all dead. Asked how long ago it had happened she answered that she could not remember, and that she had not been present personally, but had heard of it from those other sisters who were present, and she had seen the child either on the day itself that he was healed or the following day.

19. She also said that neither she, nor any other sister could ever fully tell of the holiness and greatness of the life of Lady Clare of blessed memory, unless they should be especially inspired by the Holy Spirit. Even when she was most gravely ill, Saint Clare never ceased her accustomed prayers.

20. How the monastery was liberated from the Saracens by the prayers of Saint Clare.

Sister Benvenuta told how on one occasion when Assisi was at war, some Saracens had scaled the wall of the monastery and climbed down into the cloister. The holy mother the Lady Clare was then very ill, but she raised herself in bed and called the sisters comforting and reassuring them. Then she prayed, and the

Lord liberated the monastery and the sisters from their enemies, and those Saracens who had already entered departed.

21. She also said that because of the graces and virtues given by God to the Lady Clare, all considered her a saint.

22. She told how most especially the blessed Mother loved poverty, and neither Pope Gregory nor the Bishop of Ostia* could ever persuade her to receive any possession; indeed blessed Clare had sold all that was hers and given it to the poor. Asked how she knew these things, she replied that she was present and heard the Pope asking her if she would not receive and hold some possessions, and that Pope came in person to San Damiano.

23. She also said that the Mother Saint Clare knew by spiritual insight that one of the sisters, Andrea by name, was afflicted with scrofula in the throat; one night this sister squeezed her throat so tightly with her own hands that she lost the power of speech, but immediately Saint Clare, knowing what had happened, sent another sister to help and minister to Sister Andrea.

Witness 3

1. Sister Philippa, the daughter of Messer Leonardo de Gislerio, nun in the monastery of San Damiano declared on oath that four years after Saint Clare had entered the religious life, she herself entered the same religion owing to the preaching of Saint Francis; and because Saint Clare spoke to her of how Our Lord Jesus Christ was born and suffered and died on the cross for the salvation of mankind she felt great compunction at this thought and consented to enter religion and together with Saint Clare to do penance. And she was with the Lady Clare always until her death, that is for about thirty-eight years.

2. She said that the sanctity of the blessed Mother's life, and the virtue of her behaviour were so great that neither she nor any other sister could fully explain them. As the Lady Clare had been chaste from her infancy, so she was when the Lord called her, and so remained. And neither she nor any of the other sisters had the slightest doubt concerning the sanctity of the Lady Clare. Even

---

* Cardinal Rainaldo dei Conti d'Anagni, afterwards Pope Alexander IV.

before she entered religion she was reputed a saint by all who knew her, and this because of the great honesty of her life, and because of the many virtues and graces given her by God.

3. Of the conversation of Saint Clare in the monastery.

This witness said that ever since the Lord called the Lady Clare into religion He greatly increased all her virtues and graces, and she was most humble and devout, most benign, a great lover of poverty, and having deep compassion for the afflicted. She was assiduous in prayer, and all her conversation and speech turned on the things of God, and neither her ears nor her tongue were ever inclined to worldly things.

4. Saint Clare ever tormented her body with harsh clothing, and sometimes she wore garments made of boar's hide or horse hair; and she had one tunic, and one cloak made of common "lazzo." Her bed was made of vine twigs, and with this she was content for a long time.

5. She also afflicted her body by eating nothing three days in the week, on Monday, Wednesday, and Friday; and on the other days she fasted on bread and water.

6. Notwithstanding all this, she was always gay in the Lord, and her life was entirely angelic; and the Lord had given her such grace that often when the sisters were ill she made the sign of the cross over them and they were healed.

7. Sister Philippa told how the blessed Mother had especially the gift of many tears because of her great compassion for her sisters and all those who were afflicted; but especially she wept copiously when she received the Body of Our Lord Jesus Christ.

8. When asked how she knew these things she answered that she was the third sister to join the Lady Clare, and that she had known her from childhood, and had always been with her and seen these things.

9. She told of how the blessed Mother despised herself with the deepest humility, and she placed herself below all the other sisters, and willingly served them, washing the seats used by those who

were infirm with her own hands, and washing the feet of the lay sisters. And once while she was washing the feet of a lay sister of the monastery, she wished to kiss them, but the sister withdrew her foot hastily and in doing so struck the holy Mother on the mouth. This however did not disturb her humility, and she kissed the sole of the foot of that same lay sister. Asked how she knew this, she said she had been present and seen it.

10. How a Sister was cured of a fistula.

When the witness was asked which of the sisters had been cured by blessed Clare with the sign of the cross, she said that Sister Benvenuta of Madonna Diambra had for twelve years suffered from a grievous sore under her arm called a fistula, and she was cured when the Lady Clare signed her with the cross after reciting the Lord's Prayer.

11. Sister Amata, another sister of the same monastery, was seriously ill with dropsy and fever with a very swollen belly; but when she had received the sign of the cross from the blessed Mother and been touched with her hands, the following morning she was fully cured, and her body reduced to the normal size of a healthy person. Asked how she knew this, Sister Philippa said she had been present when the blessed Mother made the sign of the cross and touched Sister Amata, and from having been ill for a long time she was cured by the next day.

12. Of Brother Stephano, Sister Philippa confirmed the testimony of the aforesaid Sister Benvenuta.

13. She also said that the blessed Mother's love of poverty was so great, that when the begging brothers brought back whole loaves as alms for the monastery, she would reprove them saying, "Who gave you these whole loaves?" And she said this because she preferred to receive in alms broken loaves instead of whole ones.

14. The Blessed Mother could never be induced to receive any possessions either from the Pope nor from the Bishop of Ostia. She held the Privilege of Poverty that had been granted to her in great honour and reverence, guarding it with much care, fearful lest she should lose it.

15. How Saint Clare cured a small child of fever.

Sister Benvenuta also told how a child of Messer Giovanni, the son of Maestro Giovanni, procurator of the sisters was gravely ill with fever and was thus brought to the blessed Mother Clare, and after being signed by her with the cross he recovered. Asked how she knew this, she answered that she was present when the child was brought and when the blessed Mother touched him and made the sign of the cross. Asked if the child had fever when he arrived and whether she had seen him cured, Sister Philippa answered that he appeared to be feverish, and everyone said he was in a fever; afterwards the child left the monastery and she did not see him again, but his father told her that the child was immediately cured.

16. How Sister Andrea was cured of scrofula.

The witness also described how Sister Andrea of Ferrara was suffering from scrofula of the throat, and Blessed Clare knew by means of the spirit that this sister was grievously tempted by the desire to recover. One night Sister Andrea was below in the dormitory, and she pressed on her throat so hard with her own hands that she lost her voice. This was revealed to the blessed Mother by the Spirit, and she instantly called Sister Benvenuta who was sleeping near her and said: "Go down quickly to the dormitory where Sister Andrea is grievously ill: warm an egg and give it to her to swallow, and when she is again able to speak, bring her to me." This was done, but when the blessed Mother wished to know from Sister Andrea what had happened she did not wish to tell it. Then the blessed Mother told her exactly all that had befallen; and this was recounted among the sisters.

17. How Saint Clare liberated a Sister from deafness and the monastery from the Saracens.

The witness also described how the Lady Clare had cured a sister named Christiana from deafness in one ear from which she had long suffered.

18. At a time when Assisi was at war the sisters greatly dreaded the incursion of the Saracens and Tartars and other enemies of God and Holy Church, and the blessed Mother comforted them saying: "My sisters and daughters do not fear because God will be with

us and the enemies will not be able to harm us. Trust in Our Lord Jesus Christ and He will preserve us; and I will be your hostage so that no hurt shall touch you; should our enemies come so far put me in front of them." One day when the enemy had advanced, for they wished to destroy Assisi, some of the Saracens scaled the wall and penetrated into the cloister of the monastery, so that the sisters were greatly alarmed. But the holy Mother comforted them all, and she despised the forces of the enemy saying, "Do not fear, they will not be able to harm us." Having said this she had recourse to her customary prayer; and the force of her prayer was so great that the enemy Saracens departed having done no harm as though they had been driven away, and they touched no one in the house. Asked how she knew this Sister Philippa answered, "because I was there, present." Asked on what day and in which month this had happened, she said she had forgotten.

19. She also told that when Vitale d'Aversa was sent by the emperor with a great army to besiege Assisi, everyone was sorely afraid; and it was told to the Lady Clare that the city was in sore danger since Vitale had declared that he would not leave until he had conquered it. Having heard all this the Lady Clare trusting in the power of God called together the sisters, and ordered ashes to be brought which she strewed upon her own head, which she had uncovered, and then she strewed them on the heads of the sisters, and commanded them all to go pray that the Lord God might deliver the city. And so it was done; and in the following night Vitale departed with all his troops.

20. This witness also told how when the blessed Mother lay dying one Friday evening she began to speak thus: "Go in peace for thou wilt have a good escort, and this escort will be He Who created thee, Who sanctified thee, and after creating thee Who put in thee His blessed Spirit, Who has always watched over thee as a mother watches over a beloved child." Then she added, "Blessed be Thou, O my Lord, Who hast created me." She said many other things, speaking of the Blessed Trinity so subtly that the sisters could not well understand her.

21. This witness said to a sister who was standing by, "You who

have a good memory, remember what our Mother says"; and the Lady Clare heard these words and said to all the sisters who were present, "You will remember what I am now saying as far as He allows it Who now causes me to speak."

22. Another sister, named Anastasia, asked the Lady Clare to whom she was addressing the above said words, to which she replied, "I was speaking to my soul."

23. And the witness added that throughout the night preceding the day when she passed from this life, the blessed Mother admonished the sisters speaking to them. After which she made so beautiful and holy a confession that she, Sister Philippa, had never heard the like. And the Lady Clare made this confession because she feared to have in some way offended against the faith promised at her Baptism.

24. While she was so ill the Lord Pope came to visit her, and she then said to the sisters: "O my daughters, thank the Lord God for me, because all the heavens and earth cannot suffice to praise God for me since today I have received Him in the Blessed Sacrament and have also seen His Vicar." Asked how she knew these things, Sister Philippa said that she was present and saw them all. When asked how many days this was before the death of the Lady Clare, she replied, "Very few."

25. She also told that Lady Clare was so assiduous in contemplation that on Good Friday while absorbed in the Passion of the Lord, she remained insensible all that day, and most of the following night.

26. Regarding the miracle of the oil, this witness confirmed the testimony of the aforesaid witnesses.

27. When asked about the sisters who had been healed from infirmities, she said that others had also been healed but had since died.

28. Regarding the prophecy of future things.
Sister Philippa also declared that the Lady Clare had told the sisters that while her mother was with child of her, she entered

a church and stood before the cross. While she was earnestly praying God to help and protect her in childbirth, she heard a voice which said, "Thou wilt give birth to a light which will greatly illuminate the whole world."

29. The Lady Clare also told that once she had seen Saint Francis in a vision and she was bringing him a jug of hot water and a towel for wiping the hands and with this she was ascending a long stairway, but so easily that it was as though she walked on the level earth. When she reached Saint Francis, he bared his breast, saying: "Come, take and drink." And as she did so . . . the substance was so sweet and delightful that she could not describe it . . . and what was in her mouth seemed to be such pure shining gold that she saw her own reflection in it, as in a mirror.

30. Of the marvellous hearing of Saint Clare.

The Lady Clare also told that in the night of Christmas Eve she being kept in bed by her grievous infirmity, and unable to go to the chapel, the sisters having gone as was their wont, she remained alone. Then she sighed, "O my Lord God, here I am alone with Thee in this place." And at once she heard the organ and the responses and all the Office of the Friars in the church of Saint Francis as though indeed she had been present there.

31. This witness reported these and many other miracles of sight and hearing of the Lady Clare who was the first Mother and abbess of the monastery of San Damiano, and the founder of this Order. She was of noble family and birth, rich in all the goods of this world; and she so loved Poverty that she sold all that she had and gave to the poor. And she loved this order so dearly that she would not depart from the least part of its observance even when she was ill.

32. At the end of her life she called together all her sisters and commended to them the Privilege of Poverty. She earnestly desired to have the rule of the Order approved in a Papal Bull, saying that if she could but kiss the seal of that Bull she would then be well content to die. And it happened as she desired, for when the Brother brought the sealed Papal Letter although the

blessed Mother was very near to death, she took it in her hands and placed it on her mouth and kissed it. The next day the Lady Clare passed from this life to God, shining indeed without a shadow, without any stain of sin, and so she passed into the eternal light. And this is believed by all her sisters and all who knew her and recognised her sanctity.

Witness 4

1. Sister Amata of Messer Martino of Coccorano, a nun in the monastery of San Damiano, declared on oath that she had been twenty-five years a nun in this Order, and knew Saint Clare who had exhorted her to enter religion: saying that she had asked of God this grace, that Sister Amata might not be deceived by the world into remaining in secular life. The witness told how she was the niece of Saint Clare who had been to her as a mother.

2. She knew the blessed Mother s life and had heard how she had been converted through the exhortation and preaching of Saint Francis and because of this had entered religion. But even while she was still in the world she was reputed a saint by all who knew her because of the many virtues and graces given her by God, and these were known to all.

3. After her entry into religion Sister Amata had been constantly with the blessed Mother, and thus knew the sanctity of her life and conversation and this sanctity was manifested through the gifts and graces God had given her, and which could only be explained in this way, for she possessed all virtues, complete chastity, benignity, mildness, compassion towards her sisters and towards many others.

4. She was assiduous in prayer and contemplation, and when she came from prayer her face seemed more shining and beautiful than the sun, and her words were of an indescribable gentleness so that her life seemed entirely celestial.

5. She was so frugal in her use of food that it seemed as though she must be fed by angels. She afflicted her body by fasting every Monday, Wednesday, and Friday when she ate nothing, while on the other days of the week her food was bread and water. So she

continued until Saint Francis ordered her to eat something every day, including those days when she commonly ate nothing. For the sake of obedience she therefore ate a little bread and water.

6. As regards her bedding and clothing this witness confirmed what had been said by Sister Philippa.

7. How a Sister was cured of fever, a cough, and dropsy.

Sister Amata also told how when she was grievously ill with fever, a cough, dropsy, and a pain in her side, Saint Clare made the sign of the cross over her and she was instantly cured. When asked what words the blessed Mother had said, she answered that having laid her hands upon her, Saint Clare had prayed to God that, if it were to the profit of her soul Sister Amata might be freed from her infirmity. And immediately she was cured. Asked how long she had been ill, she replied thirteen months, and she had had no relapse. At the time when the blessed Mother cured her, she was so swollen with dropsy that she could hardly bend her head, but by the merits and prayers of the saint she had been completely restored to health.

8. In like manner the Lady Clare freed other sisters from their infirmities making over them the sign of the cross. Asked who these sisters were the witness replied that Sister Benvenuta of Madonna Diambra had a sore under her arm which was so large that five fingers could be put in it, and this she had endured for about eleven years. When the Lady Clare made the sign of the cross over her, she was freed from this evil. Asked how she knew, she answered, from what came out of the sore. She never again suffered from this ill. Asked the name of this illness, she said it was called a fistula.

9. How another sister was cured of a cough.

The same witness told how Sister Cecilia was afflicted with a terrible cough and, as soon as she began to eat, it seemed as though she would suffocate. One Friday the blessed Mother gave her a small piece of cake which she took in trembling, eating it for obedience since so she was commanded. And she never suffered again from that cough. Asked how long Sister Cecilia had had the cough, the witness answered that she did not remember, but she thought it was for a long time.

10. How a Sister was cured of a deaf ear.

Sister Cecilia also told how Sister Christiana had been deaf in one ear, even before she entered the monastery. When Saint Clare touched her ear making the sign of the cross, her hearing returned. She did not remember the cases of the other sisters, although a number of them had been cured of various ills.

11. How a child was healed of a growth on its eye.

Sister Cecilia further told of a child from Perugia who had a growth which covered one eye; he was brought to Saint Clare who touched it, making the sign of the cross and then said, "Take the child to my mother Ortolana (for she was also in the monastery of San Damiano) and let her sign him with the cross." This was done and the child was cured, and Saint Clare declared he had been cured by her mother, while Madonna Ortolana said that her daughter had healed him, so each attributed this grace to the other. Asked how long the child had lived with this defect on his eye, the witness said that she had seen him with it when he was brought to the monastery to Saint Clare; she did not know him previously, nor had she seen him again after his cure for he immediately left the monastery; she herself had been enclosed in the monastery all the aforesaid years.

12. Asked about the humility of the blessed Mother, she confirmed the testimony of Sister Philippa.

13. Asked about the blessed Mother's love of poverty and prayer, she again confirmed what had been said by Sister Philippa.

14. She also told how the sisters feared the coming of the Saracens, Tartars, and other infidels, and prayed their Mother that she should pray to the Lord to defend the monastery. The blessed Mother answered: "My daughters and sisters do not be afraid for the Lord will defend you. I will be hostage for you, and if it is necessary and the enemy come to the monastery place me before

them in front of you." By the prayer of Saint Clare the sisters, the monastery, and all it contained remained unhurt.

15. Of the siege and liberation of the city of Assisi, Sister Amata confirmed what had been said by Sister Philippa.

16. Of the miracle worked by the blessed Mother Clare, of her vision of the breast of Saint Francis, of the miracle of Christmas Eve and of all these things Sister Amata confirmed what had been said by Sister Philippa; but she added that she heard that during that Christmas Eve the blessed Mother had also seen the Crib of Our Lord Jesus Christ.

17. Sister Amata also said that great good had been provided by the Lord when He ordained that the foundress of the Order should be so holy, for indeed in the blessed Mother no defect could be observed, but rather she was seen to be filled with every virtue and grace, and even while she was alive all who knew her considered her a saint. She was noble by birth, but far more noble in her observance of holy religion and of the rule of her order, of which she would never neglect anything even when she was ill, and thus in sanctity she ordered her own life and that of her sisters for about forty years.

18. The blessed Mother loved her sisters as herself, and before and after her death they always venerated her as a saint and as the Mother of all the Order. Sister Amata added that Saint Clare's sanctity and kindness, her virtues and goodness far surpassed anything that she could know or tell.

19. Sister Amata also told how on the Friday, very shortly before Saint Clare's death she was alone with her, and the blessed Mother said, "Do you see the King of Glory as I do?" And she repeated this several times, and within a few days she died.

20. She also told how she had heard that a woman from Pisa had been liberated by the Lord from five evil spirits through the merits of Saint Clare, and those spirits acknowledged that the prayer of the blessed Mother consumed them as with fire. The woman had come to San Damiano into the parlour where it is allowed to speak with the sisters in order to give thanks to God,

and to the Blessed Mother. Asked how long ago this had happened, Sister Amata replied about four years.

Witness 5

1. Sister Christiana of Messer Christiano of Parisse, a nun in the monastery of San Damiano, declared on oath that she had been long deaf in one ear, and had tried many medicines which were all unavailing. At length Saint Clare made the sign of the cross over her head and touched her ear which was immediately opened and she heard perfectly. Asked how long ago, she answered that it was about one year in either June or July, but she did not remember which day.

2. She said that she was quite unable to describe the sanctity of Saint Clare, and the excellence of her conduct; and she firmly believed that the blessed Mother was filled with all graces and virtues and every good work, so that her holiness exceeded that of any other woman after the Blessed Virgin Mary. But of all this Sister Christiana could not possibly speak.

3. Regarding the healing of Sister Benvenuta, Sister Christiana confirmed what had been said by Sister Amata.

4. This witness also said that seven years were not yet completed since she entered the monastery.

5. She told how once a heavy door fell on the blessed Mother at which Sister Angeluccia called out in terror for she was quite unable to lift the door by herself, and she feared that it had killed the blessed Mother who was imprisoned beneath it. Thus she and other sisters came running to the place, and the door was so heavy that it took three brothers to lift it and put it back in its place; and yet the blessed Mother had remained unhurt and that door had seemed to her as light as a cloak. Asked how long ago this had happened, she replied about seven years in July during the octave of Saint Peter.

Witness 6

1. Sister Cecilia, daughter of Messer Gualtieri of Spello, a nun in the monastery of San Damiano, on oath declared that she had

always heard the fame of the sanctity of the Lady Clare formerly abbess of this monastery and for about forty-three years she had lived among the sisters. Sister Cecilia had entered this religion three years after the Lady Clare herself had entered it through the preaching of Saint Francis; and she had been exhorted to do so by the Lady Clare and Brother Philip of holy memory. Thus for forty years she had been under the holy rule of the Lady Clare, whose life was entirely praiseworthy and marvellous, and she, the witness, was quite insufficient to speak fully of such holy conversation.

2. God had elected the Lady Clare to be the Mother and principal Abbess of the Order in order that her example should confirm the other sisters of all the monasteries of the Order in their observance of this holy religion, and that she should watch over the flock; and certainly she was most diligent in her exhortations to the sisters, as in her care for them and she had compassion upon all those who were infirm, being solicitous to serve them, submitting herself most humbly to the least lay sister, and always holding herself as of no account.

3. She was most vigilant in prayer, and sublime in contemplation, and once when she came from prayer her face was most unusually illuminated, and from her mouth emanated a great sweetness.

4. In prayer she shed most abundant tears, and with the sisters showed much spiritual joy. She was never disturbed, and taught the sisters with great benevolence and kindness; but when it was necessary she diligently reproved them.

5. She never considered her own body; in earlier days she treated herself most severely both as regards her bed and her clothes; and in food and drink she was so sparing that her life seemed entirely angelic, and in this way her sanctity was known to all who knew her or had heard of her. Asked how she knew these things, Sister Cecilia answered that she had lived with the blessed Mother for about forty years, and had seen her holy life and conversation, which would never have been possible had the Lord not given her these abundant graces, and many others besides which adorned the Lady Clare but of which she, Sister Cecilia, could not speak.

6. She also told how the blessed Mother was so fervent in spirit that she would willingly have endured martyrdom for the love of the Lord; and this was apparent when five brothers were martyred in Morocco which, when the blessed Mother heard of it, she wished to start off herself, which had caused the witness to weep. This happened before the blessed Mother became infirm. Asked who was present at that time, she answered that the other sisters were all now dead.

7. Of the blessed Mother's humility, of the harshness of her bedding and garments, her abstinence and fasting, Sister Cecilia confirmed all that had been said by Sister Philippa. She added that the blessed Mother washed the seats of the infirm with her own hands, and that sometimes in those seats there were vermin; but the Lady Clare said she was not conscious of any evil smell, but rather of fragrance.

8. The witness also told how the Lord had given the blessed Mother the gift to heal by the sign of the cross, and she had cured the Sisters Amata, Benvenuta, Christiana, and Andrea of their infirmities as had been recounted by Sister Philippa, and she, Sister Cecilia, had been cured as had been testified by Sister Amata.

9. She had seen other people brought to the monastery to be healed by the blessed Mother, who made the sign of the cross over them thus liberating them from their ills. Sister Cecilia, however, could not name these people, and she had never seen them either before or after they were healed for she had been continuously enclosed in the monastery.

10. Of the blessed Mother's love of poverty, of her virtue in prayer, and of the liberation of the city and monastery from the enemy Sister Cecilia confirmed the testimony of Sister Philippa.

11. She also said that in any danger the sisters were commanded by their Mother always to resort to the help of prayer.

12. She also said that she had been told by the mother of Saint Clare that before the child's birth while she was praying before the crucifix that the Lord would help her in childbirth, she

heard a voice which told her that she would give birth to a light that would illuminate the whole world. Asked when she had been told this by Madonna Ortolana, she answered that it was about the time of the death of Saint Francis (1226).

13. Sister Cecilia confirmed what Sister Philippa had said of the blessed Mother's vision of the breast of Saint Francis, except that she did not remember having heard that the nipple had remained in the mouth of the Lady Clare.

14. She also said that the Blessed Mother would never remain idle, even when she was ill, and would have herself propped up in bed and would spin. From the thread she had linen woven and corporals were made with silken cases to protect them, and these were sent to the Bishop of Assisi to be blessed after which they were distributed to churches in and round Assisi. She thought that every church had received them.

15. This witness also spoke of the Lady Clare's spirit of prophecy; and once when Saint Francis had sent five novices to be received in the monastery Saint Clare received four, but would not receive the fifth saying that she would not persevere in her vocation even if she remained in the monastery three years. However, after being greatly importuned to receive her, she consented, but the novice left after half a year. Asked who the woman was, Sister Cecilia replied that she was the Lady Gasdia, the daughter of Taccholo, and this happened during the lifetime of Saint Francis. Asked what sisters were present when Saint Clare made this prophecy, she replied that the blessed Mother's own sister Agnes was there, she who had so recently died, and other sisters whom she did not remember.

16. Of the miraculous meal.

She also told how one day the sisters had no food in the house except half a loaf, the other half of which had been sent out to the Brothers whose office it was to beg for the monastery. Thereupon the blessed Mother ordered the witness to divide the half loaf into fifty portions and to set them before the sisters seated at table. She, Sister Cecilia, had replied to the Lady Clare that if she was to divide the loaf into these fifty portions the Lord's miracle of the five loaves and fishes would have to be repeated, whereupon the blessed Mother had said to her, "Go and do what I have told you." And the Lord so increased that loaf that she was able to make of it fifty good large portions as Saint Clare had commanded.

17. Of the heavy door that fell on Saint Clare, Sister Cecilia confirmed all that had been said by Sister Christiana, saying that she too had seen it while it lay upon the blessed Mother.

Witness 7

1. Sister Balvina of Messer Martino of Coccorano, nun in the monastery of San Damiano, declared under oath that she had been in the monastery for more than thirty-three years under the rule of the Lady Clare of blessed memory, then abbess of the monastery, whose life and conversation had been adorned by God with so many gifts and virtues that it was quite impossible to give any account of them.

2. This Lady Clare remained a virgin from her birth, she was of all her sisters the most humble, and so fervent in spirit that willingly she would have endured martyrdom for love of God in defence of the faith and of her order. Before she fell ill she greatly desired to go to Morocco where she had heard that the Brothers had been martyred. Asked how she knew these things, Sister Balvina said that she had been with the Lady Clare continually and had seen and heard her great love of the faith and the Order.

3. The witness told how assiduous in prayer was the blessed Mother, in contemplation and in the exhorting the sisters. Regarding this she knew well the intention of the Lady Clare.

4. Of her humility, her virtues, her prayers, the austerity she practised both in sleeping and in clothing herself, of her fasting and abstinence, Sister Balvina confirmed what had been said by Sister Philippa except that she had not personally seen her bed of vine twigs, but only heard that she had used it for a considerable time. She had, however, seen a common table which the blessed Mother also used as a bed.

5. Of how she washed those who were infirm, Sister Balvina confirmed what had been said by Sister Cecilia.

6. She also confirmed what Sister Philippa had said of the liberation of the city of Assisi when it was besieged by Vitale d'Aversa, and the liberation of the monastery from the Saracens and other enemies, both of which were obtained by the prayers of Saint Clare.

7. Of the miracles of healing which the blessed Mother performed on her sisters through the sign of the cross, Sister Balvina confirmed what had been said by Sister Philippa. She added that Sister Benvenuta of Peroscia recovered her lost voice when Saint Clare signed her with the cross. When asked how she knew this, she answered that she had heard it from Sister Benvenuta herself.

8. She confirmed what Sister Philippa had said of the blessed Mother's love for the privilege of Poverty.

9. This witness also told how she had heard the Lady Clare tell how during Christmas Eve she heard Matins and the other Offices being celebrated in the church of San Francesco as though she had been actually present there. And the Lady Clare had added: "You all left me alone when you went to the chapel for Matins, but since I could not rise from bed the Lord Himself looked after me."

10. She also said that she had heard from the blessed Mother herself of her vision of Saint Francis, as narrated by Sister Philippa.

11. Sister Balvina further said that she was far too simple and ignorant to be able to tell of the virtues and goodness of the blessed Mother, of her humility, her benignity, her patience, and all the other virtues in which she abounded, and she, the witness, was firmly convinced that after the Blessed Virgin Mary no other woman was more full of merits than the Lady Clare. Asked how she knew this, she replied that she had indeed heard the legends of the sanctity of many other saints, but she had herself seen the sanctity of the life of the Lady Clare throughout all her own religious life, except for the period of one year and five months when the Lady Clare had sent her to a monastery in Arezzo with

another woman. Being herself the niece of the Lady Clare she had considered her aunt's life and manners with great attention, and they seemed to her very wonderful. Asked in what way they seemed marvellous, Sister Balvina answered that the abstinence practised by the blessed Mother seemed to her beyond the power of any man, but also because of many other wonderful things which God performed in and through her, as has been already described.

12. How a Sister was cured of a painful fever and abscess.

The witness added that she was once ill, and grievously afflicted all one night by a great pain in her thigh, for which she began to cry and lament. Then the Lady Clare asked what was the matter, and when Sister Balvina had told her, she immediately threw herself down on the side and laid a veil upon it from her own head and the pain was instantly cured. Asked when this had happened, Sister Balvina said more than twelve years previously: asked who was present, she answered that she was alone with the blessed Mother in a place where she habitually prayed; she had forgotten the date and the month.

13. On another and earlier occasion, she, the witness, had been healed by Saint Clare of a recurring fever and an abscess in her right breast which was so acute that the sisters thought she would die of it. This had happened twenty years before. Asked how long she had then been ill, she answered three days.

14. The witness said she had also heard of a woman whom the Lord had liberated from five evil spirits through the merits of Saint Clare. Asked whence this woman came, Sister Balvina said from Pisa as was told by the woman herself when she came to the monastery and spoke with the sisters and to render thanks to God and the blessed Mother. Asked when this had occurred, she answered about four years ago, adding that "the woman had declared that the evil spirits had said that the prayers of this saint consume us like fire."

Witness 8

1. Sister Lucia of Rome, nun in the monastery of San Damiano, said on oath that the sanctity and goodness of the Lady Clare

formerly abbess of the monastery of San Damiano were so great that she could in no way describe them. Asked how this sanctity was manifested she said in the greatness of her humility, in her benignity, her sincerity and patience.

2. Asked how long she had been in the monastery, Sister Lucia answered that if her stay there were to be measured by what she had accomplished, then it was short, but if by time, she had been there so long that she did not remember the years, for the Lady Clare had received her into the monastery when she was very small. She added that she had always seen the Lady Clare comport herself with great holiness.

3. Asked in what way this holiness showed itself, Sister Lucia replied in her maceration of her body and the great asperity of her life. In every way within her power the Lady Clare studied to please God, and she instructed the sisters in His love, and she had great compassion on the sisters both as regarded their souls and bodies. Sister Lucia added that she would have to have the wisdom of all the saints if she were to describe the goodness and sanctity that she had seen in the Lady Clare.

4. She said she had heard that many sisters had been cured of their ills through the merits of the blessed Mother, but she was not present, being ill herself.

Witness 9

1. Sister Francesca of Messer Capitano of Col de Mezzo, nun in the monastery of San Damiano, declared under oath that she had been in this monastery for more than twenty-one years having entered in the month of May when Saint Clare was abbess. She said that the holy Mother had the wisdom of Solomon and the eloquence of St. Paul, and she could never fully describe the goodness and sanctity which she had seen in her throughout this time.

2. Asked what she had especially noted in Saint Clare, she told how on one occasion the Saracens had entered into the cloister of the monastery whereupon Saint Clare had herself brought to the door of the refectory and caused the sacrament of the Body of Our Lord Jesus Christ to be carried before her in a little box. She

prostrated herself in prayer upon the ground and in tears among others prayed with these words: "Lord, look upon us Thy poor servants for I cannot guard them." Then the witness heard a voice of wonderful sweetness saying, "I will always defend thee"; whereupon Saint Clare prayed also for the city saying, "Lord, be pleased also to defend this city," and again that same sweet voice answered, "The city will suffer many dangers, but will be defended."

Then the Lady Clare turned to the sisters and said to them: "Do not be afraid; I am your safeguard and no harm will come to you, now or in the future nor at any other time as long as you obey God's commandments." And the Saracens departed without doing any harm or damage. Asked how long ago this had happened, Sister Francesca answered that she did not remember. Asked in what month, day and hour, she answered that it was in September she thought on a Friday about the hour of Tierce. Asked who was present, she answered the sisters who were in prayer. Asked whether other sisters had heard the voice, she answered that she and another sister had heard it because they were supporting the Lady Clare, but the other sister had since died. Asked how she knew that the other sister had also heard the voice, she answered, "because she told me so." Saint Clare had gathered all the sisters together that same evening and commanded them that nothing was to be said of all this during her lifetime. Asked who the other sister was who had since died, she answered, Sister Illuminata of Pisa.

3. Sister Francesca also told of another time when the Lady Clare was told that the city of Assisi was about to be given up into the hands of the enemy, and she called the sisters together saying: "We have received great good from this city, therefore we must pray God to save it." She then commanded the sisters that early on the morrow they should gather round her, which they did. Then the Lady Clare ordered ashes to be brought, and laying aside her veil she strewed them on her own head, bidding the sisters do likewise. Then she commanded the sisters that they should all go to the chapel to pray, which they also did, and the following morning the enemy army departed, disbanded and defeated. And since that time the city of Assisi had been free from any foreign domination.

During that day of prayer the sisters fasted on bread and water, and some of them ate nothing at all. Asked when this had happened, Sister Francesca answered that it was in the time of Vitale of Aversa.

4. She also told how once during the calends of May she had seen a most lovely child in the lap of Saint Clare standing in front of her body. His beauty was beyond all description, and at the sight of Him, she, the witness, felt a marvellous sweetness pervade her whole being, and she firmly believed that this Child was the Son of God. She also told how she had seen two marvellous wings, luminous as the sun above the head of Saint Clare, and sometimes they were raised in the air, and sometimes they covered all her head. Asked whether others had seen this, Sister Francesca answered that only she had seen it, and she had never revealed it to anyone; neither would she have revealed it now had it not been for the honour of so holy a Mother.

5. She also told how through her prayers and the sign of the cross, Saint Clare had cured Sister Benvenuta of Madonna Diambra of the sore under her arm, Sister Christiana of deafness in one ear as has been testified by Sister Philippa and by Sister Christiana herself.

6. She told how on another occasion she saw the son of Messer Johanni of Assisi brought to Saint Clare because he was ill with scrofula and fever, and she touched him and made the sign of the cross over him and he was cured. Asked how she knew this, she answered that the child's father had said in the parlour that he had been cured instantly; she, the witness, did not see the child before he was brought to Saint Clare, but she saw him come back afterwards to the monastery quite well. Asked how old the child was, she said five: when asked the name of the child, she said she did not know it.

7. Sister Francesca also told how she had been very ill with such pain in her head that it affected her memory, and when the blessed Mother lay dying she made a vow to her, and was instantly cured, neither had she felt any pain again. Asked how

long she had suffered in this way, she answered, for more than six years.

8. She also told that once when Saint Clare was ill and could not rise from her bed, she asked for a certain cloth, and there being no one at that moment to bring it, a little cat of the monastery started to drag the cloth along the floor as best she could to bring it to Saint Clare, who seeing this said to the little cat: "O you bad one, you don't know how to carry it; why do you drag it along the ground in that way?" Then the little cat, seeming to have understood those words, began to roll up the cloth so that it no longer touched the floor. Asked how she knew this, she said that Saint Clare herself had told her of it.

9. Sister Francesca said that she had herself counted fifty pairs of corporals made from the thread spun by Saint Clare; and these were distributed to churches as the other aforesaid sisters had described.

10. She also related how when the sisters thought Saint Clare to be near death the priest brought her the Communion of the Body of Our Lord Jesus Christ, and at that moment the witness saw a wonderful light over the head of the Lady Clare, and the Host appeared to her transformed into a most beautiful little Child. And after the blessed Mother had received It with her habitual great devotion and many tears, she said these words: "All the heavens and earth could not worthily praise our Lord God for what He has granted me this day." Asked whether any of the other sisters had seen this, Sister Francesca answered that she did not know; she only knew what she had seen herself. Asked when this had taken place, she said about the feast of Saint Martin three years ago. Asked at what time of day, she replied that it was in the morning after Mass.

Witness 10

1. Sister Agnes, daughter of Messer Oportulo of Bernardo of Assisi, nun in the monastery of San Damiano, declared under oath that she had entered the monastery as a small child, and at that time the Lady Clare made use of a cilice of knotted horse hair. She

once lent it to Sister Agnes for three days who found it so harsh that she could in no way endure it.

2. She said that she was quite unable to describe the humility, benignity, the patience, the greatness of the holy life and virtue which she had observed in the Lady Clare during all her life in the monastery. She said that to her it seemed that there was nothing in the Lady Clare that was not entirely good, nothing that could be reprimanded; on the contrary that in every way she was entirely to be commended as a saint. Asked how she knew this, the witness replied that she had been under the care of the Lady Clare for about thirty years.

3. She said that in the evening after Compline the Lady Clare would remain a long time in prayer, shedding many tears. When she was well, she was in the habit of rising again to pray at midnight when she woke the sisters silently by touching them. She prayed especially at the hour of Sext for she said that was the hour when Our Lord was crucified.

4. She also said how Saint Clare afflicted her body through fasting. Asked how she knew this, she answered again because she had been present.

5. She also told how whenever the Lady Clare saw any sister suffering temptation or tribulation she would call her secretly and with tears console her, sometimes throwing herself at the sister's feet. Asked how she knew this, she answered that she saw several whom the Lady Clare had thus consoled, and one of them told her how the blessed Mother had thrown herself on the ground at her feet. Asked the name of this sister, she said it was Sister Illuminata of Pisa, who had since died.

6. She also said that the humility of the Lady Clare was so great that she washed the feet of the sisters and lay sisters. And once while she was washing the lay sisters' feet, wishing to kiss them as was her custom, one of the lay sisters accidentally hit her on the mouth, at which the Lady Clare rejoiced and kissed the sole of that foot. Asked how she knew this, Sister Agnes answered, "because I saw it." Asked when it had happened, she said on one Thursday of Lent.

7. Sister Agnes also said that for most of the time that she was in the monastery Saint Clare had a mat for her bed, and a little straw under her head, and she was content with this. The witness knew this from having seen it. Before her entry into the monastery she had heard that the Lady Clare had slept on vine twigs; but after she became ill, at the command of Saint Francis she made use of a mattress stuffed with straw.

8. She also told how the Lady Clare loved to hear the word of God; and although she had never studied letters, nevertheless she liked to hear learned discourses. Once when Brother Philip of Atri of the Friars Minor was preaching, she, Sister Agnes, saw a most beautiful Child of about three years near to the Lady Clare. Then she prayed fervently in her heart that she might not be deceived in this matter, and in her heart she heard the words: "I am in the midst of them." Thus she understand that the Child was Jesus Christ, who is ever present among those who preach and those who listen as is their duty. Asked how long ago this had happened she said about twenty-one years. Asked what had been the time of year, she said in that week soon after Easter in which the words are sung "Ego sum Pastor Bonus." Asked who was then present, she replied the sisters. Asked whether any of the other sisters had seen the Child, the witness replied that one of them had said to her, "I know you have seen something." Asked how long the Child remained in that position, she answered that it had been for the greater part of the sermon; and she added that it had appeared as though the Lady Clare was in the midst of a wonderful radiance and was no longer like a material being, but had the splendour of the stars. She, Sister Agnes, was filled with an inexplicable sweetness when she saw this apparition. A short while after this she again saw the Lady Clare in the midst of the greatest splendour, not the same colour as before, but all rosy, as though it were sending out sparks of fire, and it surrounded the Lady Clare and covered all her head. And wondering what this could be Sister Agnes heard, not by a voice, but in her own mind, the words: "Spiritus Sanctus superveniet in te."

9. She also said that it was believed that the monastery had been saved from the Saracens, and the city of Assisi liberated from

its besieging enemies through the virtue of the prayers of Saint Clare. She, Sister Agnes, saw the Mother Saint Clare praying for this intention most humbly with many tears, her hands joined and her eyes turned upwards to Heaven.

10. She told also that when Saint Clare was dying, she exhorted the sisters to pray, and she, the witness, recited the prayer to the Five Wounds. Saint Clare spoke very low, but as far as they could understand, the Passion of Christ was continually on her lips together with the holy Name of our Lord Jesus Christ. And almost the last word said by the blessed Mother to Sister Agnes was, "Pretiosa in conspectu Domini mors sanctorum ejus."

11. She also told how once when the Lady Clare had washed her, the witness', feet, she had urgently begged to be allowed to drink the water, and it had seemed to her indescribably sweet. Asked if any other sister had tasted it, she said no, and that the blessed Mother had immediately thrown it away in order that no one should taste it.

Witness 11

1. Sister Benvenuta of Madonna Diambra of Assisi, a nun in the monastery of San Damiano, declared under oath that she had suffered from sores under her arm and in her breast which are commonly called fistulas; and five fingers could be put into this fistula, it having five heads. She had endured this for twelve years, and one evening she went to the blessed Mother Clare in tears asking to be heard. Then the same kind Mother, moved by her usual pity got up from her bed, and prayed on her knees to the Lord. When she had finished praying she turned to the witness, and having first signed herself with the cross, she then made the sign of the cross over her Sister Benvenuta, and touched the sores with her naked hand, saying the Our Father. Thus she, the witness, was healed of those sores which had seemed incurable. Asked how long ago this had happened, she answered that in the last September it had been two years; and she had never again felt any pain.

2. She said she had been in the monastery more than twenty-nine years, always under the rule of the blessed Mother Lady

Clare, who had taught her to love God above all things; then secondly she had taught her to confess her sins thoroughly and often, and thirdly she taught her always to have in mind the Passion of Our Lord.

3. Of the wonderful gathering of the celestial court during the happy death of Saint Clare.

During the night of the Friday to Saturday, which was the third before the death of the Lady Saint Clare, the witness with other sisters were sitting round the bed, weeping for the death of such a Mother; no one spoke but the Lady Clare began the commendation of her own soul saying: "Go in peace for thou wilt be well escorted for He Who created Thee has provided for thy sanctification, and after He had created thee, He infused into thee His holy Spirit, and He has ever guarded thee as a mother does her little child." And when a sister named Anastasia asked the blessed Mother to whom she spoke, she answered, "to my blessed soul."

4. Then Sister Benvenuta began diligently to consider of the great and marvellous holiness of the Lady Clare; and while she was thus meditating it seemed to her that the whole celestial court was preparing to honour this saint. Especially the most blessed Virgin Mary was preparing the garments for this new saint; and while she, Sister Benvenuta, was absorbed in this thought and contemplation she saw all at once with her bodily eye a great multitude of white robed virgins with crowns on their heads who came entering by the door into the room where lay the Mother blessed Clare. Among these virgins there was one unspeakably greater than the others, and beyond all words more beautiful, and she had on her head a more wondrous crown than any; and above the crown there was a golden round vessel like a thurible from which came such a splendour that it illumined the whole house. This virgin drew near to the bed of the holy Lady Clare, and she who was the greatest among them covered the bed with a veil which was so fine that although she was covered with it, yet the Lady Clare was still plainly visible. Then the greatest among the virgins inclined her face over the face of the holy virgin blessed Clare, bending over her so that the witness could not rightly distinguish

one from the other; and this being done, they all vanished. Asked whether she was asleep or awake at that time, the witness answered that she was wide awake and that it was evening tide as has been said. Asked who else was present, she answered that several sisters were there, and some were awake while others slept: she did not know whether any of these had seen what she saw, because until now she had never revealed it to anyone. Asked when this happened and what day, she answered that it was on the Friday evening, and that the holy Lady Clare died the following Monday.

5. Sister Benvenuta also said that all she had said of the sanctity of the Lady Clare was true; and however much she related of this sanctity it would never be sufficient, and that after the blessed Virgin Mary she did not believe there had ever been a more holy woman than the Lady Saint Clare. She was chaste and humble, burning with the love of God, assiduous in prayer and contemplation, harsh to herself in food and clothing, and wonderful in fasting and vigils; many indeed wondered how she could live on so little food. She had great compassion for the afflicted, and was benign and liberal towards all the sisters: all her conversation was of God, and she would neither speak nor hear of worldly things. In the ordering of the monastery she was beyond all words provident and discreet. When asked how she knew these things, Sister Benvenuta answered, "because I was continually with her all the twenty-nine years that I was in the monastery under her; and I saw these things, and if necessary I could give greater details about them."

Witness 12

1. Sister Beatrice of Messer Favorone of Assisi, a nun in the monastery of San Damiano, declared under oath that she was the carnal sister of the Lady Clare of blessed memory whose life from childhood had been entirely angelic, for she always preserved her virginity. And she was so assiduous in all holy works that her good fame was spread abroad among all who knew her.

2. Of the conversion of Saint Clare.
Sister Beatrice said that when Saint Francis had heard the fame of the Lady Clare's sanctity, he preached to her several times, and

the Lady Clare listened willingly to his words, and renounced the world and all earthly things, and went and gave herself up to the service of God as quickly as she could.

3. Therefore she sold her own heritage, and part of the heritage of her, Sister Beatrice, and gave it to the poor.

4. After this Saint Francis shore her head before the altar in the church of Saint Mary, called of the Porziuncula; and he then took her to the church of San Paulo de Abbatissis.* When her relations tried to drag her away from thence, the Lady Clare grasped the altar cloth, and uncovering her head showed them it was shorn; and in no way would she consent to leave that place, nor allow herself to be removed, nor to return with them.

5. After that Saint Francis with Brother Philip and Brother Bernard took her to the church of Sant' Angelo in Panso where she stayed a short time and was then taken to San Damiano in which place the Lord brought other sisters into her order. Asked how she knew these things, Sister Beatrice answered that being the Lady Clare's own sister, she had seen some of these things herself, and the others she had heard from the Lady Clare and from others. Asked how long ago this was, she replied about forty-two years.

6. Of the conversation of Saint Clare in the monastery.

Sister Beatrice also told that while she was abbess of the aforesaid monastery, the Lady Clare governed her order with the greatest holiness and prudence, and God performed so many miracles through her, that all who know of her life hold her in honour as a saint. Asked in what this sanctity was manifested, the witness replied in her virginity, her humility, her patience and benignity, in correcting when necessary, but admonishing the sisters with gentleness, in the instancy of her prayer and contemplation, in her fastings and abstinence, in the asperity of her bedding and garments, in her contempt for herself, in her fervent love of God and desire for martyrdom, and above all in her love of the privilege of Poverty.

7. When asked how she knew all these things, Sister Beatrice answered: "Because I myself saw all that she did being her sister

* The Benedictine convent at Bastia.

and I was with her in the monastery for about twenty-four years. Before this I lived and conversed with her as my sister." The witness added that she could never tell all the goodness that was in the Lady Clare.

8. When asked what miracles God had performed especially through the Lady Clare, Sister Beatrice answered that she had healed several sisters by signing them with the cross; and besides this there were numerous other miracles as for instance when she defended the monastery against the Saracens and the city of Assisi against the enemies that besieged it by her prayers: and this is commonly believed. When asked how she knew this, the witness replied that she had seen the Lady Clare at prayer after which the Saracens departed hurting no one and doing no damage to the monastery. After this prayer the following day the whole army departed which was encamped about the city of Assisi.

9. Asked about the healing of the sisters from their infirmities, Sister Beatrice answered that Sisters Benvenuta and Christiana and others were healed by the Lady Clare. Asked how she knew this she answered that she had seen them first ill and afflicted until the time when the blessed Mother made the sign of the cross upon them and prayed when they were cured. And afterwards she saw that they were well.

Witness 13

1. Sister Christiana of Messer Bernardo di Suppo, a nun in the monastery of San Damiano, declared under oath, confirmed all that Sister Beatrice had said of the holy conversation and manners of the Lady Clare, who, she also said had left her home in a truly wonderful way. Fearing that she might be prevented from departing, Saint Clare would not leave by the door that was in general use, but she went to another door which had been blocked up with heavy wooden bars and a stone column to prevent it from being opened. It would have taken many men to remove these obstacles, yet the Lady Clare did so with the help of Jesus Christ and opened the door. All who saw that opened door next morning were astounded that such a feat could have been performed by any girl. Asked how she knew this, Sister Christiana answered that she was

in that house at the time, and she and the Lady Clare had been together before, and she had always known what concerned her, for she lived with her in Assisi. Asked how long it was since this had happened, she answered forty-two years and perhaps rather more. Asked how old the Lady Clare was at that time, she answered, that it had been said she was eighteen.

2. She also said that in her father's house the Lady Clare was always considered virtuous and saintly: and in the next month of May it would be thirty-four years since she, the witness, had entered the monastery where she had been subject to the Lady Clare, who had made the whole monastery illustrious by her virtues and the holiness of her life, and she had ever inculcated the manners and virtues which are required from consecrated women.

3. Sister Christiana said she could speak fully and truthfully if she were asked concerning any special virtue of the Lady Clare; who above all else was consumed with a burning charity and loved her sisters as herself, and if ever she heard of something unpleasing to God she was moved to great compassion and hastened to try to correct it. Because she was so holy and so filled with virtues, God had wished that she should be the first Mother and Mistress of her order; and she defended the order and the monastery so valiantly against the contagion of sin that her memory will be eternally held in honour. The sisters are all convinced that she, their Mother, is now praying to God for them in heaven who on earth governed them with such prudence, benignity, and vigilance, and strengthened them in religion and in their resolution of poverty. When asked how she knew all this, Sister Christiana answered that she had lived in the monastery for the above mentioned period with the Lady Clare, had seen these things, and had been familiar with what concerned the blessed Mother.

4. She also said that she had never heard of any other woman to equal the Lady Clare who indeed seemed to surpass any woman in the world in her fasting and abstinence, in the harshness of her clothing and penances as in her prayers. She added that she knew these things because she had seen them.

5. Of Sister Benvenuta's liberation from the fistula she confirmed

what that sister had herself said and she also was present when this cure took place.

6. She was also present when Sister Amata was healed of dropsy and confirmed what that sister had said.

7. She also confirmed what Sister Christiana had said of her own cure.

8. She confirmed what Sister Philippa had said concerning the cure of Sister Andrea of Ferrara.

9. She also confirmed what Sister Philippa had said of Saint Clare's defence of the monastery against the Saracens, and how the monastery was preserved; also of her prayer for the city of Assisi when it was besieged by enemies. Sister Christiana added that she was present when the blessed Mother called the sisters together and commanded them to pray.

10. She also told how when the blessed Mother lay mortally ill she never ceased praising God, and admonishing the sisters to observe the rule in perfection, and to the love of poverty. Asked how she knew this, she answered that very often she had been present.

11. Speaking of the Lady Clare's sale of her heritage, Sister Christiana said that her own relations would have given her more money than others; but she would sell nothing to them, and preferred to sell to others in order that the poor should not be defrauded. She sold all that came to her by inheritance and distributed the money to the poor. Asked how she knew this, the witness said, "Because I saw it and heard of it."

Witness 14

1. Sister Angeluccia of Messer Angeleio of Spoleto, a nun in the monastery of San Damiano, under oath declared that she had been twenty-eight years in the monastery of San Damiano and throughout her sojourn there she had been subject to the Lady Clare of blessed memory, and had seen such proofs of her immense goodness that it is indeed possible to say of her what could be said of any saint in Paradise.

2. Asked in what this goodness consisted the witness said that when she entered the monastery the Lady Clare was ill, but notwithstanding this, she would rise at night and keep vigil in prayer with many tears; and this she also did in the morning about the hour of Tierce.

3. She, the witness firmly believed that the prayers of the Lady Clare had saved the monastery from the Saracens on the occasion when they had already penetrated into the cloister. On another occasion she had saved the besieged city of Assisi from the enemy.

4. Sister Angeluccia also said that Saint Clare was pre-eminent in her humility, her benignity towards the sisters, her patience and constancy in tribulation, in her austerity of life, in the meagerness of her food and clothing, and in her charity towards all. She was prudent in governing and exhorting the sisters who were subject to her, and when she reproved them it was with much grace and gentleness, and many other good and holy things could be said of her, beyond all power of understanding or expression. There was far more sanctity in Saint Clare than the witness could ever express; and in her the love of poverty was supreme. Asked how she knew these things, Sister Angeluccia said, "because I was with her throughout that time, and I saw the holiness of her life even as I have said."

5. No one among the sisters doubts that God worked many miracles through the Lady Clare even during her life, as has been already said. Asked how she knew this, the witness replied that she had seen Sister Benvenuta healed of her sores when the Lady Clare with her own hand made the sign of the cross upon her. And she had heard how many other sisters and strangers had been healed in the same way.

6. She, Sister Angeluccia, had also been present when the monastery door fell onto the Lady Clare, and thinking that she must surely have been killed the sisters set up a great cry. But the Lady Clare remained unharmed, and said she had not felt any weight from the door which lay upon her although it was so heavy that it took three brothers to replace it. Asked how she knew this, she replied that she had been present and saw it. Asked how long ago this

had happened, she answered about seven years; asked what day, she replied one Sunday evening during the octave of Saint Peter. It was she, the witness, who had first set up the cry that brought the sisters running to the spot, and they found the door still lying on the Lady Clare since Sister Angeluccia was powerless to move it by herself.

7. She also told of the wonderful and glorious death of the Lady Clare: and how only a few days previously she had spoken of the Blessed Trinity and had spoken divine words with such subtlety that even the very learned would hardly have been able to understand her; and the Lady Clare said much else besides this. Asked what she had said, the witness replied that her words had been already reported by Sister Philippa.

8. Sister Angeluccia also told how Saint Clare had once heard the antiphon being sung, *Vidi aquam egredientem de templo a latere dextro,* and it caused her much joy and she always bore it in mind; and always after eating and after Compline she had holy water brought for herself and the sisters and she said to them: "Sisters and daughters you must always remember and keep in mind that holy water which came from the side of Our Lord Jesus Christ when He hung on the cross."

9. The witness also said that whenever the blessed Mother sent the lay sisters outside the monastery, she admonished them that they should praise God for every beautiful green and flowering plant they saw; and that for every human being they saw, and for every creature, always and in all things God must be praised.

Witness 15

1. On the 28th day of the month of November in the infirmary of the monastery and in the presence of Brother Marco, Sister Philippa and the other sisters, Sister Balvina of Porzano, nun in the monastery of San Damiano, speaking under oath told fully of the sanctity of Saint Clare's life, and of her great goodness.

2. She also told that she, the witness, had seen the holy Mother lying under the door which had fallen on top of her, and which had not yet been raised. She recounted how Saint Clare had said that she had felt no harm from the weight of the door which had

not seemed to her heavier than her own cloak. She said that door was extremely heavy and that she and the other sisters had come running at the cry of Sister Angeluccia and that all feared that the blessed Mother might be dead. Asked how long ago this had happened, she said about seven years.

On the same day, the 28th of November, in the cloister of San Damiano in the presence of Messer Leonardo, archdeacon of Spoleto, Don Jacopo, parish priest of Trevi, accompanied by Messer Bartolomeo, Bishop of Spoleto, and Brother Marco of the order of the Friars Minor, chaplain of the monastery, all the nuns enclosed in the monastery of San Damiano were assembled and this because certain of the nuns had sworn to bear witness to the truth and had testified concerning the life, conversion, and conversation of the Lady Clare of blessed memory, and concerning the miracles which were reputed to have been performed through her merits. In view of this the Lady Abbess Sister Benedetta with all the other nuns of the monastery of San Damiano declared unanimously in the presence of the venerable Father the Lord Bartolomeo, Bishop of Spoleto, that all the holiness that can be ascribed to any saint after the Blessed Virgin Mary can be found in and ascribed to the Lady Clare of blessed memory, their former abbess and most holy Mother. And to this her sanctity they were all ready to testify and to add their sworn witness to that of the others. This they were prepared to do since they had seen her marvellous conversion, and during all the time they had spent with her in the monastery they had seen the sanctity of her life, and her angelic conversation. Human words would never be sufficient to explain these things.

Witness 16

1. On that same day in the church of San Paolo in Assisi in the presence of the venerable Father the Bishop of Spoleto, and present also Andriolo de Bartholo, Jannello de Benvenuto Lucchese, and several others, Messer Ugolino de Pietro Girardone, Knight of Assisi, under oath spoke of the life, conversion and conversation and miracles of the Lady Clare of blessed memory. He said that Saint Clare was of a very noble family of Assisi, that Messer Offreduccio of Bernardino was her grandfather, and his son, Messer Favorone, her father.

2. The Lady Clare was a virgin, and while living in her father's house was esteemed for her most virtuous behaviour and she showed herself gracious and kind to all. As Saint Francis was the founder of the order of Friars Minor which order with the help of God he governed, so this holy virgin Clare was chosen by God to found the Order of the enclosed ladies; which order she governed in all holiness and goodness and to this all bear witness.

3. He also said that as is generally known, the holy virgin Clare entered into religion through the preaching and admonition of Saint Francis.

4. He also told how he, the witness, had separated from his wife by name the Lady Guidutia, and had sent her home to her parents, and had remained without her for more than twenty-two years; indeed he had always refused to receive her back into his house although many times religious persons had admonished him to do so. At last Saint Clare sent him a message that she had been told in a vision that Messer Ugolino was speedily to take back his wife and by her beget a son who would be a joy and consolation to him; and the witness was much distressed by this message. Nevertheless within a few days he began ardently to desire his wife, and fetched her back and received her from whom he had for so long been separated. And even as Saint Clare had said he begot a son by his wife who was still alive, and was his joy and consolation.

5. Asked whether he had known the Lady Clare while she lived in her parents' house, he replied yes, and that he had seen her virtuous and holy behaviour even as he had already said.

6. Asked how he knew that Saint Clare had entered religion through the preaching of Saint Francis, he answered that this was of public knowledge; and he had also heard how Saint Francis had shorn her head in the church of Our Lady of the Porziuncula; and that since she had entered the monastery of San Damiano he had always heard what was obvious and known to all that her sanctity and goodness in her Order was that of any saint in Heaven.

In that same place, and at that same hour in the presence of the witnesses Messer Angelo di Pelcio and Bonamantia Barbieri and before the aforenamed Lord Bishop, the Lady Bona de Guelfuccio, Raniere de Bernardo, and Pietro de Damiano under oath spoke of the life, conversion, conversation, and miracles of Saint Clare.

Witness 17

1. The Lady Bona de Guelfuccio of Assisi declared that she had known Saint Clare while she still lived in her father's house; and she too lived in that house and had much intercourse with her. The great sanctity of the Lady Clare's life before and after she entered religion had firmly convinced the witness that the Lady Clare had been sanctified even in her mother's womb. She would send the food which it was thought she ate herself to the poor; and she, the Lady Bona, had repeatedly been the bearer of it.

2. The Lady Clare was always esteemed by all to be a most chaste virgin, and she was most fervent in spirit as to how she could best serve and please God.

3. She the witness had repeatedly accompanied the Lady Clare to talk with Saint Francis, and they did this secretly in order not to be seen by her family. Asked what Saint Francis had said to them, she replied that he always preached that the Lady Clare should be wholly converted to the Lord Jesus Christ, and Brother Philip had done the same. And she listened to them willingly, and consented to all that they said. Asked how long ago this took place, she replied more than forty-two years; since the Lady Clare had been that time in religion.

4. The Lady Bona also said that when Saint Clare entered into religion, she was about eighteen years old, a prudent girl who always remained at home; and she kept herself hidden for she did not wish to be seen, and so she contrived that those who passed by the house should not see her. She was kindhearted and attended to all good works. Asked how she knew these things, the witness answered: "because I lived with her."

5. Asked how the Lady Clare had been converted, the Lady Bona said that Saint Francis had shorn her head in the church of Santa Maria of the Porziuncula; and this she had heard because she was not present, having gone to Rome to keep Lent.

6. She also told how the Lady Clare, while still at home, had induced her, the witness, to go and visit the church of Saint James (of Campostella) because the Lady Clare being herself so full of grace wished that others should be the same.

7. The Lady Clare while still in the world had also given her money with the command that she should take it to those who were working in Santa Maria of the Porziuncula in order that they might be able to buy some meat.

8. The witness said that the sanctity of Saint Clare was so great that her heart was full of many things for which she could never find words because all that Saint Clare ever said was a lesson to others.

Witness 18

1. Messer Ranieri de Bernardo de Assisi declared under oath that he had no doubt that the Lady Clare of blessed memory was a saint in heaven, and he was convinced of her sanctity. If anyone doubted this of her, then it could be believed of nobody. He could sooner doubt that our faith is groundless than doubt her holiness. This was so because he had known her as a child in her father's house; and from her earliest years she was busied with holy works as though she had been sanctified in her mother's womb.

2. Since she was of a beautiful countenance the question of her marriage was discussed; and many of her relations begged of her to consent to accept a husband, but she would never agree to this. He, the witness, had often urged her to consent, but would not even hear it spoken of, and the more he spoke, the more she urged him to despise the world. Asked how he had come to know all this, he replied that his wife was related to the Lady Clare, and therefore he was on familiar terms with her family and was often in the house and saw her good works.

3. Asked what these good works were, he answered that she fasted and prayed, and gladly gave alms to her utmost possibility. And when she was sitting among those of the household, she always wished to speak of the things of God; and as soon as she could she had her head shorn by Saint Francis. Her relations wished to

remove her from San Paolo (in Abbatissis) but they could in no wise succeed for she did not wish it, and uncovered and showed them her shorn head, and thus they had to leave her.

4. The Lady Clare belonged to the most noble families of Assisi, both through her father and her mother. Asked how he knew these things, the witness replied that they were of public knowledge throughout the district.

5. He also said that when the Lady Clare went to live in San Damiano holy as she was, she taught her daughters the way of sanctity that thus they might serve God, and this is seen today in these her daughters.

6. All the citizens firmly believe that the monastery was defended, and the city liberated from its foes by the prayers and merits of the holy Lady Clare.

7. Asked how long it was since the Lady Clare entered religion, he answered, "more than forty years."

Witness 19

1. Pietro de Damiani of the city of Assisi, under oath, said that he and his father were neighbours of Saint Clare, of her father, and of all the members of her family. He had known the Lady Clare while she was still in the world, and also her father, Messer Favorone, who with the others of his house was noble and great and powerful in the city. The Lady Clare was noble, of noble birth and most virtuous conversation: and there were seven knights in her family all noble and powerful. Asked how he knew this, he said he had seen them because he was their neighbour.

2. At that time the Lady Clare was but a child, but she was considered to lead a spiritual life. Her father and mother and her relations all wished her to marry magnificently in accordance with her rank with some great and powerful lord: but she who was then a girl of about seventeen years could in no way be induced to do so because she wished to preserve her virginity and to live in poverty as she afterwards did having sold all her inheritance and given the proceeds to the poor. She was esteemed

most virtuous by all. Asked how he knew this, he answered that being her neighbour he knew that no one could ever persuade her to take heed of worldly things.

Witness 20

1. On the 29th day of November in the church of San Paolo in the presence of Messer Leonardo, archdeacon of Spoleto, Don Jacopo, the parish priest of Trevi, as in that of the Lord Bishop of Spoleto, Johanni de Ventura of Assisi on oath declared that he frequented the house of the Lady Clare while she was still a child in her father's house, because he was a familiar friend of her family.

2. The Lady Clare was then about eighteen and belonged to all that was most noble in the city of Assisi both on her father's, as on her mother's side. Her father was named Messer Favorone and her grandfather Messer Offreduccio de Bernardine: and she although still a girl was as virtuous in life and in habit as though she had already been a long time in the monastery.

3. When asked what kind of life she led, he replied that although her home was one of the greatest in the city and the life of her family very sumptuous, nevertheless she, who was served with the food of a great house, would set it aside to send to the poor. When asked how he knew this, he answered that being in the same house with her, he saw what passed, and he also believed these things because they were told him.

4. Even while she lived in her father's house the Lady Clare wore a very harsh white garment under her other clothes.

5. He said that he saw her fasting, and praying and how she was given to works of piety; and that it was believed that from the beginning she had been inspired by the Holy Spirit.

6. He also said that when the Lady Clare heard how Saint Francis had chosen the way of poverty, she determined in her heart to do the same. And thus her head was shorn by Saint Francis in the church of Santa Maria of the Porziuncula or in that of San Paolo. Then since her relations wished to bring her away from

this church of San Paolo back with them to Assisi, she showed them her shorn head. Asked how he knew this, he replied that it was common knowledge and that he had heard it spoken of.

7. After this she went to San Damiano where she became the Mother and mistress of the Order of San Damiano, and there she brought up many sons and daughters in the way of the Lord Jesus Christ which are those we see to-day.

8. He also said that it is impossible to doubt her sanctity since the Lord performs many miracles through her, as is manifest to all.

9. He also said that in this very year after the death of the Lady Clare he saw a mad stranger from beyond the Alps, a man possessed by the devil who was bound with ropes and they brought him to the tomb of the Lady Clare. Asked how he knew this, he replied that he saw the man while he was under this infirmity of madness, and saw how there, at the tomb of Saint Clare he was immediately cured. Asked at the invocation of what saint the man had been healed, he replied that it was at the sepulchre of the Lady Saint Clare; and that this is notorious and known to all. Asked in what month and day this happened, he replied that he thought it was in September but he did not remember the date. Asked who was present, he replied that all the folk in the piazza saw the madman and went with him to the tomb of the Lady Saint Clare.

Finis. Deo gratias. Amen.

THE BULL OF CANONIZATION OF
THE VIRGIN ST. CLARE

Alexander, Bishop, servant of the servants of God to all the venerable Brothers, Archbishops and Bishops, health and Apostolic Benediction.

Clare, who shines through her radiant merits, is now shining in Heaven in the light of glory, and on earth through sublime miracles. Her own high and unfaltering institution illuminates this world while the full grandeur of the eternal reward shines in Heaven and magnificent proofs testify to Clare's virtues which dazzle the eyes of mortal men. On earth Clare was granted the privilege of the strictest poverty, and in Heaven she is rewarded with inestimable treasures, and all the faithful bring her the tribute of universal devotion and immense honour. The fullness of the divine light shines on Clare and the stupendous miracles that she works illuminate her in the eyes of all Christian people. O Clare, thou art enriched with uncounted shining treasures; even before thy conversion thou didst shine; after that conversion thy brilliance was enhanced; thou wast resplendent in the life of the cloister, and when this earthly life had passed thou dost shine in utmost brightness. In Clare the world sees an untarnished mirror of example; she has carried the fragrant lily of her virginity into the celestial garden, while in this world we experience the manifest help of her protection. O admirable and blessed light of Clare! the more we study her earthly work, the greater splendour is revealed in all her actions. While living she sparkled; after her death she radiates light; she shone on earth, and now is resplendent in Heaven. How great is the power of this light! How vehement the brightness of such splendour! On earth this light was enclosed within the sacred precincts, and yet its rays were seen far beyond;

she lived in a strict monastic circle, and yet her light was diffused in the whole world; she restricted herself within, yet she was manifested to those outside. Clare hid herself; and her life is known to all; Clare was silent; yet the fame of her was everywhere heard; she remained in her cell, yet she was preaching to the city. Neither is this to be wondered at, for so shining and brilliant a light could not hide its own brightness, or prevent it from illuminating the house of the Lord. A vase filled with such fragrance could not be hidden, and the sweetness of its scent filled the house of God. Within the narrow walls of her cell, she broke the alabaster vase of her own body, and the fragrance of her sanctity has filled the whole Church.

From her childhood and while still a girl in the world she was intent to enter upon the path of purity and thus to pass through this changing and impure world; she ever guarded the treasure of her chastity with unstained modesty; she was always given to works of charity, so that her name was beloved and praised by all both far and near. Blessed Francis, hearing the praise of her virtues, soon began to exhort her that she should dedicate herself to the perfect service of Christ. She listened willingly to his holy words, for already she desired to hold the world and all earthly goods in contempt and to serve God alone in voluntary poverty, and she was prompt to satisfy this, her fervent desire. All that she possessed of value she sold and distributed in alms to the poor in homage to Christ.

Since she also desired to fly from the distractions of the world, she took refuge in a country church where she received the sacred tonsure from the hands of the same blessed Francis, and having been put by him in another church for safety, with persevering force she resisted her relations when they tried to take her with them; she embraced the altar, and clinging to the altar cloths, she uncovered her shorn head to show that since she had become the bride of God in all purity of heart, she could not be dragged away from His service. At last by the care of Blessed Francis, she was brought to the church of Saint Damian outside her native city of Assisi; and God, wishing to be honoured through the cult and love of His most holy Name gave to Clare several companions. In this place there originated the worthy and holy order of the

Damianites, now known throughout the world; following the exhortations of the same Blessed Francis, Clare began this new and holy observance; she was the first and steadfast foundation stone of this great religion, the first stone of this sublime building.

Noble by birth, but still nobler by conversion, through this rule of extraordinary sanctity, she preserved the virginity she had so jealously guarded. Her mother, by name Ortolana, who was also entirely given to holy works, not long afterwards followed the example of her daughter, and entered into religion; and here Ortolana, this excellent gardener, who had cultivated so wonderful a plant in the Lord's Garden, finally ended her days.

When a few years had passed, at the insistence of Blessed Francis, Blessed Clare took over the ruling of the monastery and the sisters. This was truly the high and noteworthy tree whose spreading branches bore many sweet fruits of religion in the field of the Church; and many followers hastened from all parts, and are still hastening to enjoy the shade of those branches and their delectable fruits.

Thus Clare was the new woman in the valley of Spoleto who opened a fresh fountain of living water for the benefit and restoration of souls, and this water, carried in little streams throughout the territory of the Church, has prospered in reviving religion. Clare too is that splendid candle of sanctity shining in the Lord's temple, and many hasten to kindle their own lamp at this light. In the field of faith, Clare planted and cultivated the vine of poverty from which are gathered most wholesome and copious fruits. And in the field of ecclesiastical humility, she prepared a garden adorned with all the flowers of poverty from which come forth the flowers of every virtue.

In this citadel of religion, this tower of strict abstinence, the generous refreshment of spiritual food is dispensed; Clare was the foremost among the poor, the leader of the humble, the mistress of the continent, the abbess of the penitent; she governed the monastery and family entrusted to her with most diligent care and prudence, in the fear and service of the Lord according to the perfection of religion, she was ever vigilant in duty, prompt in the performance of her office, cautious in exhorting, unfailing in teaching; in correcting she was moderate, temperate in ordering, admirably compassionate, discreet in keeping silence, prudent in speech and in all that concerned the wise government of the monastery, she was more desirous to obey than to command, more anxious to honour others, than to be honoured herself. For others her life was a school of doctrine and wisdom; and in this living book others learnt the path for their own lives.

Clare walked in this world, but her soul moved in Heaven; she was a vessel of humility, a tower of chastity, a flame of charity, in her goodness was gentleness, she sustained others by her patience, she was a maker of peace, mild in word and in action, loving and kind to all. Then, when her body was consumed by suffering her spirit was strengthened; and since everyone having overcome an enemy feels more courageous, so she would lie on the bare ground or on vine twigs, with a hard bit of wood for her pillow, and one only tunic with a poor cloak of rough material. Thus she clothed her body and veiled her head most poorly, and beneath her outer garments on her bare flesh she wore a most harsh string shirt woven with horsehair. She was very austere in food and drink, and her abstinence was such, that for many years on the second, fourth and sixth days of the week, she took no food to support her body; on the other days she so reduced the quantity of what she ate that all marvelled how she could live on so little. Often she kept vigil, and continued absorbed in prayer in which she spent the greater part of the day and night; she was troubled by incessant illness so that she could not rise unaided for any bodily exertion, and needed the help of her sisters. She would then cause herself to be raised on her bed, and with a support behind her shoulders she worked with her own hands in order not to be idle even in illness, and she would then spin the finest thread for linen from which she made many corporals for the Holy Sacrifice of the altar and which she distributed to the churches of the Assisan hills and valley of Spoleto. Especially she was the undaunted lover of poverty; and this virtue was so precious to her heart, she was so anxious to possess it, her love for it was so burning that she embraced it ever more ardently, and for nothing in the world would she ever loosen her hold upon this beloved poverty; no argument ever availed to persuade her into consenting that her monastery should hold any possession, even when Pope Gregory, Our predecessor of happy memory, would willingly have made sufficient provision for the material needs of the sisters.

So great and wonderful a light cannot be covered without showing the rays of its own splendour, and thus even during her lifetime the virtue of her sanctity shone through many and various miracles. Thus one of the sisters of the monastery recovered her speech which had long been lost; another was cured of dumbness, another of deafness; simply by the sign of the cross she cured a sister ill of a fever, another suffering and swollen with dropsy, another of a fistula, and many others troubled by various ills. She also cured a Friar Minor of madness.

Once when there was no drop of oil in the monastery she sent for the Brother whose office it was to beg for alms; she took a jar and having washed it she placed it empty near the door of the monastery so that the brother should take it with him to have it filled but when he went to fetch it, he found it full, and this thanks to the divine charity of God.

On another day when there was but one half loaf in the monastery to feed all the sisters, Clare ordered that it should be divided into minute pieces and given to the sisters. But He Who is the Bread of life and provides food for the hungry so multiplied that bread in the hands of the sister who was dividing it, that it sufficed to be divided into fully fifty portions which were then dispensed to the sisters who already were sitting at the table.

Through these and other stupendous miracles Clare revealed even during her life the pre-eminence of her merits. When too she came to the end of her life, a white robed chorus of blessed virgins, their heads adorned with shining crowns, and in their midst one more beautiful and majestic by far than the others, appeared and entered the cell where Clare lay and they advanced and surrounded the poor bed and comforted and consoled her with careful kindness.

After she had died an epileptic was brought to her tomb for his legs were helpless so that he could not walk; and there his legs were straightened with a sound heard by all, and he was healed of both his infirmities. Many who were deformed and helpless from illness also came, others suffering from madness and terrible fits at her tomb regained perfect health. One man who had lost the use of his right hand from a blow recovered it through the merits of this saint; another who had become blind was led to the tomb by a guide, and his sight was restored so that he departed unaided. Through these and other wonderful miracles this blessed virgin has become celebrated, and the prophecy heard by her mother when with child has been fulfilled in the daughter, for that mother had heard the words, "that she would bring forth a light which would shine in the whole world." Holy Mother Church rejoices that she has produced and formed such a daughter, who, herself the mother of many virtues has brought forth many disciples through her own example, and has formed them as perfect servants of Christ. Let all the company of the faithful rejoice because the Lord and King of Heaven has chosen their sister and companion for His bride, and has taken her into His wonderful temple and surrounded her with so great glory; and in Heaven too the company of the saints is rejoicing for the marriage feast of the King's bride.

It is only seemly that a virgin exalted by God in Heaven should be universally venerated by the Church on earth; and after diligent and careful research, and rigorous examination and discussion as to her sanctity of life and miracles, it has appeared manifest that her wonderful actions are already known to those far away. Therefore We, after the common advice and with the common consent of all Our Brothers and Prelates attached to the Apostolic See, confiding in the divine Omnipotence and by the authority of the blessed Apostles Peter and Paul and by Our own authority We consider Ourselves in duty bound to inscribe her name among those of the holy virgins.

Therefore We give notice to your community, and by these apostolic letters We command you to celebrate the feast of this virgin worthily and with devotion on the eve of the Ides of August, and to cause this feast to be celebrated with equal devotion by all your subjects in order that we may merit to have this kind and merciful protectress before the throne of God. And in order that the multitude of Christian people should hasten to her tomb with increased zeal and that her feast may be celebrated with ever growing solemnity, We offer, by the mercy of God, and the authority of the Blessed Apostles Peter and Paul, each year an Indulgence of one year and forty days to all those, who with real contrition after Confession shall humbly and with reverence visit the tomb of this virgin and implore her protection on the day of her feast or in any other day within the octave.

Given in Anagni on the day of the 26th of September in the first year of Our pontificate (1255).

BIBLIOGRAPHY OF WORKS CONSULTED

Acta Sanctorum, August 12 and March 6.

Legenda Sanctae Clarae Virginis, ed. Pennacchi (Assisi, 1910).

Tommaso da Celano, *La Leggenda di Santa Chiara d'Assisi* (Sancasciano, 1926).

—— *Le Due Leggende di San Francesco d'Assisi,* ed. Fausta Casolini (Milano, 1923).

S. Bonaventura, *Vita di San Francesco,* ed. Batelli (Sancasciano, 1906).

La Leggenda dei Tre Compagni, ed. Lazzeri (Firenze, 1923).

Lo Speculum Perfectionis, ed. P. Sabatier (Assisi, 1905).

Acti B. Francisci et Sociorum ejus (Paris, 1905).

Sacrum Commercium (The Lady Poverty), ed. Carmichael (London, 1901).

Fioretti di San Francesco (Firenze, 1922).

A New Fioretti, ed. John Moorman (London, 1946).

Saint Francis of Assisi, Legends and Lauds, ed. Otto Karrer (London, 1947).

Cronaca dei XXIV Generali, Analecta Francescana (Quaracchi, 1897).

Opus Conformitatum, Bartolomeo Pisano, Quaracchi, *Analecta Francescana* (1906, 1912).

Liber de Laudibus, Bernardo de Besse, *Analecta Francescana,* Vol. III (Quaracchi, 1897).

Regula Sanctae Clarae, Seraphicae Legislationes (Quaracchi, 1897).

Testamentum Sanctae Clare (Quaracchi, 1897).

Annales Minorum, Luke Wadding (Rome, 1731).

Vie de Saint Francois d'Assise, P. Sabatier (Paris, 1931).

Etudes Inedites, P. Sabatier (Paris, 1932).

Life of Saint Francis of Assisi, Fr. Cuthbert, O.S.F.C. (London, 1912).

The Writings of Saint Francis, Fr. Paschal Robinson (London, 1906).

San Francesco d'Assisi, Johannes Joergenson (Rome, 1919).

Vita di San Francesco, Salvatore Attal (Livorno, 1931).

Frate Elia, Salvatore Attal (Roma, 1936).

Nuova Vita di San Francesco d'Assisi, Arnaldo Fortini (Milano, 1926).

Assisi nel Medio Evo, Arnaldo Fortini (Roma, 1940).

Vita di San Francesco d'Assisi, P. Facchinetti, O.F.M.Cap. (Milano, 1926).

Vita di Santa Chiara, V. Locatelli (Quaracchi, 1854).

Vita di Santa Chiara, P. Z. Lazzeri (Quaracchi 1920).

De Origine Regularum Ordinis S. Clarae, P. L. Oliger, in *Arch. Franc. Hist.,* Vol. V, 1912.

Il Processo di Canonizzazione di Santa Chiara, P. Lazzeri, in *Arch. Franc. Hist.,* Vol. XIII, 1920.

Letters of Saint Clare to Bl. Agnes of Bohemia, ed. Walter Seton, British Society of Franciscan Studies (Aberdeen, 1915). Also ed. P. Oliger, *Arch. Franc. Hist.,* Vol. XII, 1919.

The Writings of Saint Clare of Assisi, Fr. Paschal Robinson, in *Arch. Franc. Hist.,* Vol. III.

The Life and Legend of the Lady Saint Clare, Balfour (London, 1910).

Life of Saint Clare, Fr. Paschal Robinson, O.F.M.

Saint Clare of Assisi, E. Gilliat–Smith (London, 1914).

Storie d'Assisi, A. Cristofani (Assisi, 1875).

Storia di San Damiano in Assisi, P. Bracaloni, O.F.M. (Assisi, 1919).

L'Umbria Francescana Illustrata, P. Cavanna, O.F.M. (Perugia, 1910).

Per una nuova vita di Santa Chiara d'Assisi, P. Z. Lazzeri.

Vie de Sainte Claire d'Assisi, Mons. Richard: ed Pennacchi (Assisi, 1900).

La Gloriosa Santa Chiara di Assisi (Napoli: Sorrento, 1894).

Sorella Chiara, Albina Henrion (Torino, 1925).

Santa Chiara d'Assisi, Fausta Casolini (Milano, 1921).

Les Origines de l'Ordre de Sainte Claire, P. René de Nantes, O.S.F.C. (Paris, 1912).

Sainte Claire d'Assise, Maurice Beaufreton (Paris, 1926).

L'Esprit de Sainte Claire, P. Exupere, O.S.F.C. (Paris, 1912).

Figurines Franciscaines, G. Goyau.

Santa Chiara d'Assisi, P. Leopoldo de Chérancé (Italian edition — Milano, 1903).

The Princess of Poverty, Fr. M. Fiege, O.S.F.C. (Evansville, 1909).

De Originis S. Clarae in Flandria, Fr. D. De Kok in *Arch. Hist. Franc.*, Vol. VII, 1914.

Vita Breve di Santa Chiara, T. Locatelli (Assisi, 1882).

La Beata Ortolana d'Assisi, P. C. Ortolano da Pesaro (Roma, 1904).

Santa Chiara d'Assisi, P. Leone Bracaloni, O.F.M. (Milano, 1949).

Il Protomonasteri di S. Chiara in Assisi — Storia e Cronaca (1253–1950), Fausta Casolini (Garzanti, 1950).

Index

Agnes, sister of Clare, letter of, to Clare, 60; pursued by family, 37

Agnes of Prague, begs for privilege of poverty, 106

Assisi, Catharists in, 26; Charlemagne's conquest, 8; Civil War in, 22; Clare born in, 19; description of, 1; description of Lombards in, 7; Francis born in, 16; Francis' talk of, 27; Frederick Barbarossa in, 14; Frederick II perhaps born in, 19; history of, 1–16; Hohenstaufens driven from, 21; invasions of, 1–16; martyrs in, 2; peace with Perugia, 25; return of Clare's family to, 25; St. Rufinus of, 3; in twelfth century, 17; under interdict, 26; war with Perugia, 25

Benediction of St. Clare, 178

Bull of Canonization of St. Clare, 231 ff

Cardinal Ugolino, first letter to Clare, 54; friendship with Francis and Clare, 54; Rule for Poor Ladies, 56

Cause of Canonization, 179 ff

Clare, St., attitude regarding Friars, 83; at Bastia, 35; birth of, 19; building of Church in honour of, 137; burial in San Giorgio, 135; canonization of, 136; Christmas ecstasy, 129; confidence in Elias, 115; consecrated by Francis at Porziuncula, 35; contact with first companions, 78; correspondence with Agnes of Prague, 101–112; death of, 134; description of, 28; devotion to Blessed Sacrament, 95; devotion for holy water, 93; devotion to the Passion, 90; discovery

of body, 138; episode of Saracens, 118; family of, 20; finding of Rule of, 138; first community at San Damiano, 39; first meeting with Francis, 31; gift of miracles, 89; growth of Order, 51; her clothing, 48; her cousins, Bona and Pacifica Guelfuccio, 22; her first miracle, 46; iconography of, 137 f; influence of Francis on, 32; insistence on poverty, 89; instruction to Sisters, 88; joined by Agnes, 36; lament for Francis, 75; last days, 132; leaves home, 34; letter to Ermentrude, 113; love of flowers, 97; love of penance, 49; love of poverty, 45; love of sermons, 83; makes shoes for Francis, 70; miracles at tomb, 135; moved to Sant' Angelo in Panso, 36; moves to San Damiano, 38; nieces join community, 87; outward signs of sanctity, 96; in Perugia, 22; power of healing, 93; pursued by family, 35; receives ratification of poverty, 134; relations with fellow citizens, 53; saves Assisi, 119; testament of, 126; testimony in canonization of, 180 ff; trust in God, 45; upbringing of, 25; vision of Francis, 77; visited by Cardinal Rainaldo, 129; vocation of, 33; writes Rule for Poor Ladies, 125

Elias, builds Church of St. Francis, 116; connection with Frederick II, 117; death of, 130; excommunication of, 117; position of, 116; retires to Cortona, 123

Elizabeth of Hungary, contact with Franciscans, 58

241